Hotel Ponce de Leon

UNIVERSITY PRESS OF FLORIDA

Florida A&M University, Tallahassee
Florida Atlantic University, Boca Raton
Florida Gulf Coast University, Ft. Myers
Florida International University, Miami
Florida State University, Tallahassee
New College of Florida, Sarasota
University of Central Florida, Orlando
University of Florida, Gainesville
University of North Florida, Jacksonville
University of South Florida, Tampa
University of West Florida, Pensacola

HOTEL PONCE DE LEON

The Rise, Fall, and Rebirth of Flagler's Gilded Age Palace

LESLEE F. KEYS

University Press of Florida

Gainesville · Tallahassee · Tampa · Boca Raton

Pensacola · Orlando · Miami · Jacksonville · Ft. Myers · Sarasota

VIVA FLORIDA 500
1513-2013

A FLORIDA QUINCENTENNIAL BOOK

Special thanks to Flagler College and to the St. Augustine Foundation for their generous support of this work.
Printed in the United States of America on acid-free paper

This book may be available in an electronic edition.

First cloth printing, 2015
First paperback printing, 2018

23 22 21 20 19 18   6 5 4 3 2 1

Library of Congress Cataloging-in-Publication Data
Keys, Leslee F., author.
Hotel Ponce de Leon : the rise, fall, and rebirth of Flagler's gilded age palace / Leslee F. Keys.
pages cm
Includes bibliographical references and index.
ISBN 978-0-8130-6149-8 (cloth)
ISBN 978-0-8130-6499-4 (pbk.)
1. Ponce de Leon Hall (Saint Augustine, Fla.)—History. 2. Flagler, Henry Morrison, 1830–1913.
3. Flagler College—History. 4. Saint Augustine (Fla.)—History. 5. Historic buildings—Florida—Saint Augustine. 6. Saint Augustine (Fla.)—Buildings, structures, etc. I. Title.
F319.S2K49 2015
975.9'18—dc23
2015010511

The University Press of Florida is the scholarly publishing agency for the State University System of Florida, comprising Florida A&M University, Florida Atlantic University, Florida Gulf Coast University, Florida International University, Florida State University, New College of Florida, University of Central Florida, University of Florida, University of North Florida, University of South Florida, and University of West Florida.

University Press of Florida
15 Northwest 15th Street
Gainesville, FL 32611-2079
http://upress.ufl.edu

To gifted architects Roy Eugene Graham and Herschel Shepard—
teachers, mentors, friends

The historic monuments of a people may be regarded as the features of its countenance, through which is revealed the soul of that people.

Thomas Hastings, *Six Lectures on Architecture*

CONTENTS

ILLUSTRATIONS

ACKNOWLEDGMENTS

The genesis of this book dates to May of 2005 when I accepted a position as Flagler College's first historic preservation staff member. My research on the Hotel Ponce de Leon, or "the Ponce" as the building is affectionately known, began immediately. The former hotel was being considered for National Historic Landmark status at the time, a distinction it achieved officially the following year. The research on the College's historic campus complemented my fundraising responsibilities there. The subjects covered in this book are an outgrowth of that process.

Thank you to Flagler College administrators William T. Abare Jr., Ed.D., president, and Alan Woolfolk, Ph.D., vice president for academic affairs, for their support and encouragement. Similarly, thank you, colleagues at the University of Florida: Christopher Silver, Ph.D., dean, College of Design, Construction and Planning; Roy Eugene Graham, FAIA, Beineke-Reeves distinguished professor; Herschel Shepard, FAIA, professor emeritus, Department of Architecture; Kathleen Deagan, Ph.D., distinguished research professor emeritus of anthropology; and John Nemmers, archivist, Smathers Libraries.

Many people assisted with this book. They include Michael Gallen, Peggy Dyess, Brian Nesselrode, and Jolene Dubray at the Proctor Library, Flagler College; Matthew Armstrong of the Smathers Libraries at the University of Florida; Bob Nawrocki and Charles Tingley at the St. Augustine Historical Society Research Library. Joy MacMillan, executive director of the St. Augustine Foundation, facilitated use of that organization's records. Dana Ste. Claire, executive director of the St. Augustine 450th

Commemoration at the city of St. Augustine, provided access to primary sources related to the community's early historic preservation efforts and the city's 400th anniversary activities. Sincere appreciation is extended to the St. Augustine Foundation for supporting the book's publication.

Archivists at academic institutions throughout the United States helped with sources that strengthened this project: Paul Israel, director and general editor of the Thomas A. Edison Papers at Rutgers University; Janet Parks, curator of drawings and archives, Avery Library, Columbia University; Joanne Archer, Special Collections librarian, Hornbake Library, University of Maryland Libraries; Ellen Welch, Albert and Shirley Small Special Collections Library, University of Virginia; and David Kessler, Special Collections librarian, Bancroft Public Services, University of California, Berkeley. The staff at the Jefferson Building of the Library of Congress gave me a personal tour of the rooms with murals by Maynard and provided background on the construction of the building.

Steven Brooke, of Steven Brooke Studios in Miami, who spectacularly presented the design and details of the Hotel Ponce de Leon through his photographs, generously provided some of those images. The book is the better for your efforts.

Additional images were provided from a variety of repositories with assistance from Kristen Gurciullo in the Florida Photographic Collection at the State Archives of Florida; Wendi Goen, archivist at the Arizona State Library; Christina Moretta, photo curator for the San Francisco Photographic Archives Collection at the San Francisco Public Library; Laurie Austin and Stephen Brannelly in Audiovisual Archives at the John F. Kennedy Presidential Library and Museum in Boston; Stacey Erdman, Digital Collections curator at Northern Illinois University; Becky Hartke and Joe Enos with the National Pastime Museum of Major League Baseball; and John Conway, historian, Sullivan County, New York.

Ruth Hawkins, director of the Hemingway-Pfeiffer Museum and Educational Center in Piggott, Arkansas, and Carey Baughman, historical resource specialist with Orange County Parks at Helena Modjeska's home Arden, assisted with research about their sites. The front desk staff at historic hotels that were mentioned in the text graciously allowed me to ask questions, explore their buildings, and photograph the public spaces.

Finally, thank you to my family who encouraged me in this endeavor. Most important, my heartfelt gratitude to Thom McDonald who shared many of the trips to visit grand hotels, indulged my questions and curiosities over the years, and proofread this document. Any shortcomings in the work remain mine.

ABBREVIATIONS

BCSR	Biltmore, Campbell, Smith Restorations, Inc.
CHDC	Carrère and Hastings Digital Collection, George A. Smathers Libraries, University of Florida, Gainesville
COSA	City of St. Augustine
CU.MARK	Mark Twain Papers, University of California, Berkeley
FCA	Flagler College Archives
HSAPB	Historic St. Augustine Preservation Board Archives
IFACS	International Fine Arts Conservation Studio, Inc.
JMP	John Morris Papers
NACR	National Advisory Committee for Restoration
NSCDAFL	National Society of The Colonial Dames in America in The State of Florida
SAHRPC	St. Augustine Historical, Restoration and Preservation Commission, Inc. and St. Augustine Restoration, Inc.
SAHSRL	St. Augustine Historical Society Research Library
SAF	St. Augustine Foundation
UFDC	University of Florida Digital Collections, George A. Smathers Libraries, University of Florida, Gainesville

Hotel Ponce de Leon

Introduction

The Hotel Ponce de Leon, an imaginative and exuberant expression of the Gilded Age fascination with art and architecture, is recognized as one of Florida's and the nation's most iconic and historically important structures. The building has held this status from the time that Standard Oil cofounder Henry Flagler opened it in 1888 and throughout the subsequent eighty years that it operated as a resort owned by him and then his heirs. In addition, the hotel anchored downtown St. Augustine and served as the social and cultural center of the region.

Flagler College was founded in 1968, in part as a means to ensure preservation of the building with an economically viable use. Establishment of the college paralleled adoption of the National Historic Preservation Act of 1966. The law set as policy what had been a limited social movement for more than a century. This is the context that enabled retention of the formal hotel and fostered its transformation into the principal building on the new college's campus.

In the next half century, Flagler College bolstered its rising academic standing with a campus emphasizing high quality architectural facilities and amenities created within a framework of historic preservation. In 2018, Flagler College will mark its fiftieth anniversary. In addition to celebrating this institutional milestone, the college will showcase a campus that demonstrates the realized potential of integrating contemporary uses in historic buildings.

Today, known as Ponce de Leon Hall and the keystone of the Flagler College campus, the former Hotel Ponce de Leon maintains a national and international reputation for its engineering and architectural attributes, its decorative and fine arts collections, and its role as one of Florida's most authentically preserved heritage tourism destinations. Equally notable, the campus is acknowledged as one of the country's most attractive college settings, principally due to the architectural gem that serves as its centerpiece.

This work explores the interwoven stories of the Hotel Ponce de Leon and Flagler College within the context of architecture, social history, and historic preservation. These stories provide a compelling and unique opportunity to understand important chapters in the history of Florida and, by extension, the United States. As St. Augustine hosted an international tourism audience when Henry Flagler opened the Hotel Ponce de Leon, so Flagler College is showcasing to an international audience the preserved hotel as part of St. Augustine's 450th anniversary and the college's 50th anniversary.

Henry Morrison Flagler and John D. Rockefeller founded Standard Oil, forging a business partnership and friendship that lasted nearly half a century. In 1882, twelve years after they started the corporation, Flagler began a second career developing the southernmost frontier of Florida with a string of resort hotels along the Atlantic coast, linked by his Florida East Coast Railway (FEC). He invested in a steamship line that provided service to Cuba and the Bahamas. He funded portions of the Atlantic Intracoastal Waterway through Florida and started an electric company that is recognized today as Florida Power & Light (FP&L). He developed cities to host his hotels. He bricked streets, installed sewers, constructed trolley systems, fostered arts and culture, and hosted sporting events in Florida. This second career spanned thirty years, concluding in 1912 with completion of the Overseas Railway to Key West.

The Hotel Ponce de Leon in St. Augustine was Flagler's first Florida venture and stands as the flagship of his empire. Known throughout its history as "the Ponce," the five-building complex incorporated state-of-the-art construction, technological innovations, and modern conveniences, all to satisfy his discerning guests' most extravagant wishes. In 1909, with construction of his railway through the Florida Keys well under way, Flagler maintained that construction of the Ponce had been his greatest challenge.

The Ponce stands as the only building in the world to incorporate the talents of a team of artisans, craftsmen, and inventors who were responsible for its construction and decoration. This is an ambitious statement; however, the principals, more than a dozen men, came together to undertake this project exclusively.

Young New York architects John Merven Carrère and Thomas Hastings led the team. The Ponce, their new firm's first commission of what would be more than 600 projects, is considered their most creative effort. They were assisted by their former École des Beaux Arts atelier partners Bernard Maybeck and Emmanuel Masqueray. Maybeck left the firm after completion of the Ponce and established a successful architectural practice in California. Carrère died in a traffic accident in 1911 shortly before completing the architectural firm's final effort, the New York Public Library. These actions precluded the full complement of men from working together again.

With construction of the Ponce, Connecticut-based builders James McGuire and Joseph McDonald completed the nation's first major cast-in-place concrete structure. Northerners William Kennish and William Hammer served as engineers for the project. Inventor Thomas Edison's direct current dynamos and thousands of electric lights brought St. Augustine its first and the nation's largest incandescent lighting plant at that time.

Artisan Louis Comfort Tiffany designed the interiors and the seventy-nine stained glass windows. The project came early in his glassmaking career and before he achieved international renown. Also, master craftsman Maitland Armstrong participated in the glass creations. Auguste Pottier and William Stymus, founders of New York's long-standing interiors firm, orchestrated the elaborate marble wainscoting and floors, carved woodwork, and opulent furnishings. Their protégé Virgilio Tojetti and renowned muralists George Maynard and Herman Schladermundt created the decorations of the grand rooms.

These men were emerging leaders in their professional fields before and, in part, because of their participation in the project. They were socioeconomically linked with connections to New York and New England, connections that reinforced the importance of their collaboration on Flagler's hotel. The Ponce was completed shortly before the World's Columbian

Exposition of 1893 held in Chicago. Many of the talented men who honed their skills in construction of the Ponce demonstrated their heightened abilities to an international audience at the Exposition.

Flagler commissioned Carrère & Hastings and retained McGuire and McDonald to build a second hotel immediately south of the Ponce. The Hotel Alcazar provided guest rooms and incorporated recreational opportunities, including a casino, swimming pool, and steam baths. Diagonal to the southeast of the Ponce, Flagler acquired a third hotel and renamed it the Hotel Cordova. Together the trio of hotels hosted guests from the United States, Canada, and Europe.

The resorts anchored St. Augustine's downtown and revived a depressed post–Civil War economy in a city that had relied on tourism for most of the nineteenth century. In addition, Flagler's investments spurred development of nearby neighborhoods known today as the Model Land Company, Lincolnville, the Abbott Tract, and North City. Flagler's investments inspired development beyond the city limits and at the beaches. He established recreation and athletic competitions as leisure activities for his hotel guests and for the greater St. Augustine community. This took place during the same time that intercollegiate athletics and professional sports teams were being developed nationally.

As the nineteenth century concluded, the Ponce operated as a resort hotel for the wealthy who traveled the Eastern United States. They traveled from New England or Long Island, from eastern or midwestern cities. They journeyed through Newport or Jekyll Island to enjoy the sunny climate of Florida. By the turn of the twentieth century, Florida had become a preeminent national and international vacation destination. St. Augustine, with its European appearance and heritage, served as the gateway.

In 1929, the Stock Market Crash jeopardized the operation of the Ponce, forced closure of Flagler's other two hotels, and threatened the economic viability of St. Augustine. During the Depression of the 1930s, attempts to market the community as a heritage tourism destination helped the hotel and the city survive. This effort partnered the National Park Service, Florida State Government, Carnegie Institution of Washington, D.C., and private organizations such as the St. Augustine Historical Society, the National Society of The Colonial Dames of America in The State of Florida, and the Woman's Exchange. Though the program did not reverse the economic downturn, the program set the stage for future efforts.

The Ponce continued as a hotel. The building evolved from its position as a luxury resort for tourists to an expanded role as the social center for northeast Florida. Fewer guests used the hotel rooms, but the grand spaces continued to serve as the backdrop for sumptuous feasts and festivities.

Beginning in late 1942, the hotel became the founding headquarters for the Coast Guard Reserve. This new function enabled the massive concrete structure to remain in use and introduced a new population to St. Augustine, military service men and women. Thousands of soldiers and officers were trained on the Ponce grounds and in the hotel building. They returned with their families as tourists after World War II to enjoy the city.

The nineteenth and early twentieth centuries witnessed an interest in patriotism and heritage, as evidenced through limited successes with the preservation of historic buildings. Arguably, the most well-known story is the rescue of Mount Vernon, led by Ann Pamela Cunningham. Her all-volunteer organization, the Mount Vernon Ladies Association of the Union, raised $200,000, or about $6,000,000 today, to purchase the property after three failed governmental attempts. The Ladies Association continues to own and operate George Washington's homestead. The saving of Philadelphia's Independence Hall, Thomas Jefferson's Monticello, Newport's Touro Synagogue, and Andrew Jackson's Hermitage are other early examples.

In the initial decades of the twentieth century, successes were achieved in preserving collections of historic buildings in Charleston, New Orleans, San Antonio, Alexandria, Williamsburg, Winston-Salem, Georgetown, and Nantucket. Historic villages were developed, including Mystic Seaport, Williamsburg, Greenfield Village, and Plymouth Plantation. The Association for the Preservation of Virginia Antiquities and the Society for the Preservation of New England Antiquities preserved properties with a shared geography and history.

The New Deal programs during the Great Depression included the Historic American Buildings Survey (HABS) that retrained unemployed architects to document historic properties. St. Augustine's Spanish colonial architecture and its Flagler-era hotels were recorded. HABS chronicled more than 35,000 properties that help to illustrate the history of the nation.

In 1947, in the aftermath of World War II, the United States was focused on domestic construction projects. The American Institute of Architects was beginning preparations for its centennial anniversary a decade later. Architects, historians, and city planners, recognizing that this post-war era would result in dramatic changes to the nation's built environment, prepared a record of nationally important buildings. The Ponce figured prominently as one of only two Florida properties to be included. The other property was Frank Lloyd Wright's Florida Southern College.

During the 1950s, in anticipation of St. Augustine's 400th anniversary, an international public-private partnership was created to oversee prepa-rations. The partnership included member nations of the Pan American Union, a new means of strengthening economic and political ties between the United States and its neighbors in the Western Hemisphere. St. Au-gustine's celebration took place in the early 1960s, culminating on the an-niversary of September 8, 1965.

St. Augustine's 400th anniversary served as the motivation for a major program of physical changes to the city that reinforced its Spanish colonial heritage. About fifty properties were reconstructed, most of which were north of the Plaza de la Constitución. Infrastructure improvements en-hanced the historical ambience of the community. By this time Flagler's Hotel Alcazar was operating as the City Hall and Lightner Museum. The Hotel Cordova had reopened as the St. Johns County Courthouse and administration building. The Catholic Church constructed a new church at the Mission de Nombre de Dios and erected a cross to honor Pedro Menendez and the 1565 landing site.

Simultaneously, the United States experienced one of the nation's most tumultuous eras. As St. Augustine became immersed in activities related to the commemoration of its 400th anniversary, so, too, the city became embroiled in national events. The city served as the location for the final chapter in the Civil Rights movement as challenges were made to the ra-cial segregation in St. Augustine and throughout the South. Part of that history was made at the Hotel Ponce de Leon.

In addition, student demonstrations against the Vietnam War be-ing held at colleges throughout the nation introduced questions about the practicality of establishing a new college during such a volatile time. Though most of the demonstrations were peaceful, they represented the unrest of the era and the changing nature of the nation.

Flagler College experienced growing pains as an educational institution and in trying to fit an educational framework into a Gilded Age hotel. Hotel rooms became dormitory rooms. Hotel security and administrative offices were used for similar functions by the college. The Dining Room, renamed the Dining Hall, served as the cafeteria. The Artists' Studios housed executive offices for the FEC before becoming classrooms and faculty offices. The library moved three times to meet campus needs.

In honor of the centennial anniversary of the Ponce in 1988, the college implemented an ambitious restoration campaign overseen by a national advisory committee composed of many of the country's foremost architects, museum directors, and conservation experts. Chaired by Lawrence Lewis Jr., Henry Flagler's great-nephew and Flagler College's founder, the committee developed a program that guided preservation efforts and remains in place today.

Restoration focused on the Grand Parlor, Dining Hall, and Rotunda, with all three carefully returned to their Gilded Age splendor. Preservation efforts continued as did incorporation of historic buildings into the campus. The college acquired buildings that shared a history with the Ponce. In 2013, Flagler College completed restoration of the Ponce with a dramatic rehabilitation of the Solarium, flanking fourth floor wings, and roof terraces. The effort was completed to coincide with the 125th anniversary celebration of the Hotel Ponce de Leon's opening and the 500th anniversary of the explorer for whom the hotel was named.

Throughout this lengthy process, the college served as a resource for best practices in historic preservation and documentary research. Working with the unique materials in the Ponce—poured concrete, Portland cement mortar, terra cotta, asphalt, and Argentine pine—afforded opportunities to learn and understand preservation techniques and procedures. The college supported these efforts, retaining national and international experts to ensure the highest quality effort. Today, Flagler College is considered by experts to be a national leader and the strongest of Florida's academic institutions committed to historic preservation.

In 2012, the Florida chapter of the American Institute of Architects celebrated its 100th anniversary with a listing of the state's "Top 100 Places." Contemporary buildings were favored by member architects. However, with overwhelming public support the Ponce reinforced its reputation as a Florida icon. Photographs of the building are featured regularly in state, national, and international publicity. The building's design, detailing, and polychromatic coloring have provided a dramatic setting for films beginning with silent movies more than a century ago and continuing to the present day.

In 2013, the state of Florida commemorated the 500th anniversary of Spanish explorer Don Juan Ponce de Leon's landing on the east coast of present-day Florida. In 1885, St. Augustine inaugurated an annual festival commemorating his discovery. The city's event closed the winter tourist season in Florida and in 1888 resulted in the opening of a grand hotel named for the explorer.

The Ponce was constructed during the post–Civil War era that emphasized architecture, engineering, technology, and fine craftsmanship. The building's restoration, a process spanning nearly half a century, represents a demonstrable commitment to preservation and conservation values that developed nationally during the same time frame. Thus, the building contributes to the understanding of the historic preservation movement in the United States since the passage of the National Historic Preservation Act of 1966.

Today, the Hotel Ponce de Leon remains as Henry Flagler's most enduring legacy, stands as one of the nation's most remarkable buildings, and serves as a testimonial to Florida's emphasis on tourism. The building anchored the city's downtown from the time it opened in 1888. After more than 125 years, the building continues to command the skyline, attracting many thousands of visitors to experience the art and architecture of the Gilded Age and a unique college campus.

The Men Who Mentored a Masterpiece

As John D. Rockefeller Sr. strolled through the streets of St. Augustine, Florida, he contemplated development of this small coastal city. His visit in December of 1883 to the historic Spanish town came at the suggestion of Henry Flagler, Rockefeller's longtime friend and cofounder in Standard Oil. Flagler and his bride Ida Alice were honeymooning in St. Augustine and invited Rockefeller and his wife, Laura, to accompany them. Also, the couples celebrated Flagler's new business investments in Florida, which he had begun the year before, shortly after creation of the Standard Oil Trust.[1]

In St. Augustine, Dr. Andrew Anderson and New York tobacco baron George P. Lorillard entertained the couples at Markland, Anderson's estate a block west of town. Both men were promoting investment in St. Augustine. Lorillard Villa, located at St. George and Hypolita Streets, featured an elaborate Victorian residence identified by its striking windmill that pierced the skyline of the former Spanish city. The property commanded the commercial downtown and foretold a new period of development for the city.[2]

A few weeks later, two more northerners, Thomas Edison and his wife Mary, made their second of three consecutive winter sojourns to St. Augustine. While staying at the Magnolia Hotel, Edison heard tales of an enormous shark that had eluded capture for years. He chartered the Magnolia and its Captain Whitney, embarked with Mrs. Edison and some friends, and went fishing. Shortly after they entered open water, the shark appeared. Edison threw out a line of insulated electrical wire attached to an electric battery. Some three hours later, he captured the fifteen-foot, 700-pound animal. The following day newspapers nationwide reported the story of the electric bait and the demon shark.[3]

Louis Comfort Tiffany, New York interior decorator and glass artisan, had collaborated with Edison on several projects. He visited St. Augustine with his family during this same era. While in the city Tiffany painted local scenes, including two sites south of the plaza, a date palm tree and the courtyard façade of the Segui-Kirby Smith House (now the St. Augustine Historical Society Research Library). Two views featured Fort Marion (Castillo de San Marcos), *Carriage Waiting beside a Wall* and *An Old Fort at St. Augustine, Florida*. In April of 1883, Tiffany introduced the latter work and *A Study in St. Augustine* at New York's National Academy Museum and School of Fine Arts' annual exhibition.[4]

The convergence of these northeasterners in St. Augustine in the 1880s signaled a new chapter in the ancient city's colorful history. Flagler wrote this chapter with help from his business associates and some talented men, including Edison and Tiffany. Launched with a resort hotel, ultimately Flagler was credited with the creation of modern Florida and as the father of Florida tourism. More than his many successes with Standard Oil, his legacy was development of the southernmost frontier of Florida. In 1933, fifty years after Rockefeller's first visit to the sunshine state, he reminisced, "He [H. M. Flagler] undertook, single handed, the task of building up the East Coast of Florida. He was not satisfied to plan a railroad from St. Augustine to Key West—a distance of more than six hundred miles, which would have been regarded as an undertaking large enough for almost any one man—but in addition he has built a chain of superb hotels to induce tourists to go to this newly developed country."[5]

By the time that the Rockefellers and the Flaglers wintered in St. Augustine, the men had been business partners for fifteen years, since 1867 when they founded Standard Oil. By the 1880s they controlled the oil industry. Their business relationship mirrored an equally close friendship. They proved to be inseparable and undefeatable, friends and business partners. The men lived near each other, first on prestigious Euclid Avenue in Cleveland. Then the families moved to New York where they lived across the street from each other at Fifth Avenue and 54th Street on Manhattan's fashionable Millionaire's Row.[6]

On January 10, 1870, Rockefeller and Flagler and three other Ohio businessmen formed the Standard Oil Company. The youthful Rockefeller, thirty years old, and his brother William, twenty-eight, served as president and vice president, respectively. Flagler, the senior partner at age forty, served as secretary-treasurer and was the legal mind of the company as well. Samuel Andrews and Flagler's brother-in-law Stephen V. Harkness held minority financial interests.[7]

On January 2, 1882, Flagler celebrated his fifty-second birthday with Rockefeller and seven other men by creating the Standard Oil Trust. That action concluded Flagler's direct participation in daily operations of Standard Oil, though he continued to assist Rockefeller with policy and legal decisions. He remained as a company trustee until 1911 when the U.S. Supreme Court found the company to be a monopoly in violation of U.S. antitrust laws and dissolved the corporation.[8]

Also in 1882, Flagler began to diversify his business interests. Railroad entrepreneur Henry Bradley Plant enlisted Flagler, Henry Sanford, and eight other northern businessmen, incorporating the Plant Investment Company (PICO) in Plant's home state of Connecticut. The corporation served as a legal mechanism through which the partners developed Florida. Flagler and Plant maintained a personal friendship and several business partnerships focused on promoting the nation's southernmost frontier, Florida.[9]

Though Plant had resided in Georgia for many years, 1882 marked the thirtieth consecutive year that he had wintered in Florida. His inaugural visit in 1853 by steamship from Savannah to Jacksonville to improve his wife's health had included a buggy excursion southward along the Old King's Road, present-day U.S. Route 1, to St. Augustine. In 1879, Plant began investing in Florida land and railroads. His passion for development continued over the next two decades. When Plant died in 1899, he left a legacy that included 2,000 miles of Georgia and Gulf Coast railroads, steamships, towns, villages, and hotels: the Tampa Bay Hotel and the Inn at Port Tampa, the Belleview Biltmore Hotel near Clearwater, the Hotel Kissimmee, the Hotel Seminole near Winter Park, and the Ocala House.[10]

In 1870, along the St. Johns River in what was south Florida, Henry Sanford founded a town to which he gave his name. Over the next decade, he developed Sanford, built infrastructure along the waterfront, and maintained the citrus grove Belair. In 1881, Sanford's friend and fellow Connecticut businessman Hamilton Disston bought 4,000,000 acres of Florida from the state government. Two years later, Disston incorporated the town of Kissimmee west of Sanford. PICO's first investment in Florida was the acquisition of the South Florida Railroad that linked Sanford and Kissimmee.[11]

Additional PICO members included Baltimore businessmen and close friends William Thompson Walters and Benjamin Franklin "Frank" Newcomer of the Northern Central Railway. Newcomer served as president of the Union Railroad Company and as a director of the Philadelphia, Wilmington and Baltimore Railroad Company. These two men merged interests into the Atlantic Coast Line Company, now CSX Railroad.[12]

PICO partners included Edward B. Haskell, co-owner of the *Boston Herald* and an investor in the South Florida Railroad. Also participating was New Yorker Morris Ketchum Jesup, banker, philanthropist, patron of the Metropolitan Museum of Art, and president of the American Museum of Natural History. Connecticut railroad executive George H. Tilley joined. Plant included his Connecticut family members, his half-brother Horace P. Hoadley, and his brother-in-law Lorenzo Blackstone, a banker, railroad developer, and politician. Plant's other brother-in-law and personal attorney was Judge Lynde Harrison, a business investor and career legislator.[13]

The PICO members and their colleague Disston shared several characteristics. None served in the Civil War; all benefitted from the conflict. Each achieved business success, amassed wealth, exerted political influence, patronized the arts, and enjoyed an elite social status. Collectively, they controlled rail lines and transportation enterprises. They based their empires in northern cities. Yet, the active partners spent time in Florida and reveled in these experiences. Their impact on Florida remains unparalleled.[14]

Their investments in the southernmost frontier began at the time when that frontier began at Orlando and terminated at the Florida Keys. In 1845, Florida had become the nation's twenty-seventh state, without a physical survey of the entire land area. The coasts had been explored and featured sparse settlements. The interior, known for a time as the Mosquito Coast, described aptly the swampland that predominated. The largest cities by population were Key West, St. Augustine, and Pensacola.

In 1892, after Flagler and Plant were well established in Florida, they formed another business arrangement. On June 22, the summer after Henry Plant opened the Tampa Bay Hotel and the year before Flagler opened his Royal Poinciana Hotel in Palm Beach, the men forged an alliance to control rail transportation in Florida. They secured the bounds of their Florida empires.[15]

Transportation interests brought the men together and became one of their most important ventures. In fewer than twenty years, PICO controlled thousands of Florida's 8,725,000 acres devoted to railroads, including lines that ran the length of the state. They shared business connections via railroads that crossed the nation to the Pacific coast as well. Their vast transportation network carried commercial cargo and industrial materials. Equally important, the routes brought wealthy northerners and Europeans to Flagler's, Plant's, and Sanford's hotels.[16]

Paralleling rapid expansion of railroad lines throughout the United States and across Canada was a movement to use property near rail lines for development of resorts for wealthy travelers. Hundreds of resorts were built in elaborate architectural designs, featured modern technology, and included contemporary comforts. They dotted the Atlantic and Pacific coasts, the waterways and mountains east of the Mississippi River, and the western mountain ranges of the United States and Canada.[17]

Some hotels built during this era continue to operate as hotels today and illustrate the geographic diversity of the trend. They include the Driskill Hotel (1886), Austin, Texas; Hotel Monteleone (1886), New Orleans, Louisiana; Grand Hotel (1887), Mackinac Island, Michigan; Grand Hotel (1887), Block Island, Rhode Island; Hotel del Coronado (1888), Coronado, California; Banff Springs Hotel (1888), Banff, Canada; Hotel Jerome (1889), Vail, Colorado; the Brown Palace (1888–1893), Denver, Colorado; the Copper Queen Hotel (1898–1902), Bisbee, Arizona; and the Mount Washington Hotel (1899–1901), Bretton Woods, New Hampshire. Many shared clientele who traveled between the hotels to enjoy the varied tourist seasons throughout the year.

PICO's incorporation and Henry Flagler's financial investment in St. Augustine coincided with the development of these Gilded Age hotels. As investors nationally recognized that the west and Florida were ripe for development, Flagler realized that St. Augustine's location, climate, and

European ambience provided the small town with a unique position in the coastal South.[18]

In early 1885, the Flaglers and Rockefellers returned to Florida. The Flaglers arrived in Jacksonville on February 19, staying at the St. James Hotel before heading to St. Augustine on February 25. Both couples stayed at the new San Marco Hotel located just north of the City Gate. The property afforded views toward Fort Marion and Matanzas Bay. Opened in 1884 by Bostonian Isaac Cruft and managed by veteran New England hotelier O. D. (Osborn Dunlap) Seavey, the San Marco satisfied northerners' expectations for luxurious accommodations supported by nearby arts, culture, and recreation. After Cruft's death in 1889, his heirs sold the San Marco Hotel to Standard Oil partner Pennsylvanian William Warden whose winter "castle" was located north of Fort Marion and diagonally across the street from the hotel.[19]

Beginning in 1875 with New Hampshire's Maplewood Hotel, Cruft established his reputation as a summer resort developer. Located in the White Mountains in a landscaped setting replete with formal gardens, the hotel afforded luxury and comfort during July and August, the season there: "With a capacity of over 350 people, the interior contained several new dining rooms and parlors, a large hall with stage, game rooms, an ample lobby (office), and over 130 bedrooms, each lit with gas and connected to the office by ingenious speaking tubes."[20] By 1886, under Cruft's ownership, the advertised Palace Hotel of the Mountains expanded to serve more than 500 guests. The site included a hunting park, an observatory, a farm that provided food for the hotel, and a freshwater reservoir. In addition to the Maplewood, Seavey managed Cruft's first Florida resort, the Magnolia Springs Hotel in Green Cove Springs west of St. Augustine. As did many New York industrialists, the Standard Oil cofounders enjoyed summer vacations in the White Mountains. Cruft's and Seavey's reputations may have inspired the Standard Oil partners' choice of lodging and, possibly, influenced Henry Flagler's decision to embark on a new career developing resorts in Florida.[21]

Providing luxury accommodations for travelers had begun before the Civil War and exploded with popularity as the nation rebuilt after the war. Flagler capitalized on his business connections and social network to raise the standards for resort development. He had maneuvered Standard Oil

FIGURE 1.1. St. Augustine hosted the Ponce de Leon Day celebration, recognizing the Spanish explorer who christened the land "La Florida" in 1513. Ponce de Leon Day celebration 1909, St. Augustine Historical Society Research Library.

masterfully to a position as the nation's most successful company. He set out to achieve equally unparalleled success with the development of Florida resorts and railroads.

In March 1885, as St. Augustine's winter season concluded, the Flaglers prepared to return to New York. The Rockefellers had already done so, though perhaps regrettably for at least half of the couple. Rockefeller noted in a business letter to Flagler dated March 17, St. Patrick's Day, that the temperature that morning in New York was fourteen degrees, cold, and windy. Assuming that Rockefeller used the railway mail service, the modern method for delivery of correspondence, the letter would have required about three days travel time on a newly launched route from New York City through Charlotte, North Carolina, to Jacksonville, Florida. The information would have reached Flagler shortly before the end of his warm, sunny vacation.[22]

To close the winter season in grand style and pay homage to the famous Spanish explorer, St. Augustine launched the inaugural Ponce de Leon Festival on March 27, 1885, and drew the largest attendance in the city's history (fig. 1.1). Considering the crowds that attended, most likely the Flaglers enjoyed the festivities.

Three days later, Henry Flagler bought his first parcel of Florida land, part of Dr. Andrew Anderson's Markland. With this purchase he reinforced his ties to PICO and launched his own real estate empire. With Anderson's help, Flagler gained title to an entire block immediately west of the center of St. Augustine. To achieve his vision, he had buildings moved and redirected filled portions of Maria Sanchez Creek.[23]

At this same time another development was in its embryonic stages, one that would further Flagler's ambitions. In March 1885, several New York industrialists began development of a resort enclave, the legal arrangements for which were finalized the following December 9. The Jekyl Island Club is located on the island near Brunswick, Georgia, 110 miles north of St. Augustine and easily accessible by rail. Club members adopted the "Jekyll" spelling in 1929. Members enjoyed the winter months at the club, then went to Florida, typically in February. Flagler's ties to the club included family members and business colleagues, such as J. P. Morgan, William Rockefeller, William K. Vanderbilt, Edward Stephen Harkness, and Morris Ketchum Jesup. Designers for Jekyl's buildings belied New York connections. Flagler recommended architect Charles Gifford, designer of several Jekyl Island buildings, for work on White Mountain resorts. In St. Augustine, between 1899 and 1901, Gifford orchestrated a Beaux Arts transformation of the coquina stone plantation house at Markland for Flagler's friend Dr. Anderson.[24]

Upon his return to New York City in April 1885, Flagler chose a new firm founded by two young architects as designers for his St. Augustine hotel. John Merven Carrère was twenty-six years old, and Thomas Hastings Jr. had just turned twenty-five. In 1877, Flagler had joined West Presbyterian Church in New York City where Thomas Hastings Sr. served as pastor. Hastings Jr., a lifelong New Yorker, enjoyed a reputation for attention to details, "ironclad integrity, serious purpose, exacting thoroughness, and a measure of personal dullness."[25]

An intertwined series of familial connections between Flagler, Hastings, and the Benedict family added to the intricacy of the relationship. On the professional side, Flagler knew of Hastings' training at the École des Beaux-Arts and Carrère and Hastings' work for the firm of McKim, Mead & White. In October 1883, Flagler had retained that firm to redesign his newly acquired country house. The forty-room residence was set on a twenty-eight-acre spit of land known as Satan's Toe at the end of the Orienta Point peninsula in Mamaroneck, New York. Hastings designed the library. Following the building's complete renovation, Flagler renamed the property Lawn Beach.[26]

John Merven Carrère's strengths included developing and implementing large-scale concepts. Born in Brazil to a French father and Scottish mother and boarding-school educated in Switzerland, his cosmopolitan background made him an effective diplomat negotiating with clients, suppliers, and employees. He kept projects moving in contrast to Hastings' introverted, detail-oriented personality that thrived on orchestration of elaborate architectural designs. In 1894, after the close of the Columbian Exposition, Carrère's architectural abilities were recognized. He was offered the position of supervising architect for the United States Government. He declined, possibly as his firm was busy with commissions in the northeastern United States and in Florida. Both men enjoyed the recognition that their talents, skills, and contacts fostered.[27]

Flagler's decision to give the new Carrère & Hastings firm its first major commission resulted in a building that remains recognized as the firm's most original and unique creation. More than a century later, the remarkable design, construction, and detailing of the Hotel Ponce de Leon continue to garner praise. The building has been acclaimed as the nation's most monumental and unique building of the era.[28]

The assignment of orchestrating grand spaces for guests to assemble, dine, dance, enjoy recreation, and listen to music added to the challenge. The architects were unfamiliar with hotel design. Later, Hastings recalled that the complexity of the building and success of the design were the result of the great length of time spent planning before the contractors broke ground for the foundation.[29]

McGuire and McDonald's experience was limited to frame construction. Recognizing the newness of monolithic concrete and his builders' unfamiliarity with the material, Flagler revised his original proposal to the architects. He requested more than a mere sketch. The Carrère & Hastings firm designed the five-building complex and served as construction supervisors. The partners oversaw selection of materials and the use of techniques and processes. Hastings is credited with details on the exterior and interior. Particularly for this time period, the architects' level of participation was unusual. They elevated the importance of resort hotel design and construction. The architects displayed an unparalleled talent to design large spaces and a unique ability to work with concrete construction well ahead of their contemporaries. Also, the architects adapted the Renaissance vocabulary learned in Paris to challenges in the United States.[30]

Both Carrère and Hastings spent significant amounts of time in St. Augustine and Jacksonville to fulfill the myriad of tasks necessary to complete the construction. In addition to launching the firm, Carrère benefitted from an enhanced personal life from his time in the region. In 1886, he married Marion Dell of Jacksonville, daughter of Seminole War military commander Colonel Charles Dell.[31]

In 1900, Thomas Hastings married Helen Benedict, reinforcing the complex and longstanding Flagler-Hastings-Benedict family connections. Earlier, his brother Frank had married her cousin Caroline Fanning, and her brother Frederick Benedict had been married to Flagler's daughter Jennie Louise who died in 1889. In 1901, Carrère & Hastings designed Flagler's spectacular residence for Flagler's third wife and new bride, the former Mary Lily Kenan. Thanks to Flagler and Kenan descendants, the palatial marble Whitehall (1901–1903) overlooking Lake Worth has been preserved as the Henry Morrison Flagler Museum.[32]

Flagler's patronage of Carrère & Hastings continued after completion of the Ponce. The firm designed more buildings for Flagler, including several in St. Augustine that remain in a high state of preservation: the Hotel Alcazar (1887–1889) now the Lightner Building, Grace [United] Methodist Church (1887), and Flagler Memorial Presbyterian Church (1889–1890) with the Flagler family mausoleum addition (1906). They designed Flagler's residence Kirkside (1893), which was demolished in 1950. The Carrère & Hastings firm designed Flagler's hotels throughout Florida's east coast.

With completion of Flagler's St. Augustine's hotels, the architects' reputation as hotel designers was established. By 1888, the firm had been retained to design a major addition to the Waumbek Hotel in the White Mountains at Jefferson, New Hampshire. Theirs was the first of several transformations that enabled the building to become one of the nation's most luxurious hotels. Though more regimented architecturally than the

Ponce, the firm's Laurel-in-the-Pines hotel opened in 1891 in Lakewood, New Jersey, and reaffirmed their skill in designing resorts.[33]

Carrère and Hastings participated in the World's Columbian Exposition of 1893 in Chicago, designing the Walter Baker and Co. pavilion that overlooked the lake in the Manufactures area. A few years later, Carrère chaired the Pan-American Exposition held in Buffalo in 1901 and designed the McKinley Monument erected there in 1907, memorializing the president who was assassinated during the Exposition. The architectural firm designed more than 600 buildings, including the Jefferson Hotel (1895) in Richmond, Virginia, the Cannon House and Russell Senate Office Buildings (1903–1908) in Washington, D.C., and the New York Public Library (1897–1911).[34]

Carrère died in a traffic accident shortly before completion of this last project. Hastings continued using the firm name until his death in 1929. In 1912, Hastings was appointed chair of the team responsible for the Pan-Pacific Exposition of 1915. His Tower of Jewels at 435 feet high was the centerpiece of the construction. Though McKim, Mead, & White was the more prominent firm, many experts consider the protégés Carrère and Hastings to have been the more talented partnership.[35]

The Carrère & Hastings firm's ties to Flagler continued after their patron's death in 1913. Dramatically, Hastings expanded the firm's Beaux Arts repertoire with the design in 1922 of the thirty-one-story Standard Oil Company building at 26 Broadway in New York City for John D. Rockefeller, Jr.[36]

In 1928, Hastings designed a small classical Greek theater for Robert Worth Bingham of Louisville, Kentucky. At the same time Hastings designed the Louisville Memorial Auditorium, a project Bingham influenced as well. In 1908, the Carrère & Hastings firm had designed a country house east of Louisville for James Ross Todd, a property with which Bingham was familiar. In 1916, the recently widowed Bingham married the former Mary Lily Kenan, a sweetheart from his University of North Carolina days. She was an older sister of his friend William Rand Kenan Jr., and she was the widow of Henry Flagler. The Binghams spent part of their short marriage at her Carrère & Hastings–designed residence, Whitehall, where they entertained friends and family, including Thomas and Helen Hastings.

Mary Lily Flagler Bingham died nine months after the marriage at age 40. Shortly before her death she added a codicil to her will giving Bingham $5 million with which he purchased two newspapers from Henry Watterson, the *Louisville Daily Journal* and *Louisville Morning Courier*. Watterson and Hastings worked together on Perry's Victory Memorial completed in 1921. The U.S. Congress commissioned the project for the centennial anniversary of the War of 1812. As did Henry Flagler, Watterson wintered in Florida and shared friendships with President and Mrs. Cleveland, writer and actor Joseph Jefferson, and actress Helena Modjeska.[37]

Carrère & Hastings added staff architects who assisted with the Hotel Ponce de Leon and, upon its completion, enjoyed successful careers. Bernard Maybeck and Emmanuel Masqueray joined the firm in its early years. Both headed west from New York to less developed sections of the United States where they honed their skills, Maybeck to California and Masqueray to Minnesota. Training at the École des Beaux-Arts and the popularity of World's Fairs and similar events launched each architect to prominence in his own right in the late nineteenth century.

For decades, scholars have debated architect Bernard Maybeck's contributions to the Ponce. Recent research and newly discovered primary source documents lend additional credence to the important relationship between the architect and the building. Maybeck joined the Carrère & Hastings' firm in 1886, during the building's construction. Hastings and Maybeck had studied together in the atelier of Jules Andre at the École de Beaux-Arts in Paris. Following completion of the St. Augustine projects, Maybeck moved westward, first to Chicago where he attended the Columbian Exposition. Then in California he enjoyed a rich and lengthy career and was recognized as one of that state's five most influential architects.[38]

In 1952, preservation architect Frederick D. Nichols interviewed the frail 91-year-old Maybeck. Nichols followed that interview by corresponding with him through his wife, Annie White Maybeck, and noted that Maybeck was particularly proud of his work on the Ponce. Years later, Nichols orchestrated restoration of Thomas Jefferson's Monticello and the University of Virginia Rotunda. Also, a quarter century after his interview with Maybeck, Nichols served on the national committee that oversaw restoration of the Hotel Ponce de Leon's Dining Room. Perhaps he enjoyed the opportunity to help preserve Maybeck's early work.[39]

FIGURE 1.2. View of Dining Room, facing south. The main hall features elaborately carved woodwork, decorative murals, and stained glass. Library of Congress,
Prints & Photographs Division, HABS. Reproduction Number: HABS FLA,
55.SAUG, 45-7.

Years apart in their writing, Flagler's biographer Edward Akin and Carrère & Hastings' expert Laurie Ossman credited Maybeck with design and
construction for the Ponce. Other Maybeck scholars, his contemporary
Jean Murray Bangs and the architect's protégé Kenneth Cardwell, authors
Sally Woodbridge and Richard Reinhardt strongly championed Maybeck's importance to the Ponce. Reinhardt in particular cited as evidence
of Maybeck's participation the fanciful and exuberant decoration in the
Dining Room and the central dome with its flanking terraces (fig. 1.2).[40]

During Maybeck's lifetime, Wayne Andrews prepared a social history for the American Institute of Architects' centennial anniversary and

FIGURE 1.3. Tower of Jewels by Thomas Hastings was the centerpiece of San Francisco's Panama-Pacific International Exposition in 1915 and is considered to be one of the greatest examples of Beaux Arts design. San Francisco History Center, San Francisco Public Library.

declared that the Ponce was Carrère & Hastings' most creative design. The striking use of brick and concrete to create a polychromatic effect is particularly effective. Concrete authority Carl Condit enthusiastically echoed that the materials, textures, and colors "give it a playful and exotic quality that suggests the hand of an imaginative architect. The commission went to Carrère and Hastings, but the real author was Bernard Maybeck, then a designer with the New York firm."[41]

California architect Mark Wilson shared a friendship with Maybeck's daughter-in-law and had access to newly discovered family papers. In his 2011 biography he cites as verification of Maybeck's pivotal role in the design details from the family records and signed sketches published in *American Architect and Building News* at the Ponce's opening.[42]

Maybeck's father, Bernhardt Maybeck, chief architectural woodcarver with the New York interiors firm of Pottier & Stymus, oversaw fabrication and installation of the Ponce's elaborate wood ornamental architectural elements. His son's fondness for the creative and vigorous use of wood throughout his architectural career reflects his work with his father in New York and St. Augustine.[43]

Maybeck remained lifelong friends with Hastings. The latter was president of the American Institute of Architects when, in January 1912, he was appointed to the Architectural Commission for the Panama-Pacific Exposition. Maybeck had chaired the Department of Architecture at the University of California–Berkeley. His creative designs for the Palace of Fine Arts were accepted enthusiastically by the Architectural Commission. Writing in 1965 after the New York World's Fair, architectural historian

FIGURE 1.4. Bernard Maybeck's Palace of Fine Arts is the one building remaining from the Exposition and was creatively updated for its 100th anniversary in 2015. San Francisco History Center, San Francisco Public Library.

Marcus Whiffen recognized Hastings' Tower of Jewels (fig. 1.3) and May-beck's Palace of Fine Arts (fig. 1.4) as two of the nation's four best repre-sentative examples of Beaux-Arts Classicism.[44]

Carrère and Frenchman Emmanuel Masqueray participated in Charles-Jean Laisné's atelier while at the École. Masqueray possessed a talent that was identified early and cultivated for creating picturesque representations of buildings. In 1887, Carrère invited Masqueray to join the firm. Though titled a "draughtsman," his artistic skills provided an advantage to the firm and gained him personal success as well. Francis Swales, writing shortly after Masqueray's death, noted the importance of his renderings of the Ponce to the architect's career.

Masqueray prepared watercolors of the façade as part of the record for the construction and the architectural marketing of Carrère & Hastings. One of the watercolors featured the completed front elevation of the build-ing. A second watercolor highlighted the east section of that elevation, and the third showcased the elaborate entrance. Masqueray remained with Carrère & Hastings until 1892. Over the next several years his work with other firms focused on designs and renderings for the World's Columbian Exposition in Chicago (1893) and the Louisiana Purchase Exposition in St. Louis (1904). He is most noted for his elaborate designs of churches and cathedrals, both Roman Catholic and Protestant, in Minnesota and Kansas.[45]

In 1881 Boston hotel investor Isaac Cruft had retained New England shipbuilder James McGuire to rebuild the fire-ravaged Magnolia Hotel along the St. Johns River steamship route at Magnolia Springs (now Green Cove Springs), eighteen miles west of St. Augustine. In 1884, satisfied with the result, Cruft hired McGuire and his new partner, another New Eng-lander, Joseph A. McDonald, to build the San Marco Hotel north of St. Augustine's City Gate. Flagler employed the "Macks" to construct his St. Augustine hotel (fig. 1.5). In 2007, during restoration of the marble and mahogany men's room located off the main lobby, a print advertisement for "McGuire and McDonald" was found behind the brass upper hinge at the entry door.[46]

Following construction of the Ponce, Flagler employed McGuire and McDonald for construction of the Hotel Alcazar and other St. Augustine buildings, including residences built as ancillary structures to the hotels.

FIGURE 1.5. Construction of Dining Room Rotunda. Construction of the vaulted ceiling in the main hall of the Dining Room and the curved venido wings illustrated the challenging nature of the construction. The rectangular facilities building has framing to accommodate another section of poured-in-place crushed coquina concrete. Photocopy of an undated photograph (original in files of Hotel Ponce de Leon), Library of Congress, Prints & Photographs Division, HABS, Reproduction Number: HABS FLA, 55.SAUG, 45-12.

The Osborn Seavey (Union Generals') House reflected the polychromatic appearance of the hotels and served as the residence for the general manager. Ponce de Leon Cottage (Thompson Hall) was built as half of a pair of twin cottages provided for guests who preferred privacy beyond that available in the hotels. Casa Amarylla (Wiley Hall) and its accompanying Power Plant (Palm Cottage) were constructed in 1898 and served the hotel physician. McGuire and McDonald maintained an office in the Ponce, reaffirming readily available and high quality services to the hotels' owner and his guests.[47]

Flagler retained the duo to expand the Hotel Ormond (1891), construct Palm Beach's Royal Poinciana (1895) and The Breakers (1905), Miami's Royal Palm (1897), and Nassau, Bahamas' The Colonial (1899). The architects and builders joined together for construction of Henry Flagler's Palm Beach mansion, Whitehall, completed in 1902, and for the Flagler mausoleum addition to Memorial Presbyterian Church in 1906. Their skills increased as did Flagler's confidence in their abilities and his resorts moved southward down the Atlantic coast.[48]

McGuire remained based in St. Augustine, overseeing repairs to Flagler's buildings. In 1891, Flagler added the Valencia Hotel to his St. Augustine holdings, entrusting the construction and then the ownership to McGuire. In contrast, McDonald joined the migration down the east coast of Florida to Miami. There he purchased hotels and related businesses. He served on boards of directors and as an elected official, and participated in the community.[49]

Assisting McGuire and McDonald was engineer William Kennish Jr., who was credited with demonstrating significant engineering talents for the many creative and pioneering construction methods and materials used on the Ponce. He had worked on the Erie Canal and prepared the concrete used in the construction and testing of the Hanover Portland cement used in the Ponce (fig. 1.6). At the same time he was employed in the construction of the hotel, he served as chief inspector for the 70-foot-tall concrete plinth, or base, in New York Harbor on which the pedestal and Statue of Liberty would stand and be dedicated in October of 1886. Also, Kennish and William Hammer oversaw the hydraulics for artesian well drilling. Kennish recognized the importance of the underground springs in and around St. Augustine and the possibilities of using the water as a power source. Five years later, as he was preparing to patent a number of his inventions, he died suddenly, cutting short his engineering contributions, while adding importance to his work on the Ponce.[50]

Over the winter of 1882–1883 interior designer Louis Comfort Tiffany celebrated completion of two major commissions by vacationing in St. Augustine with his ailing wife Mary and their children. In 1881, at the request of President Chester A. Arthur, Tiffany redecorated a suite of state rooms in the Executive Mansion, which was renamed the White House

FIGURE 1.6. The Hotel Ponce de Leon facing King Street before construction of the central dome and towers. Additional sections of the building to the north await construction as well. Hotel Ponce de Leon, construction of corner towers, St. Augustine Historical Society Research Library.

in 1901. Also in 1881, author Samuel Clemens and his wife, Livy, retained Tiffany's interior design firm to transform their home in Connecticut.[51]

During this same period the artist's father, jeweler Charles Lewis Tiffany, commissioned the prestigious architectural firm of McKim, Mead & White to design a residence for his family in New York City. In 1883, in the midst of that construction, Thomas Hastings joined that firm. Also at about that time, the younger Tiffany dissolved his Associated Artists business and founded Louis C. Tiffany and Company. He worked with the architects in creating the interiors of his parents' house.[52]

FIGURE 1.7. This grouping of art glass windows is half of a pair that flanks the central staircase and visually directs the visitor from the Lobby floor to the Mezzanine. Reproduced with permission from Steven Brooke Studios.

In 1880, Louis Tiffany worked with Thomas Edison on Steele MacKaye's Madison Square Theatre. James Steele MacKaye is most well-known for orchestrating Buffalo Bill's Wild West Show and for establishing the nation's first acting school, later the American Academy of Dramatic Arts. Then, in 1884, Tiffany collaborated with Edison on the creative lighting scheme for MacKaye's Lyceum Theater in New York that opened the following spring as the nation's first fully electrified theatre. Several months later, Tiffany and Edison joined Hastings and the team responsible for the creation of the Ponce. Tiffany's biographer Robert Koch credited the designer's influence, writing "it was likely that the industrialist had consulted with the artist before making his first move."[53]

The Ponce serves as a rare example of Tiffany's work. He is credited with decorative plaster ceilings and the eleven Austrian crystal chandeliers in the Grand Parlor, known now as the Flagler Room. During this era he was known for his interiors; his original glass designs were just beginning. Koch recognized Tiffany as responsible for the interiors and the stained glass used in the hotel.[54]

Tiffany's contributions included windows flanking the main entry doors, along the staircases leading from the Rotunda to the Dining Room (now Dining Hall), and on either side of the west entrance to the Dining Room (fig. 1.7). The classical designs of the clerestory windows in the rectangular main section of the Dining Room and their companion windows framing the curved *venido,* or welcoming, rooms that flank the Dining Room provide remarkable light and complement the murals on the walls and ceilings. Even minor spaces received treatment: both sides of the baggage entrance and the north side of the carriageway. Tiffany created a total of seventy-nine stained glass windows for the building.[55]

At the conclusion of the construction, Tiffany returned to New York. In 1888, he exhibited The Old Governor's House at St. Augustine, Florida, in the Indianapolis Art Association's annual show. In 1905, his creation, Cornelius and the Angel, was gifted to Trinity Episcopal Church located a block east of the Ponce. Over the decades he enjoyed Florida winters and continued to paint images there as well. Beginning in 1921 he built a winter home, Comfort Lodge, on Brickell Avenue in Miami. He celebrated his 80th birthday on February 18, 1928, on Miami Beach. Tiffany's Miami residence was destroyed in the Labor Day Hurricane of 1935 and sold by his estate shortly thereafter to benefit the Tiffany Foundation.[56]

From late April through May of 1887, as construction on the Hotel Ponce de Leon concluded, Tiffany enlisted his friend and colleague Maitland Armstrong to orchestrate installation of the Dining Room windows. This collaboration emphasizes the creative and energetic nature evident throughout the Ponce, reinforcing the unique and important contributions of the artists. Regarding design of the windows, Armstrong's biographer and stained glass artisan Robert O. Jones contended that the windows evidence the work of multiple talented artisans. The circular windows flanking the front doors feature Moorish designs typical of Tiffany. Armstrong's designs with Renaissance motifs are reflected in the Dining Room's half-round clerestory windows that sport flaming urns (fig. 1.8).[57]

Armstrong strengthened his ties to Northeast Florida with this project and shortly thereafter established his own stained glass studio. Since 1869, his older brother Gouverneur Armstrong had spent time at Hibernia on the west bank of the St. Johns River, about 25 miles inland from St. Augustine. There he became friends with the Fleming family. In 1878, Margaret Fleming built a small church on part of the former plantation, and the elder Armstrong participated as church treasurer. Maitland Armstrong & Company provided four windows that resulted in the tiny mission Episcopal church achieving a reputation for remarkable stained glass windows.[58]

Over the next several years, Armstrong expanded his artistic talents. He participated on the planning team for the World's Columbian Exposition in Chicago in 1893 with fellow Ponce artist George W. Maynard. Upon his brother's death in 1899, Armstrong inherited and then acquired additional acreage at Hibernia. He and his wife enjoyed time there over the next three decades. Between 1900 and 1910 Armstrong created windows for St. Augustine's Trinity Episcopal Church. The congregation included numerous Fleming relatives and their cousins, and prominent St. Augustine residents, including the Fatios, Dunhams, and Colts.[59]

During the winter of 1884–1885 Thomas Edison returned to St. Augustine for his third visit. This time his daughter Marion (nicknamed Dot) and his friends Ezra and Lillian Gilliland accompanied the recently widowed inventor. The sojourn to St. Augustine followed a trip to New Orleans for the World Industrial and Cotton Centennial that featured some

FIGURE 1.8. Ten windows in a clerestory illuminate the murals in the main hall of the hotel Dining Room. Their cauldron pattern is credited to artisan Maitland Armstrong. Reproduced with permission from Steven Brooke Studios.

of Edison's telephone inventions. In late March, the group returned to New York, a few days before St. Augustine closed its winter season with the inaugural Ponce de Leon Day celebration.[60]

During at least one of Edison's trips to St. Augustine, he visited Franklin Smith at his new home, the Villa Zorayda. He corresponded with Smith's family for many years. As an inventor Edison was impressed particularly with concrete as a new building material. Afterwards he invested considerable time and money in the use of concrete for housing and furniture. Also, he improved the composition of Portland cement.[61]

In 1886, newly remarried to Mina Miller, Edison returned to Florida, this time to the warmer Gulf climate of Fort Myers, where he and Gilliland had bought thirteen acres of waterfront land the previous year. There they built winter homes, and Edison constructed a laboratory. Edison remained a part-time resident of Florida throughout his lifetime. In addition to his lengthy stays at his Gulf coast property he traveled via the Florida East Coast railroad the length of the state, from Jacksonville to Key West.[62]

The Edison United Manufacturing Company supplied steam power and electricity to the Hotel Ponce de Leon (fig. 1.9). Thomas Hastings' older brother, Frank S. Hastings, served as a chief executive officer after a tenure as secretary and treasurer, and he may have influenced the decision to choose Edison. The Ponce was operated by four Babcock and Wilcox boilers and an equal number of forty-five kilowatt direct current steam dynamos. These were powered by three Armington & Sims engines produced in Providence, Rhode Island. Each of the smaller 60 horsepower engines powered an Edison 640-light dynamo, with the larger 125-horsepower engine driving a pair of No. 16 dynamos.[63]

Edison's chief assistant William J. Hammer oversaw "completion and starting of the 8,000-light plant of the Ponce de Leon Hotel at St. Augustine, Fla., which at that time was the largest isolated incandescent lighting plant ever constructed."[64] This statement was made in 1909 and appears to reflect additions over time to the original lighting system. Lights were located throughout the building in the public spaces, the hallways, and the hotel rooms. This convenience had become the custom in fine hotels since 1882 at New York's Hotel Everett. Company records dated May 1, 1888, state that 2,000 lights were added to achieve a total of 4,100 for the Ponce and Flagler's second hotel, the Alcazar.[65]

Carrère & Hastings designed the 100 gilded papier-mâché lions' heads light fixtures added in 1893 to the friezes framing the Rotunda and Dining Room. The lights enabled greater appreciation of the ceiling decorations and were a dramatic addition to the dark woodwork of the friezes. These fixtures replaced the metal chandelier, consisting of two electrified hoops. Electrification added the Hotel Ponce de Leon to a prestigious list of modern buildings in the United States.[66]

In 1883, George Willoughby Maynard, Carrère, and Hastings worked together on a project designed by architect Stanford White in Baltimore. Maynard, a preeminent painter and muralist, rejoined the architects to work on the Ponce. There he created the allegorical female figures in oil on plaster on the ceilings of the Rotunda and in the Dining Room. Two

FIGURE 1.9. Rear view of the Hotel Ponce de Leon, from Flagler Memorial Presbyterian Church. A polychromatic brick and concrete smokestack identified the Edison Boiler Building that housed the equipment for the steam power and lighting that illuminated the hotel. Photo taken between 1880 and 1897 by William H. Jackson, Library of Congress, Prints & Photographs Division, Reproduction Number: LC.DIG.det.4a03451.

series of figures representing the Four Seasons: Spring, Summer, Fall, and Winter adorn the latter. In the Rotunda the standing and seated figures alternate encircling the ceiling. Standing figures represent the Elements: Earth, Air, Fire, and Water. Seated figures depict the Exploration series: Adventure, Discovery, Conquest, and Civilization (fig. 1.10).[67]

After the Ponce opened, Maynard went to Chicago, serving on lead architect Daniel Burnham's planning team for the World's Columbian Exposition. In 1897, Maynard traveled to Washington, D.C., gifting to the nation reproductions of the Exploration series. They adorn the ceiling in the

FIGURE 1.10. Muralist George Willoughby Maynard's works decorate the elaborately detailed lobby of the hotel. The Mezzanine features paintings by nationally renowned artist Martin Johnson Heade. Photo taken between 1880 and 1897 by William H. Jackson, Library of Congress, Prints & Photographs Division, Reproduction Number: LC.DIG.det.4a03469.

FIGURE 1.11. Artisans including George Maynard and Herman Schladermundt created the decorative murals in the former Hotel Ponce de Leon's Dining Room. Ponce de Leon Hall Dining Hall, Flagler College Archives.

Pavilion of the Discoverers (Southwest Pavilion) in the Jefferson Building of the Library of Congress. A quarter of a century after Maynard completed the murals in the Ponce, Carrère & Hastings adapted this series for one of a pair of elaborately adorned classical flagpole bases set on the terrace of the New York Public Library.[68]

Yet another young talent at the time of the Hotel Ponce de Leon's construction, Herman Schladermundt, assisted Maynard with the murals. Schladermundt's artistic expertise extended to stained glass, enabling him to work with his colleague Maitland Armstrong on some of the designs in the Ponce. In 1935, Schladermundt reminisced about his work as the superintendent for the decorations on the Ponce (fig. 1.11).[69]

In 1890, Carrère and Hastings added Schladermundt to their team of experts for the Central Congregational Church in Providence, Rhode Island. There he executed the elaborate mural paintings in the apse, one of the many remarkable interior features of the building. A few years later the artists worked together on the Agriculture Building at the World Columbian Exposition and on the Library of Congress. Arguably, Schladermundt's greatest effort in St. Augustine was the creation of the stained glass windows for the Memorial Presbyterian Church.[70]

During the 1890s, New York's American Art Association counted all three men as officers. In 1896, during the era of work on the Library of Congress, Schladermundt moved to the Bronxville artist colony where he joined a friend and colleague, Ponce artist Otto Bacher.[71]

A family of artists, the Tojetti family, originally of Rome, arrived in San Francisco in 1871. Patriarch Domenico Tojetti received commissions from popes and decorations from kings before accepting a teaching position in 1867 at the Guatemala Academy of Fine Arts. Mrs. Emilia Tojetti became a noted art patron, and their daughter Emilia enjoyed a reputation as an accomplished pianist. Sons Virgilio and Eduardo gained fame as painters, also. All three men achieved reputations for their romantic allegorical subjects.[72]

In 1875–1876, the three Tojetti men were chosen to work on California railroad baron Leland Stanford's palatial San Francisco Italianate-style residence. Specifically, they worked under the direction of William Stymus and his New York interior design firm of Pottier & Stymus. This exposure to both the East and West Coast elite launched their successful careers in the United States.[73]

Virgilio Tojetti studied in Paris with painters William-Adolphe Bouguereau and Jean-Leon Gerome. He exhibited in New York, Philadelphia, and Boston. A few years after completion of the Stanford mansion he moved to New York, where he was recognized for his work on several Pottier & Stymus projects. He worked on several hotels, including the Fifth Avenue, Hoffman House, and Savoy. In Boston and Providence, he decorated the Keith's Theatres. His residential commissions included work for Cornelius Vanderbilt.[74]

About 1890, Thomas Edison's second wife, Mina, commissioned Tojetti to paint a canvas mural on the ceiling of the den of their home, Glenmont, in Llewellyn Park in West Orange, New Jersey. Featured in an article in *The Decorator and Furnisher* shortly after its completion, the author noted the theme of music and science presented with female figures and playful

FIGURE 1.12. Frescoes, one in each of the four quadrants of the Grand Parlor, are rare examples of the Italian-born artist Virgilio Tojetti's work. Most of the buildings that featured his paintings have been demolished. Reproduced with permission from Steven Brooke Studios.

cherubs. A tour of Glenmont on June 17, 2011, verified the signature "V. Tojetti," which is the form used by Virgilio Tojetti for the painted canvases in the Grand Parlor of the Hotel Ponce de Leon.[75]

Most of the Fifth Avenue mansions were demolished in the early twentieth century to make way for a skyline dominated by high-rise buildings. Tojetti's mural at Glenmont is a rare example of his work in the New York area. The collection of four murals in the Ponce is remarkable for their number, their high quality of detail, and their location—the southern United States (fig. 1.12).[76]

The prestigious New York interiors firm of Pottier & Stymus orchestrated the interior details and furnishings for the Ponce. As early as the Philadelphia Centennial International Exposition of 1876, the firm included Henry Flagler as a client, along with fellow industrialists William

Rockefeller, George Westinghouse, Leland Stanford, and Mark Hopkins. The firm designed U.S. Treasury rooms for President Andrew Johnson and a suite in the Executive Mansion for President Ulysses S. Grant. French-born Auguste Pottier learned the woodcarving craft in his native country then immigrated to the United States in 1847. A decade later he and William Stymus worked for the same furniture making firm. In 1859, they established the New York-based Pottier & Stymus. Their strength was the interrelated use of three elements: color, pattern, and woodwork. By 1876, they employed 700 men and achieved gross sales of more than $1,000,000. The Pottier & Stymus firm was known for lavish woodworking. Bernard Maybeck apprenticed with the firm briefly before his father arranged for him to study furniture design in Paris with Pottier's brother.[77]

Pottier and Stymus were known for meticulous record keeping. On March 1, 1888, their building burned and destroyed all of the company records. These included records for the Hotel Ponce de Leon and earlier H. M. Flagler work.[78]

For completion of the Leland Stanford residence in 1875–1876, William Stymus moved to California and listed himself in the San Francisco city directory as an architect. A number of designs introduced in that mansion became components of the firm's trademark motifs and details, including the enthusiastic use of extravagant and exotic materials in elaborate patterns.[79]

Photographs of the Stanford residence include elements used throughout the next decade and adapted in Flagler's hotel. Classical themes, seasons, days of the week, continents, all were representations included in the Stanford mansion and in the Ponce. In particular, the Rotunda and the Mezzanine share similarities: "At the center of the second floor, a brass railing encircled the open well and allowed anyone standing at that railing or below a view of lunettes and pendentives that resembled baroque frescoes."[80]

On May 1, 1887, construction of the Ponce was completed, with interior finishes, details, and furnishings installed over the next several months. As the year 1887 came to a close, Flagler prepared to open to the world his resort hotel built on the edge of a tiny Spanish colonial city. Flagler's investment and the efforts of the cadre of New York artisans, craftsmen, and inventors changed St. Augustine and Florida forever.

2

✦⸙✦

"The Modern Wonder of the Ancient City"

Henry Flagler brought Thomas Hastings to St. Augustine in his private railroad car in May of 1885 to see the Spanish colonial city and begin the design for a grand resort hotel. Over the next half year, Hastings and his partner John Carrère returned to St. Augustine numerous times, creating a vision for a European masterpiece that satisfied Flagler's wishes, exceeded his guests' expectations, and launched the architects' careers (fig. 2.1).

The resulting symmetrical design reflected Carrère's and Hastings' Beaux-Arts educations and was enhanced by their exposure to Spanish and Moorish architecture. They embraced themes from palaces and fortresses, including Granada's Alhambra, Seville's Real Alcázar, and Zaragoza's Aljaferia. They emulated churches, notably Seville's cathedral and Segovia's San Martin and San Esteban.[1]

To accomplish Flagler's vision required relocation of several buildings on the site and the construction of new structures. The Grace Methodist Church was built immediately north of the hotel site and reflected the Ponce's rich design mixture of pearl gray concrete and red brick detailing in its polychromatic construction. Anderson Cottage, a two-story frame dwelling built by Dr. Anderson's family about 1875 for a winter guest house, was moved from King Street to Sevilla Street on the Markland property to accommodate a Palm Garden west of the Ponce.[2]

Flagler had become interested in the use of concrete, which had been used in limited fashion for residential construction in California between 1860 and 1879. Also, hurricanes that struck St. Augustine in the summers of 1882 and 1885 may have influenced his decision, and the three in the

FIGURE 2.1. The principal façade of the Hotel Ponce de Leon, including the Alameda Gardens across King Street to the south, provided an inviting setting for visitors to enjoy the winter season in St. Augustine. Photo taken in 1902 by William H. Jackson, Library of Congress, Prints & Photographs Division, Reproduction Number: LC.DIG.det.4a09451.

summer of 1886 may have reinforced his selection of materials. Flagler had St. Augustine's native coquina shells incorporated into the concrete mix. The shellstone was obtainable from an Anastasia Island quarry nearby. The coquina shell material had been used on the Castillo de San Marcos and many of the extant Spanish colonial dwellings. In 1883, Bostonian Franklin Smith experimented with mixing concrete and crushed coquina shells. Satisfied with the results, Smith used the material for his residence Villa Zorayda, located directly south across King Street from where Flagler would choose to locate the Ponce.[3]

Flagler was familiar with Smith's efforts. Carrère and Hastings developed the scheme that enabled the material to be used for the hotel, a much larger scaled and more elaborately designed project: "Technologically advanced, the buildings employed concrete-wall construction at a time when the material was virtually experimental."[4] The exceptional span of the Dining Room ceiling, the four-story concrete-topped central dome, and the two towers required robust iron reinforcing as did the support headers over doors and windows. The balance of the hotel complex was constructed of unreinforced concrete. The cost was significant, but Flagler justified the expenditure, predicting that the building would be structurally sound a century later.[5]

Carrère and Hastings became comfortable with the use of concrete as a building material, and by the early twentieth century they had designed three buildings that today remain preserved and in use: Vernon Court (1898) in Newport, Rhode Island, for Mrs. Richard van Nest Gambrill, now the National Museum of American Illustration; Flagler's south Florida home Whitehall (1901–1902) in Palm Beach, now the Henry Morrison Flagler Museum; and the Murry Guggenheim Residence (1903–1905) in West End, New Jersey, now the Monmouth University library.[6]

Builders James McGuire and Joseph McDonald began the process of casting in place a mixture of concrete and crushed coquina after conducting tests on strength and compression. Once the testing was under way, William Kennish arrived from New York to serve as concrete superintendent. According to Flagler's brother-in-law William R. Kenan Jr., construction was accomplished when "eleven hundred Negroes with song leaders to pace them, tamped the mixture to ensure its solidity as the great walls rose in one piece."[7] Sarah Murray recalled in a 1934 interview her brother and former slave Prince Brown's pride in constructing the building.[8]

Each casting was performed around the perimeter and the interior structural walls for the five buildings that comprised the hotel complex. This resulted in a linear measurement of two-thirds of a mile of uninterrupted masonry wall sections without joints. For the base of the building, the recipe consisted of equal amounts of sand and concrete. Coquina was added in double that amount. The shell aggregate that framed the monolithic concrete was poured in forms to a thickness of four feet, tapering to less than half that as the building rose. The upper story walls were composed of five parts coquina and two parts sand to one part cement and poured to a thickness of between 16 and 20 inches. The structure's need to withstand hurricanes was anticipated and proved over time.[9]

The New York distributor Baetjer & Meyerstein advertised in an 1892 edition of *American Architect and Building News* regarding the "highest grade imported" Hanover Portland cement mortar used in the construction. *Engineering News and American Railway Journal* covered the use of the new materials, stating that the recipe for the concrete was 1 part cement, 2 parts sand, and 3 parts coquina. In addition to 50,000 barrels used in the Hotel Ponce de Leon, the Hotel Alcazar and Hotel Cordova received the same mortar composition.[10]

Portland cement was developed in Portland, near Dorset, England, in the early nineteenth century and became popular in the United States after its promotion at the Philadelphia Exposition of 1876. The use of large quantities of Hanover Portland Cement at the time was significant as the material was not widely used in the United States until the 1890s. By that time Portland cement was brought to the United States from a variety of European countries.[11]

Only four projects featured use of the imported mortar from Hanover. The first was the Ponce. Two more were designed by renowned architect Richard Morris Hunt: the Biltmore House (1889–1895), built by George Washington Vanderbilt in Asheville, North Carolina, and the Breakers (1893), built by his cousin Cornelius Vanderbilt II at Newport, Rhode Island. Frederick William Vanderbilt, a brother to Cornelius, was a longtime friend and business associate of Flagler. The Vanderbilts would have been familiar with and were perhaps influenced by Flagler's use of the material on the Ponce. In the early twentieth century, Flagler imported the mortar for one more project, the concrete bridge pilings that supported the Overseas Railway through the Florida Keys.

According to an 1889 article in *Engineering News* describing the construction of the Ponce, a strong day's work resulted in a five-foot vertical section of the perimeter walls being completed. Both interior and exterior walls consisted of structural concrete. In addition, wood floor beams were enhanced with corrugated concrete boxes, reinforcing the concrete connections throughout the structure. The article lauded the use of the material for its quantitative benefits as well as its qualitative characteristics.

The design and execution received praise as the first use of this simple and innovative material and for the achievement of a sophisticated result. The cost per cubic yard was $6.00, a significant savings over the use of either brick or stone.[12]

In contrast to the pearl gray of the coquina concrete formula, the 2,000,000 red bricks with matching mortar and the terra cotta provided a dramatic polychromatic effect, newly popular for the era. In the 1870s, during their early years, the firm of McKim, Mead & White experimented with adding tints to original gray terra cotta to achieve a red clay effect. Later, experts credited the architects as national leaders in this treatment. Their protégés Carrère and Hastings would have been familiar with terra cotta tinting. The Perth Amboy Terra Cotta Company of Perth Amboy, New Jersey, supplied the terra cotta.[13]

The building featured an exuberant mixture of balconies, loggias, alcoves, and arcades, detailed in brick or terra cotta. The color and ornamentation helped bring the scale of the massive monolithic concrete building to one readily appreciated by visitors. The elaborate variation in the details found throughout the building made a striking contrast to the horizontal rhythmic bands identifying the concrete pours.

Wood structural members were of Argentine heart pine in beams of three sizes, 4" × 8", 6" × 10", or 6" × 12". The material proved extremely resistant to termites. Henry Plant used this same material for the Tampa Bay Hotel a few years later. Though native U.S. heart pine, the hard center of longleaf or yellow pine trees, was readily available to both hotel builders, perhaps their choice of materials reflected the strong British influence in rail construction and availability of high quality materials in Argentina in the latter half of the nineteenth century.[14]

The complex form roof continued the polychromatic theme through the use of clay barrel tiles. Provided by the J. C. Ewart firm of Akron, Ohio, the native Summit County clay echoed the dark red of the bricks. Ewart produced brick and drainage tile as well. The majority of the barrel-shaped roof tiles remain on the Ponce after 125 years. Replacements made in 2013 were kindred spirits. The Ludowici Roof Tile Company of Lexington, Ohio, was a firm contemporary with Ewart's. The clay was geographically similar as well.[15]

The Medal Brand Roofing Felt Company of New York provided

underlayment for the roof. The company name, logo, and "1854–1886 trade mark" imprints were included on the products. The material remained in service on the Ponce until damage from the 2004 hurricanes Charley, Frances, Ivan, and Jeanne eliminated the continued functional integrity of the material. Original flashing, revealed during a reroofing in December of 2012, had been provided by the Revere Copper company of Boston, Massachusetts. The company began operation in 1801 and manufactured rolled copper shortly after that date. The material had a life expectancy of more than a century.[16]

The distinctive yellow paint that was inaugurated on the Hotel Ponce de Leon became a trademark known as Flagler yellow. The color outlined the 1,000 windows and highlighted the exterior woodwork. Flagler continued to use the color on his resorts along Florida's Atlantic coast. The color identified the Florida East Coast Railway cars as well. Gently, the red and yellow reinforced St. Augustine's ties to Spain, the flag of which was enjoying its centennial anniversary during the Hotel Ponce de Leon's construction.

The Sicilian Asphalt Paving Company of New York, under general manager Henry Bolze, provided rock asphalt as the primary component for the floors of the loggias and dome room in the Ponce. Native crushed coquina was added when the mix was in liquid form. The material was used for the Mezzanine in the adjacent Hotel Alcazar. Flagler imported 350 tons of asphalt for streets surrounding the hotels. Walkways around the hotels were composed of asphalt laid in blocks. Bolze perfected the use of asphalt in these applications and patented his innovations.[17]

Another engineering feat began in November 1886. Daniel Dull, a contractor from New York, drilled a well for Flagler's hotels and other St. Augustine properties. Securing an artesian well ensured a new, clean water supply to accommodate guests' needs and added to the exotically landscaped setting for the Ponce. Water circulated through four fountains around the property, removing minerals from the well water. Dull drilled a 12-inch diameter well with a depth of 1,390 feet by February 1887. The well provided 10,000,000 gallons of water a day and sustained pressure sufficient to shoot the water to a height of 42 feet above the well at ground level.[18]

From the fountains, water was pumped into two storage tanks in each of the Ponce's twin towers. Each tank held 4,000 gallons of water. The steam-powered pumps were located in the lower floor of the service building located beyond the Dining Room. Water stored in the two tanks ran throughout the hotel to the pistons at the basement level, which operated the hydraulic elevators.[19]

The well was sufficient to serve the Ponce and the Alcazar, including providing 82-degree Fahrenheit water for the latter's swimming pool. Well drilling continued in attempts to break through limestone for water to heat the hotels. The efforts failed. Edison's four direct current steam dynamos powered the Ponce. Three dynamos supplied power to the Alcazar.

On April 7, 1888, the Thursday prior to Easter Sunday and the end of the hotel's first season, an event took place that was related to but more important than electrification of the Ponce. William Hammer and engineer William Kennish initiated a unique experiment for Flagler. They set a turbine over one of the artesian wells and bolted an Edison dynamo to the turbine (fig. 2.2). The dynamo was designed to power 375 sixteen-candle lamps, the force necessary to operate the Ponce. A sixteen-candle lamp was the standard light measurement in the United States at the time and was equivalent to a 48-watt incandescent light bulb. Water shot out of the ground to a height of thirty-five feet in a twelve-inch diameter column. The power generated was sufficient to operate the Hotel. *Scientific American* writer H. Bradford Rockwood witnessed the event, recording the world's first electric light plant run by artesian well power.[20]

Flagler named his resort hotel for New World explorer Juan Ponce de Leon, paying homage to the discoverer of La Florida and acknowledging St. Augustine's role in preserving the nation's Spanish heritage. The city's inauguration of an annual festival in the explorer's honor reinforced the relationship. Some scholars have speculated on the similarities between the explorer's fabled search for the Fountain of Youth and Flagler's reinvigorated life investing in Florida real estate and remarrying later in life.

Local author Charles Reynolds presented a description of the Ponce that reflected the sentiments of many visitors to St. Augustine: "Standing within the sound of the surf on the Florida shore, its towers overlooking the sea, it should be named in honor of the Discoverer whose romantic

FIGURE 2.2. In 1888, engineers William Hammer and William Kennish mounted a turbine with an Edison dynamo over an artesian well. The national press recorded the world's first water-powered electric light plant at the Ponce. Photo taken between 1880 and 1897 by William H. Jackson, Library of Congress, Prints & Photographs Division, Reproduction Number: LC.DIG.det.4a03485.

quest had made his name typical of the adventurous and chimerical spirit of his age. And as the bastions and watchtowers of the Fort were significant of the military might of sixteenth-century Spain, so this new memorial, in beauty and harmony of parts, shall be a reminder of that other Spain, the mother of artists and architects and cunning craftsmen."[21]

Flagler's magnificent Spanish Renaissance Revival hotel featured distinctive architecture based on historical precedent. It stood as a functionally and physically self-contained complex and demonstrated patently conspicuous luxury. The complex of five buildings consisted of more than 270,000 square feet. With its setting, the property consumed an entire city block of seven acres. The building, advertised as fireproof construction, featured masonry walls, details, and roof, estimated to cost $2,500,000 ($62,500,000 in 2014 U.S. dollars). Some sources credit the construction at $2,000,000 with the additional $500,000 in furnishings and landscaping.[22]

The principal façade faced south onto King Street and comprised 66,480 square feet. A semicircular central entry plaza led through a pyramid-roof gatehouse featuring two terra cotta lions' heads flanking a portcullis. A central rectangular courtyard of 150 feet to a side and framed by arcaded walks and loggias afforded access from a variety of points to the U-shaped, four-story building (fig. 2.3).

Landscaping designed by Nathan Franklin Barrett emphasized the semitropical climate and included varieties of palms and traditional Southern plants, including roses, azaleas, camellias, and magnolias. The center of the courtyard featured a fountain sporting four turtles considered representative of the four seasons, and twelve frogs spouting water and symbolizing the twelve months and the hours on a clock. These elements surrounded a tall, mosaic column. The central entrance was up a short flight of steps beyond the fountain. Adjacent to the steps a low retaining wall was created from cut coquina blocks that were salvaged after a fire in 1887 burned the Catholic church nearby. This is the single example of coquina in the building. Correspondingly, the two Ladies' Entrances were accessed from walkways to the right and left of the fountain. Elaborate and imaginative expression can be found on balconies, door and window surrounds, and on the towers.[23]

Twin towers, each planned to be 165 feet in height, including the 15-foot-tall finials, anchored the interior corners of the building and flanked the

FIGURE 2.3. The primary entrance to the Hotel Ponce de Leon features the central courtyard and fountain on the approach to the polychromatic façade of poured concrete contrasted with brick and terra cotta. Library of Congress, Prints & Photographs Division, Reproduction Number: HABS FLA, 55.SAUG, 45-2.

central dome. (A 2013 field evaluation of the towers conducted by A. D. Davis Construction Company using a laser provided a vertical measurement of 163 feet.) The towers included staircases descending to the lobby floor from the hotel room corridors. Roof terraces led east or west from the upper lobby or Solarium. Each was covered in asphalt, one of the earliest uses of the newly developed material. Elaborate staircases led into the towers from which balconies were accessed, affording exceptional panoramic views of St. Augustine (fig. 2.4). Water holding tanks, two in each tower, stored 8,000 gallons of water for the operation of the elevators and to serve the guests.[24]

FIGURE 2.4. The west tower of the Hotel Ponce de Leon. Hotel guests could enjoy panoramic views of St. Augustine and its environs from either of the two towers atop the building. Photo taken between 1880 and 1900 by William H. Jackson, Library of Congress, Prints & Photographs Division, Reproduction Number: LC.DIG.det.4a28752.

The building's corners boasted hipped-roofed towers with overhanging balconies. Windows exhibited great variety, illustrating the breadth of Victorian-era glass manufacturing: casements, some with transoms, round and flat-headed sash, dormers, and stained glass. The majority of the windows featured two sashes with six panes each, which was a typical window configuration in the nineteenth century. The windows were a particularly important feature as they provided airflow, enabled appreciation of the views and fragrant aromas of the gardens, and fostered conversation among guests.[25]

A nautical theme evident on the exterior's and the interior's public spaces paid homage to Florida's French and Spanish explorers. As he landed in 1564 at present-day Jacksonville on the St. Johns River, French Huguenot explorer René Goulaine de Laudonnière claimed the land as New France and its north flowing waterway as the River of Dolphins. These creatures, as well as mermaids, mermen, and shells, decorated the building. Three-dimensional representations of the last element executed in metals highlighted the entry, doorknobs, and fences.[26]

The central entrance opened into a vestibule that provided access to the asphalt-covered loggias that led from the Ladies' Entrances. The central entrance and those leading to the loggias each feature a pair of carved Spanish motif doors set on heavy bronze hinges. For the main entrance side panels in the same design, small sidelights, and a half-round transom complete the entrance that is framed by a large half-round arch. Decorative iron balusters are set in the glass and add to the fortified appearance. Elaborate carvings flank the central entrance. A round window set in a deeply recessed frame features pieces of clear glass reminiscent of flowers. One of these is located on either side of the entrance.

Four Tuscan columns with a ribbon or egg-and-dart molding separate the vestibule from the first of the hotel's grand spaces. Each of the public spaces was distinct in design and detail. All of the spaces reflected the exuberance and variety of the Victorian era.

The vestibule opens onto a large rectangular lobby, identified on drawings as the Lounge. At the far side of the lobby, opposite the vestibule, dual staircases descend to the carriage drive, the former "pleasuring grounds," and hotel facilities. Materials featured in the lobby include Numidian pink marble wainscoting, oak wainscoting and woodwork, and Italian mosaic tile floors. The Rotunda's most defining feature, the octagonal inset framed by eight carved oak caryatids, supports a five-story central dome. George Maynard's two sets of murals with four allegorical figures in each set—the Elements and Exploration series—decorate the arches between the caryatids. Smaller, flat arches identify Spanish and French explorers of the New World.[27]

The Rotunda dome rises through the center of the building's four stories. Above the second level, twenty-four plump cherubs encircle the space, standing with their arms raised below a series of gold helmets and shell shields. Beyond the circumference of this segment of the dome, a wood paneled bench and railing provide guests, and now students, with another seating area. In the center of the space a small circular metal-framed opening affords a view to the copper cupola that topped the dome.

At the Mezzanine level, a gallery provides another gathering space. On each side of the row of south-facing casement windows that overlook the courtyard, inglenooks feature tiled walls and fireplaces with tiled surrounds and angled oak overmantels laid in a basket-weave pattern. The fire boxes are shallow for use with either coal or gas. Oak benches flank the mantels.

Above the lobby and immediately under the thirty-foot diameter dome is the 400 Rotunda. This fourth floor Solarium is a rectangular space of 2,500 square feet, the octagonal center of which features the eight large iron support beams that rise from the ground floor to culminate supporting the cylindrical concrete dome atop the building. These beams are encased within simple rectangular wood columns. A multipane sliding glass wall provides views of the courtyard, the Alameda gardens, and the Alcazar and Cordova hotels. When open, the glass wall is concealed from view from the building's exterior by the concrete balcony walls. Flanking the Solarium are roof terraces that lead to the towers and their balconies. Promotional literature of the era touted the terraces as promenades affording spectacular views of the ocean and town to the east and the state of Florida to the west.[28]

At the end of a corridor, leading west from the Rotunda, a pair of carved oak doors lead to the delicate and elaborately painted Grand Parlor (now the Flagler Room), providing striking contrast to the rich, substantial oak and marble construction of the Rotunda and Dining Room. The parlor

FIGURE 2.5. The Grand Parlor's decoration reflected the original intent as a ladies' lounge and contrasted greatly with the heavy woodwork and ornamentation of the other major rooms in the building. Photo taken between 1880 and 1897 by William H. Jackson, Library of Congress, Prints & Photographs Division, Reproduction Number: LC.DIG.det.4a03472.

side of the doors feature applied decoration. Cherubs, nautical characters, and egg-and-dart molding enhance the spaces. Ceilings of a light robin's egg blue are remarkably similar to the color that Charles Lewis Tiffany, Louis Comfort Tiffany's father, trademarked in 1845 and that continues to represent the Tiffany jewelry company. References to Ponce de Leon the explorer decorate the center salon. The 1512 date in a ceiling medallion reflects King Ferdinand's authorization of the expedition. The landing at La Florida took place in April of 1513.

The Grand Parlor, originally a room reserved for women, includes five distinct salons. A short corridor at each end of the room separates the rectangular salons and provides access to a large central rectangular space. The ceilings of each of the four small salons exhibits Virgilio Tojetti's murals painted on canvas. All four salons are framed with fluted and banded Corinthian columns, each set on a low wall. Arches with drapes, originally of red velvet, separate the four quadrants from the main salon (fig. 2.5).

The first two quadrants feature mantels with tiled hearths on the walls that abut the entry corridor. The salon nearest the courtyard features a southern exposure and includes a single door to the loggia, enabling easy access to the exterior. Flanking the mantel in that salon are two single-door entries that led to a small ladies lounge, now a handicapped-accessible women's restroom.

The main salon features a large electric clock set above the room's third mantel. The clock is embedded in a block of Mexican onyx marble that serves as the hearth surround. Opposite that wall, a pair of doors leads to the west corridor. Long multipane sash windows add natural light to that provided by the eleven crystal chandeliers spaced equidistantly throughout the Grand Parlor.

Adorning the walls were fine paintings and decorative art objects that had been acquired by Knoedler and Company of New York for Henry Flagler to be exhibited in the Ponce. New and established artists, Americans and internationals, were represented. As was the custom at the time, the frames were created to best showcase the works within them.

The Grand Parlor provided direct access to the hotel's west wing, the area that contained Flagler's private suite of rooms. This suite was used by President and Mrs. Cleveland during their five visits and by Admiral Dewey for his stay. For VIP guests such as these, the Grand Parlor was closed to other hotel guests, affording the dignitaries this space for their gathering and entertainment.[29]

A marble staircase leads from the Rotunda to the Dining Room (fig. 2.6). The marble landing at the top of the staircase features a tile inset with the final stanza of eighteenth-century English poet William Shenstone's work, "Written at an Inn at Henley" on the Thames River and purported to have been a favorite verse of Flagler's:

> Whoe'er has travell'd life's dull round,
> Where'er his stages may have been,
> May sigh to think he still has found
> The warmest welcome—at an inn.[30]

Bronze castings, created in France by sculptor Léonard Morel-Ladeuil and sold in 1887 in England, stand on pedestals and are adorned with lights. The subjects are Queen Elisabeth and Marie Stuart, Queen Elizabeth I of England and her cousin Mary Queen of Scots. The base of each is signed "Morel." They rest, one to each side of the landing, at the entry to a broad, round-arched opening. Above the arch, a pink marble balconette, adorned with carved lions' heads and "AD 1887" indicating the hotel's completion date, affords views of the landing and the Dining Room. On either side of that balconette are paintings by Georg Schweissinger, *Columbus Discovering America* and *The Introduction of Christianity to the Huns by Charlemagne*. The oak beamed ceiling features stenciled panel insets on canvas.[31]

Dual wood staircases rise from the sides of the landing to smaller landings. These latter resting spaces are lit by a triple grouping of tall, narrow round-arched Tiffany stained glass windows. Each features a cherub-adorned transom, over which is an elaborate and colorful assemblage of cornucopias overflowing with fruits, flowers, and grapes, highlighting Bacchus, the god of wine. The windows illustrate the transition from the lobby to the celebratory nature of the Dining Room. The dual staircases turn ninety degrees and rise another half story, terminating at the Mezzanine. From there, an arch in the west wall opens to a graceful oak staircase with a simple oak railing that leads to the guest rooms (now dorm rooms) and to the room under the dome.

From the marble landing, a broad corridor featuring shields of Spanish provinces leads into the Dining Room. On either side of this walkway, double doors open onto two private dining rooms, both featuring decorative Tiffany glass. Walls of stained glass windows highlight both private dining rooms. Each window measures about 9' 6" in height × 5' in width.

FIGURE 2.6. This marble staircase provided a gracious transition from the Rotunda, or lobby floor, through the arch to the Dining Room or up a flight of stairs to the Mezzanine level. Grand staircase leading to Dining Room, Hotel Ponce de Leon, St. Augustine, Flagler College Archives.

The west wall of the west private dining room is composed of four floor-length panels. A small landing adorned with an elliptical ceiling affords discreet access from the private dining room to the Rotunda and guest rooms. Light filled the space through three pairs of floor-length casement windows topped by transoms decorated with shields and filled with rows of bull's-eye glass. At the stair landing to this private entry, a half-round cauldron-pattern Tiffany stained glass window highlights the transom. A jewel tone theme predominates with a series of oval and round jewels accenting the border of the window and the urn handles and rim. The urn holds a tulip framed with leaves appearing to radiate upward from the base.[32]

The room that was considered historically and contemporarily to be the hotel's most remarkable was the 14,212-square-foot Dining Room. The structure is composed of a lower floor of poured concrete with crushed coquina shells, the material used for the entire hotel complex. The upper floors are constructed of wood framing members and support a circular clay tile roof. The interior features a wood frame ninety-foot-square room with a forty-eight-foot barrel-vaulted ceiling, and includes dramatic semicircular east and west venido, or welcoming, rooms. At either end, balconies serve as minstrels' galleries entertaining guests for dining, or dancing when the room was converted for use as a ballroom.

Resplendent in this room are forty Louis Comfort Tiffany stained glass windows. Five triple groupings or fifteen double-hung sash windows are located in each venido, for a total of thirty. They feature clear and colored glass in geometric patterns and filigree designs, with amber bull's-eye shapes in ten of the upper sashes. The windows measure about 10' 6" in height with the center window of each triple grouping measuring 6' in width. The angled windows flanking each center window measure 5' in width.[33]

Above the central rectangle, soft light is provided to the room from a clerestory of ten half-round or lunette windows, similar to the one set in the transom of the private entrance to the Dining Room. Colors in four of the windows are pink, brown, mauve, and green. Four others showcase yellow, brown, lavender, and green. The final two lunette windows include white serpentine glass at the urn rims, each with a cauldron from which ribbons of flame emerge. Four of them feature a band of glass jewels around the center portion of the urn, swirl base to the left, elongated ga-droon design in the center, and colors of pink, brown, mauve, and green.[34]

Hastings' and Maynard's murals proved to be as inspiring as Tiffany's glass. Once again, allegorical female figures predominate, as was the case in the Rotunda. Here they represent the four seasons and are accompanied by dolphins, mermaids, cherubs, and bowls of porridge. Spanish coats of arms, proverbs, and representations of galleons add to the colorful portrayal. Briefly, a two-level electrified metal hoop chandelier hung from the center of the ceiling.

Dual staircases originate in the lobby and are identified by inglenooks with wooden benches. These inglenooks flank the central marble staircase that leads through the corridor to the Dining Room. In the carriage entrance, under the marble staircase and accessed via a short stair is a massive oak door suspended on iron wheels and set in an iron track. The door slides to the left (eastward) revealing a painted sign "Baggage and Boot Room" and a ceiling of beaded board. This basement entrance is flanked by a pair of windows featuring green and amber bull's-eyes. Here, historically, luggage was transferred from carriages to Otis elevators, and from there to guest rooms. On the north side of the carriage drive, a half-round stained glass window mimics those in the Dining Room. This window features an urn flanked by shields with blue ovals. The window identified the hotel gymnasium's location. Also, a bar, workshop, and children's playroom were located under the Dining Room. During the Coast Guard's occupation of the building during World War II, an officers' hall was incorporated into the area.[35]

Beyond the Dining Room a 23,592-square-foot service facility, identified on architectural drawings as the Kitchen, housed the 12,000 square-foot kitchen and the laundry, maintenance, and printing functions for the hotel. Also, the top floor housed white male employees. The kitchen included double brick ovens, refrigerators, and a large mixer for dough that was four feet deep and five feet long. The rectangular four-story building is topped by a hipped roof. Rows of double-hung sash windows with six panes of glass in each sash were placed symmetrically along the walls of the building. Shed-roofed dormers spaced symmetrically provided light to the attic level.[36]

The Edison Boiler Building housed the boilers that required 16,000 pounds of coal daily to power the engines for the dynamos. This flat-roofed, rectangular structure was devoid of ornamentation, a striking contrast to the opulence expressed in the main building and Dining Room. Commanding the skyline at the west end of the boiler building, a 75-foot-tall conical brick chimney rested on a rectangular base and was topped by ornamental brick corbelling.

The Artists' Studios, a 10,068-square-foot structure, stood as the northernmost building in the complex. The long and narrow two-story, hipped-roofed building housed seven ateliers for visiting artists on the upper floor. Each atelier contained a corner fireplace with tiled hearth, a skylight, wood paneled wainscoting, a supply closet, windows with nautical rope trim, and canvas fabric on the walls. The ground floor featured a series of broad arched openings that afforded access to coal storage rooms. Both boilers and the multitude of hotel fireplaces used this material. The eastern-most room, fireproofed and reinforced with metal doors, contained the safe for the hotel's cash and security staff's firearms.

All of the buildings share poured concrete construction and brick and/or terra cotta trim. Clay barrel tiled roofs top the structures, with the exception of the Boiler Building, which features a flat roof with a parapet. Heavy wood trim complements the structures, most painted in Flagler yellow.

In 1889, French author Léon Paul Blouet visited the Ponce. Using his pen name Max O'Rell he pronounced, "I have almost always accepted with reserve the American superlatives followed by the traditional in the world; but it may safely be said that the Ponce de Leon Hotel, at St. Augustine, is not only the largest and handsomest hotel in America, but in the whole world. Standing in the prettiest part of the picturesque little town, this Moorish palace, with its walls of onyx, its vast, artistically furnished saloons, its orange-walks, fountains, cloisters, and towers, is a revelation, a scene from the Arabian Nights."[37]

As Flagler's hotel transformed the skyline, the small waterfront city experienced growing pains responding to the demands for improved infrastructure: paved streets, gas lines, a water system, and public safety personnel. Not possessing Flagler's resources, the city government defaulted on its financial obligations that accompanied these improvements. Increased taxes brought dissatisfaction from an electorate that already had mixed feelings about the Gilded Age changes taking place. Flagler was strong, driven, and single minded. Some townsfolk resented the loss of control to an outsider and a northerner, straining the relationship between the old guard citizenry and the upstart tourists.

Flagler's magnificent Spanish Renaissance Revival resort hotel gained a reputation as one of the most elegant and remarkable buildings of the century. The hotel featured entertainment for men and women, areas for music and dancing, a barber shop, a shoeshine stand, and numerous places to relax and enjoy the sunny climate. The Ponce charmed guests and visitors from throughout the world over the next eighty years, with the height of the hotel's glory in the first four decades. Instantly, the building achieved a reputation as the grandest hotel in the United States, illustrating a European architectural legacy merged with American modern conveniences.

3

A Spanish Renaissance Palace
in a Spanish Colonial Paradise

Early in 1888, a Pullman Palace Car Company train left New York for a thirty-hour journey to Florida. The train brought hundreds of hotel employees and Joyce's Military Band down the east coast of the United States to their ultimate destination of St. Augustine and the Hotel Ponce de Leon. Henry Flagler had recruited superb employees from New England's summer resorts, veteran staff who would bring familiarity and comfort for guests at his new Florida hotel.[1]

The train, the nation's most modern of the era, arrived in St. Augustine also bringing distinguished northern guests to experience the Sunshine State's transformation into a resort destination. Visitors included members of the New York social register, many of whom were Flagler's business colleagues and associates and had their own investments in Florida. Flagler greeted his guests and escorted them into the lobby to sign the guest register.

On Tuesday, January 10, 1888, the Hotel Ponce de Leon opened for a private party. The pleasant 80-degree day and thousands of Thomas Edison's glittering electric lights provided the backdrop for a feast in the hotel's magnificent Dining Room. The eighty guests included Frederick William Vanderbilt and William R. Rockefeller. These friends and business associates of Flagler's illustrated the importance of railroad connections to the success of his Florida business operations. Both Vanderbilt and Rockefeller served on the boards of directors of the Lake Shore and Michigan

FIGURE 3.1. Guests gathered in the Courtyard to enjoy a variety of pastimes, such as this concert in 1915, during their stays at the Ponce. State Archives of Florida, *Florida Memory*, http://floridamemory.com/items/show/147790.

Southern Railroad and the Lake Erie and Western Railroad. Vanderbilt sat on the board of the New York Central Railroad and the Chicago and North Western Railroad. Both men commissioned Carrère & Hastings to design their Long Island residences. More importantly, they and their families were members of the new Jekyl Island Club, a social linkage that would serve the Ponce well in the next few years.[2]

Two days later, on January 12, 1888, under cloudy skies and a mild 70 degrees, the Ponce opened (fig. 3.1). The public toured Flagler's remarkable hotel, the result of architects, engineers, builders, and hundreds of artisans and craftsmen. Guests noted the exotic furnishings, a $1,000 table and two others at $600 each. Carpets had cost $85,000. The 800 Dining Room chairs were manufactured at $18 each. That evening a formal celebration took place for an estimated 500 guests. Newspapers throughout the country announced the opening, initiating a publicity tradition that would carry forward for the next forty years. Activities in St. Augustine, especially at the Ponce, drew a national audience.[3]

At the time of the hotel's opening, St. Augustine was recovering from a depressed post–Civil War economy. By 1880, the city's population had more than doubled to 4,000, with three to four times that number coming to spend the winters. The city's efforts to recover included the conversion of Confederate General Edmund Kirby Smith's boyhood home into a public library, establishment of a telegraph office, and construction of the Convent of the Sisters of St. Joseph. Adjacent to the bathhouse and boat basin east of the plaza, the military authorized establishment of Florida's first yacht club, the St. Augustine Yacht Club, as a maritime defensive measure. A shell road heading north from the City Gate out of town was begun; it was named San Marco Avenue. A rail line linked St. Augustine to Jacksonville to the north and other points to the south.[4]

The thousands of winter visitors to St. Augustine hotels beginning in the late 1870s initiated a new and vibrant chapter in the history of this Spanish colonial city. In 1890, Jacksonville, the river city to the north, became Florida's largest city in terms of population, a status it retained until after World War II. The last decade of the nineteenth century marked the end of Florida as a sparsely populated, rural Southern state as many Florida cities witnessed boom periods in the early twentieth century.[5]

In addition to hundreds of hotel guests in St. Augustine at any one time, hotel employees added to the city's population in number and cultural diversity. Employees included both whites and African-Americans. Annie MacKay was a white housekeeper who worked at the Ponce for many years and was mentioned in Flagler's correspondence. Frank Thompson, in addition to serving as headwaiter, played on the Cuban Giants Negro League baseball team. The South, including St. Augustine, was segregated racially. So was the Ponce. The Kitchen was located beyond the Dining Room building in present-day Kenan Hall. White employees lived there in the upper floors. African-American men lived in a brick and frame apartment building on Cordova Street south of the Hotel Alcazar. African-American women stayed above the steam laundry building on the northwest corner of Valencia and Riberia Streets, two blocks west of the Ponce.[6]

St. Augustine residents regarded the new hotels, facilities, infrastructure, and winter residents with mixed feelings. Some citizens expressed enthusiasm; others considered the changes to be destructive to the town's uniqueness and charm. Regardless of the reaction, tourism was St. Augustine's major economic vehicle. Tourism breathed new life into the centuries-old Spanish town. Existing buildings were repaired and painted. New buildings were constructed. Colorful, subtropical plantings added to the European ambience in the city. Only the onset of the Great Depression in the 1930s challenged the strength of tourism as the economic engine in the nation's oldest city.[7]

On January 12, 1888, the same day that Flagler opened the Ponce, Jacksonville launched the Sub-Tropical Exposition. This was intended to bolster Florida's fledgling tourism market and to compete with California for winter visitors. Jacksonville architects Ellis and McClure designed the 50,000-square-foot polychromatic exposition building with towers and an electrified fountain that served as the centerpiece of the fair complex (fig. 3.2). Over the fair's four-month run, Florida and its subtropical region's life and culture were on display. The timing of the exposition paralleled that of the Ponce's inaugural season.[8]

On New Year's Day 1888, a few days before the opening of the Hotel Ponce de Leon and the Jacksonville Exposition, two business partners began another venture in Ormond Beach, fifty-two miles south of St.

FIGURE 3.2. The Sub-Tropical Exposition opened in Jacksonville on January 12, 1888, the same day as Henry Flagler's Hotel Ponce de Leon. Both events were designed to attract tourists to the southernmost frontier of Florida. State Archives of Florida, *Florida Memory*, http://floridamemory.com/items/show/37838.

Augustine. John Anderson, a native of Portland, Maine, and Joseph Price of Louisville, Kentucky, had come to Florida in the 1870s for real estate investments. They met and invested in tourism, recognizing the importance of the arrival of the railroad to the area and construction of a bridge across the Halifax River. They opened the Hotel Ormond on the east side of the Halifax River at Granada Street in Ormond Beach. Three years later, Flagler bought their hotel, hiring them as managers for the property.[9]

Both the Jacksonville and Ormond Beach ventures indicated Henry Flagler's influence on northeast Florida's tourism. Advance publicity for the Ponce had been covered in national newspapers for months. Also, all three cities were linked by rail lines. The relationship of railroad and resort development guided the sunshine state's growth for the next quarter century and ensured Henry Flagler's role as the founder of modern Florida.

Lodging rates at the Ponce were equivalent to those charged by Northern resorts, with a variation in prices depending upon the caliber of the facility. They corresponded to tariffs charged at Cruft's Magnolia Hotel in St. Augustine. The least expensive room there and at the Ponce required a daily tariff of $5. In contrast, charges for a large suite at the Ponce, including meals for a guest and a maid, were $39 per day. In current terms that amounted to $100,000 for the winter season. After a renovation in 1893, charges for a three-room corner suite for the season were $75 a day, or $250,000 in current dollars, comparable to a suite at New York's Four Seasons Hotel.[10]

Charges for more modest accommodations for one or two people were $15 to $25 per night. In the spring of 1889, one traveler chronicled his first visit. He described room number 112, a courtyard-facing suite composed of two rooms, the first of which measured about 15 feet by 12 feet. In the corner, a tiled fireplace with brass andirons included a mirrored overmantel decorated with plaster angels. Furniture was mahogany, including a writing desk, a dresser, and a chest of drawers, the latter two topped with mirrors. The desk included a built-in washstand. The furniture flanked the casement window that had a cream and green shade. The room was dominated by a table covered with a rug, as was the style of the period. Several chairs and an upholstered sofa completed the furnishings. The alcove or sleeping area, a space of roughly 10' × 12', contained the bed, a couple of chairs, and a Brussels carpet. Eight electric lights brightened the ensemble. He commented on the high quality of service as well, noting that maids straightened the room as soon as it was unoccupied. A pitcher of ice water was provided regularly throughout the day, and for overnight a single block of ice was placed in a pitcher to melt slowly. Each morning a call button brought a staff member with hot water and, if requested, fine stationery.[11]

The Ponce's carved furniture in rosewood, walnut, and mahogany was particularly impressive in the bridal suites. Appropriately, these suites featured the most luxurious furnishings and upholstery.[12]

Dozens of men and women—artists, authors, and entertainers—contributed to the ambience that resulted in an international audience that flocked to and garnered publicity for the Ponce. Many of these talented men and women shared connections in New York and the White Mountains, reinforcing the resort and railroad network that catered to the leisure class during the Gilded Age and early twentieth century. Their contributions enhanced the traveling public's experience at Flagler's hotels and left a legacy of support for the cultural arts in the community in and around St. Augustine. On December 19, 1887, less than a month before the Ponce's scheduled opening, the *New York Tribune* reported the exhibition of artwork throughout the building, complementing the architectural style of the hotel. Of note were Louis Comfort Tiffany's glass windows flanking the entrance, and in the lobby Otto Henry Bacher's drawings of the hotel entrances and Robert Frederick Blum's watercolors.[13]

Part of Flagler's vision for the Hotel Ponce de Leon and for St. Augustine as the "Winter Newport" included providing entertainment and attractions for guests, paralleling the roles played by other Gilded Age resorts. This expressed his interest in culture and the fine arts, again typical of a man of his socioeconomic status, particularly as a resort developer. Flagler's friendship with tobacco baron and art patron George Lorillard may have encouraged support for the arts. In 1885, Lorillard began construction of Tuxedo Park, a real estate enclave in New York adjacent to which the Bronxville art colony flourished. Several of the Ponce artists and artisans, including Schladermundt and Bacher, came to the colony during that era.[14]

Flagler offered salons in the Artists' Studios building, located at the north end of the linearly arranged hotel complex. Two of the first artists to

FIGURE 3.3. This gathering place above the lobby afforded opportunities to enjoy natural light from the courtyard or to appreciate some of the hotel's decoration and art collection. Mezzanine of the Hotel Ponce de Leon, Flagler College Archives.

occupy studios were friends Martin Johnson Heade and George Washington Seavey. The latter was brother to Osborn Dunlap Seavey, the Ponce's general manager. Additional artists at the hotel included Marie A'Becket, Laura Woodward, Charlotte Buell Coman, Frank Shapleigh, Felix De-Crano, and W. Staples Drown.[15]

Heade had become enamored with St. Augustine in January 1883 upon his first visit to Florida. In March, for his residence and studio, he bought and remodeled a house on the sand road leading north out of town. The following October he married Elizabeth Smith of Southampton, Long Island, and the couple moved into the house.[16]

In the Artists' Studios building, Heade received the favored west studio with two windows overlooking the broad lawn. He moved into the studio in the summer of 1887 at completion of the hotel construction. Heade's studio No. 7 was one of the most favored of the city's social scenes. He was the most prominent of the Ponce artists and achieved national acclaim. Flagler bought portraits and landscapes, numbering at least twelve for his collection. Samuel Clemens bought one of Heade's Florida landscapes. In 1886, Flagler commissioned Heade to create his two largest paintings, *The Great Florida Sunset* and *View from Fern-Tree Walk, Jamaica*, which were exhibited in the Ponce. They hung on the east wall of the Mezzanine above the Rotunda, as they are shown in photographs of the period (fig. 3.3). About 1890, in St. Augustine, Heade painted *Giant Magnolias on a Blue Velvet Cloth*, arguably his most recognized work. In 1986, the painting was gifted to the National Gallery of Art, where it is featured in prints and note cards. Heade was honored with the painting's image on a postage stamp in 2004 as part of the American Treasures Series. He was selected for his depth of work in still life and landscapes (fig. 3.4).[17]

FIGURE 3.4. *Giant Magnolias on a Blue Velvet Cloth*, 1885–95. Artist Martin Johnson Heade painted this representation of St. Augustine flora while he occupied Studio No. 7 at the Artists' Studios of the Hotel Ponce de Leon. Courtesy National Gallery of Art, Washington.

Almost half of the approximately eighty paintings acquired by Knoedler and Company to be hung in the Ponce remain on exhibit in the building. This excludes Heade's paintings, but does reflect works by artists who painted in the Artists' Studios. Some works went with Flagler to Whitehall in Palm Beach at the turn of the twentieth century or with Flagler's descendants over the years. Flagler commissioned Heade to paint at least one portrait of himself and one of Dr. Andrew Anderson. He gifted one of each to Dr. and Mrs. Anderson. Some of Flagler's paintings became part of museum or private collections.[18]

Flagler and other U.S. railroad executives recognized the emerging importance of publicity and advertising for their resorts. In the first decade of the Ponce's history, Flagler hired William Henry Jackson to take artistic photographs during the winter tourist season in St. Augustine. In addition to exceptional views of the Ponce's interiors and the city's skyline from the towers, his camera recorded lush tropical foliage in the courtyard, vines climbing concrete walls, and third-story windows sporting striped canvas awnings. Jackson had achieved national acclaim by 1883 with his inspiring depictions of the American West. Jackson chronicled Florida buildings and bucolic scenes in nearly 1,000 glass-plate negatives and transparencies.[19]

In the summer of 1871, Jackson and painter Thomas Moran were part of a U.S. Geological Survey team that documented the Yellowstone region. Their efforts led to conservation of that area as the first national park. The two men influenced protection of Yosemite, Zion, Grand Teton, and Grand Canyon through their art. Their shared experiences left a remarkable artistic legacy and fostered a friendship that lasted for more than half a century until Moran's death in 1927.[20]

In February of 1887, Moran arrived in St. Augustine, considerably less impressed with the town than he had been with the panoramic frontier in the West. However, he was charmed by St. Augustine's legend of the explorer Ponce de Leon landing on the coast nearby, but chose what he considered to be a more scenic location. He painted the explorer on Fort George Island, fifty miles to the north. Flagler acquired Moran's painting, *Ponce de Leon in Florida* (1878), for exhibition in the hotel. The work's large size, about 5.25' × 9.5', required a location that could accommodate the piece. Historic photographs of the hotel's grand spaces, with their fine and decorative arts collection displayed, eliminate the Grand Parlor and the

FIGURE 3.5. This view of the Grand Parlor features three of the Shakespearean hero-ine paintings inspired by internationally renowned Polish actress Helena Modjeska and painted by Hungarian artist Joszi Arpad Koppay. *Parlors of the Ponce de Leon*, photo taken between 1880 and 1897 by William H. Jackson, Library of Congress, Prints and Photographs Collection.

Dining Room. The Moran painting may have hung with Heade's works. A plausible location is the large unadorned wall on the west side of the Mez-zanine to the south of the guest wing entrance.[21]

A collection of eight paintings of female figures acquired for the hotel continues to adorn walls in the Ponce. Four hang in the Grand Parlor, and four hang across the Rotunda in the President's Wing (fig. 3.5). Helena Modjeska, Poland's most beloved and one of America's most-acclaimed actresses, was the inspiration. Through the 1880s she portrayed Shakespearean heroines, and Koppay used the names for his paintings that she inspired: *Rosalind, Titania, Juliet, Katherine, Ann Page, Ophelia, Beatrice,* and *Desdemona.* The paintings depict a much younger woman than the veteran actress. Her performances garnered exceptional reviews throughout Europe and the United States. She drew acclaim particularly in Boston and New York. First Lady Frances Folsom Cleveland was one of Modjeska's greatest admirers. The actress performed at the Executive Mansion during the Cleveland administration.[22]

Austro-Hungarian portrait painter Joszi Arpad Koppay, who studied in Vienna and Munich, created the works in 1885 as part of a larger romantic series. He and Modjeska each shared a friendship with Poland-born and world-renowned operatic singer Marcella Sembrich. Shortly after completing the romantic series, Koppay enjoyed favor as a court painter for the interrelated royal houses of Europe. In 1894, the family matriarch and England's Queen Victoria commissioned him to paint her granddaughter Alexandra, just betrothed to Nicholas of Russia. Having achieved fame in Europe, he was encouraged to travel to the United States. In October of 1905, Koppay arrived in New York. Over the next several years he painted on both continents. When in the United States, he maintained studios in New York and painted a variety of distinguished subjects, including Teddy Roosevelt and John D. Rockefeller Sr.[23]

Construction of the Ponce and the accompanying transportation improvements increased the attractiveness of the Spanish colonial city. Authors had been attracted to the city since at least 1827, when Ralph Waldo Emerson spent the winter there as a treatment for his tuberculosis. William Cullen Bryan visited in 1843, traveling the region and writing about his travels. In 1876, poet Sidney Lanier, employed as a travel writer, chronicled his time in the nation's oldest city. Some of the authors who enjoyed the ambience of the Ponce included Stephen Vincent Benet, Edna Ferber, John Dos Passos, Henry James, Sinclair Lewis, Somerset Maugham, and Thornton Wilder.[24]

Samuel Clemens spent the night of March 14, 1902, at the Ponce and the next night in Palm Beach on his way to a cruise leaving from Miami. Clemens and Standard Oil executive H. H. Rogers were close friends for many years. The men corresponded and enjoyed each other's company,

FIGURE 3.6. Musicians performed at Flagler's hotels, including the famous composer, conductor, and "march king," John Philip Sousa. Photo by William H. Jackson, State Archives of Florida, *Florida Memory*, http://floridamemory.com/items/show/28750.

and Clemens considered Rogers his benefactor. Quite possibly, Rogers introduced Clemens to Henry Flagler with whom the author enjoyed at least a brief correspondence relating to the author's stay at the Ponce in 1906.[25]

Music was an integral component of the hotel's ambience. Orchestras serenaded guests from the loggias or in the courtyard (fig. 3.6). Minstrels played from the galleries overlooking the Dining Room, and bands entertained after dinners. Several noted band and orchestra leaders performed. Joyce's Military Band performed at the opening of the hotel. Marching band leader John Philip Sousa enjoyed several visits to Flagler's hotels and participated in a variety of sporting activities. In 1887, the Ellis Brooks

Band received great acclaim for their introductory performance at the Minneapolis Industrial Exposition. For the following decade they played the winter seasons at all three of Flagler's St. Augustine hotels.[26]

Compositions were written and performed at the Ponce in honor of the Ponce and, at the turn of the twentieth century, for Mary Lily Kenan Flagler. Notes trumpeted, literally, throughout the courtyard. Melodies entertained guests ascending from the Rotunda into the Dining Room, and serenaded them during their sumptuous repasts.

Both the Dining Room and Grand Parlor hosted events, concerts, and balls. A New Year's Eve Ball, begun in 1888, returned to prominence when Flagler System executives and community leaders revived the event as a scholarship ball in 1967, a prelude to the opening of Flagler College the following year. The formal black-tie event continues today. Then cochair and St. Augustine mayor John D. Bailey Sr. and his wife, Peggy, have attended every year through 2012.

Beginning in 1890, ferry service connected St. Augustine to Anastasia Island, enabling visitors and residents to visit the Atlantic Ocean beaches. Tram service to North Beach provided access to the Surfside Dance Hall and Bath House and the Vilano Beach Casino. At Flagler's request, the Frank Usina family began transporting hotel guests to North Beach, where the family hosted oyster roasts. The tradition continues with the Usina family's ship *Victory III* cruising passengers on Matanzas Inlet.[27]

In the 1880s, Jacksonville, about to become Florida's largest city by population, was fostering a fledgling movie industry. Competition for business and tourism came from California, also promoted as "the Sunshine State." St. Augustine benefitted from close proximity to Jacksonville and from Henry Flagler's strong New York connections.[28]

Even after California captured the movie-making market, the Ponce played a role in U.S. movie history (fig. 3.7). Theda Bara's *A Fool There Was* (1915) and Rudolph Valentino's *Stolen Moments* (1920) are early examples. More well known is *Distant Drums* (1951), the first of several in the genre of western films during that era.[29]

Flagler's commitment to entertainment for his guests incorporated facilities located a short walk from the Ponce. He commissioned Carrère and Hastings to design a second hotel, the Alcazar, to host a casino and athletic facilities, as well as additional guest rooms. The landscaped

FIGURE 3.7. From silent movies through the "talkies" and up to the present, the Ponce has enjoyed stardom. In the 2006 movie *The Celestine Prophecy*, the former hotel is transformed into a cathedral. State Archives of Florida, *Florida Memory*, http://floridamemory.com/items/show/147793.

Alameda garden faced King Street and linked the courtyards of the two hotels. The facilities in the Alcazar included a "Russian steam bath, a Turkish bath, a gymnasium, a massage area, a bowling alley, a ballroom, playhouse, and the world's largest swimming pool . . . tennis courts and a bicycle academy."[30]

During this era, a number of sporting activities matured from amateur events to intercollegiate athletic competitions and professional sports. These included tennis, golf, and baseball. Flagler brought all three to Florida for his hotel guests.

Flagler's weeklong Tropical Championship tennis tournament, held annually in late March, drew some of the best players from the United States and England. In 1889, Flagler replaced the wood courts north of the Artists' Studios at the Ponce with asphalt courts constructed south of the Alcazar. Collegiate contenders from Columbia, Yale, and Trinity joined the competition. As an incentive, Flagler commissioned a massive sterling

FIGURE 3.8. The Fort Links golf course challenged participants to play on the grounds of Fort Marion (Castillo de San Marcos), as in this photo from 1902. State Archives of Florida, *Florida Memory*, http://floridamemory.com/items/show /27198.

silver replica of the City Gate for the winner of four tournaments. In 1887, before the Ponce opened, T. S. Beckwith of Cleveland won the inaugural tennis tournament. Over the next decade Beckwith placed first or second in several annual competitions. Beckwith's family lived on Euclid Avenue along Cleveland's "Millionaire's Row." The Rockefellers and the Flaglers had been their neighbors prior to the Standard Oil partners' move to New York City.[31]

The 1910 season opened with completion of a new tennis court on the Ponce grounds. The structure was located on the west side of present-day Kenan Hall, the building constructed to house staff and support facilities. As with many of the Ponce's activities, hotel guests and local residents participated.

St. Augustine native David Drysdale recalled that his father W. I. (Walter Irvine) Drysdale, or "Driz," excelled at several sports offered at the Ponce: tennis, golf, and baseball. He gave tennis lessons there and bested a Canadian champion in an exhibition match in the 1930s. John Fraser grew up immediately west of the Ponce. Fraser's father, John Fraser Sr., made home movies of the tennis matches a few years later. In 1955, Janis Versaggi Williams, whose family moved to Valencia Street in St. Augustine, took tennis lessons there.[32]

Beginning in 1895, the Fort Marion grounds doubled as a three-hole golf course (fig. 3.8). Soon the sport's popularity dictated a more spacious course, though perhaps not as challenging. Henry Flagler responded quickly, introducing the sport broadly at the Ponce and many of his other Florida resorts. To the west, across San Marco Avenue, the "Fort Links" attracted a competitive crowd, as had the tennis courts. Again, players from throughout the United States and the collegiate teams came to compete in winter games. Established in 1896, the University of Pennsylvania team was represented by its captain, Clayton Dixon. He competed regularly against Joseph Greaves of the Manhattan Club. By the turn of the twentieth century the *New York Times* reported the list of golfers arriving for the New Year's Cup at the Florida East Coast Golf Club.[33]

In the winter of 1885–1886 the Cuban Giants baseball team traveled to St. Augustine after completing an exhibition game in Cuba (fig. 3.9). The team featured the nation's best African-American ball players. They were

FIGURE 3.9. The winter before the Ponce opened, Henry Flagler invited the Cuban Giants to play in St. Augustine. Their string of forty wins enabled them to select the teams they wanted to play, white or African American. Original Cuban Giants—1886–1890, at Fort Marion, St. Augustine, Courtesy of the National Pastime Museum.

employees from Long Island's Argyle Hotel Athletics team and players from the Washington Manhattans and Philadelphia Orions. The Cuban Giants began a series at Fort Marion as construction started on the Ponce. Flagler invited the team back the following winter, setting a pattern that continued for the next decade and helped the team survive the off-season winters.[34]

During that first season, the Cuban Giants won forty games before suffering a loss. This string of successes elevated Negro League baseball beyond merely an entertainment. By the eve of the opening of the Ponce in 1887, the team's ball playing ability brought them national publicity and the autonomy to select their opponents, white or black. The Cuban Giants joined the Middle States League in Pennsylvania, the nation's first team of black players to join a white league.[35]

The Cuban Giants, changing members over the years, played for more than twenty years at hotels along the east coast managed by Osborn Seavey. The team toured the South each winter and played Northern teams in the summers. Team members, under the direction of Frank P. Thompson, worked as hotel staff at the Ponce and later the Alcazar. Racism remained prevalent, so players tempered the demonstrations of their athletic prowess against less competitive teams by introducing barnstorming as "comic relief" to lighten the mood and appeal to audiences' interest in entertainment. Despite the requisite antics, the Cuban Giants set the standard for African-American baseball in the late nineteenth century.[36]

During this same period, Cos Govern and Frank Thompson participated in antiracist organizations. Govern led the Hotel Brotherhood that had been founded in 1884 to address inequities among hotel workers based on race. Both men were founders of the Progressive Association of the United States of America, which fostered improvements for African-American businessmen. Thompson addressed hotel employees in the Ponce Dining Room for three-quarters of an hour, discussing racism and the South, an event reported by Govern and printed in the February 23, 1889, issue of the *New York Age*. If African-Americans could improve themselves economically, they could fare better in the white world. Though the subject matter was typical for the era, the presentation in a segregated luxury hotel for wealthy northerners was a remarkable activity.[37]

Throughout the Hotel Ponce de Leon's eighty years as a resort, countless notable people enjoyed the luxurious accommodations, entertaining pastimes, and exemplary service. Newspapers in New York and Chicago served as a social register, noting guests who were leaving the arctic temperatures of the North for the tropical climate of Florida. They brought with them the newest trends in fashion and business, displaying both at Henry Flagler's magnificent hotels.[38]

Guests at the Ponce included U.S. presidents and their cabinet members, congressmen and their aides, industrialists, and military officers. Former Civil War Union generals Martin Hardin and John McAllister Schofield visited in the early years. Andrew Carnegie, Joseph Pulitzer, George M. Pullman, J. P. Morgan, William Rockefeller, Frederick W. Vanderbilt, and John Jacob Astor lead a lengthy list of business tycoons who enjoyed Henry Flagler's hospitality.[39]

In 1900, at the close of the winter season, Admiral George Dewey and his bride of four months arrived in St. Augustine. They stayed in the Flagler suite and attended the twelfth annual Alicia Hospital charity ball. Mrs. Dewey was the former Mildred McLean Hazen, widow of General George B. Hazen, who had served as superintendent of Indian Affairs in the West. Hazen had worked with tribes in Oklahoma, the members of which were removed to Fort Marion in St. Augustine for incarceration in the 1870s. In 1892, Mrs. Dewey donated a sketchbook made by one of the prisoners and belonging to General Hazen to the Smithsonian Institution. Possibly she and Admiral Dewey visited the tourist attraction Fort Marion during their time in St. Augustine.[40]

President Grover Cleveland and his wife, Frances Folsom Cleveland, made their first of five visits to the Ponce the month after the grand opening, in February of 1888. They stayed in a suite at the southwest corner of the lobby floor at the end of the west wing. The March 20, 1889, issue of the *New York Times* described the three-room suite. The corner parlor contained an artfully tiled fireplace, a table with a top of Mexican onyx, and chairs and sofas upholstered in light gray fabric. The bedroom overlooked the hotel gardens and featured a canopied bed with a headboard, footboard, and side rails, all covered in pink brocade. The same material was used for the insets of the bureau drawer panels and as window draperies. Lace curtains and an antique lace bedspread completed the decorations. A large bathroom finished the suite. The article noted twelve electric lights.

In addition, President and Mrs. Cleveland had the use of the Grand Parlor for greeting guests. This became a pattern for dignitaries, which afforded privacy and access to the Rotunda for public addresses.[41]

Near the end of the 1895 season, when he was governor of Ohio and preparing a run for president, William McKinley stayed overnight at the Ponce. The visit reinforced his support from Flagler and fellow Republicans wintering in the town.

Ten years and six months later, on October 21, 1905, Theodore Roosevelt stayed at the hotel as part of a tour through the South. This marked the first time that the Ponce was opened outside the winter season for anyone other than Flagler or Kenan family members. The relationship between Roosevelt and Flagler was contentious. The "trust-busting" president championed government regulation of corporations, and Standard Oil was a prime candidate for such action. However, the two men's mutual interest in the Panama Canal's construction, a project of Roosevelt's, was balanced against Flagler's wariness of the president.

Roosevelt's trip came at the beginning of his second term as president and after his wife and children had visited the city, reporting to him enthusiastically about their stay. On March 17, 1905, St. Patrick's Day, Roosevelt gave his niece Eleanor in marriage to their distant cousin Franklin Roosevelt. The previous winter he and his mother, Sara Delano Roosevelt, had stayed at the Ponce following, in her assessment, unpleasant experiences on a Caribbean cruise and in Palm Beach. She commented favorably on the visit to St. Augustine. No doubt, Theodore Roosevelt had been regaled with family stories touting the features of the oldest city.[42]

Instead of greeting the president personally, Flagler sent his brother-in-law William Rand Kenan Jr. north from Palm Beach to meet Roosevelt. The president stayed in the Flagler suite and had access to the Grand Parlor. There he could have enjoyed the art collection, including the romantic series by Koppay. He would receive the artist at the White House shortly thereafter, and the result would be a portrait of the president.[43]

In letters to his daughter Ethel and son Kermit, written the following day after he departed from St. Augustine, Roosevelt commented on the beauty of the city, the old streets and new houses, and the flora and fauna. He made a speech to an enthusiastic crowd at Fort Marion, championing the social and economic equality of all men. He enjoyed a "surf bath" in the ocean at Anastasia Island. His reviews of the dinner hosted by the Board of Trade at another downtown hotel were mixed. While he appreciated the sincerity and intentions of the townspeople and his hosts, he pronounced the banquet "dreadful" and "preposterous," worsened by short speeches from community leaders. Those leaders included Governor Napoleon Bonaparte Broward and Florida East Coast Railway executive James Ingraham.[44]

Warren G. Harding, an avid sportsman, visited each year for nineteen consecutive years beginning in 1904 and concluding in 1923, a few short months before he died that August. That last winter, after he had been elected, he played several rounds of golf at the St. Augustine Links, partnering with William Rand Kenan Jr. Business included making cabinet selections before his inauguration in March 1923.[45]

Forty years later, Vice President Lyndon B. Johnson came to the city and stayed at the Ponce. In March 1963, he launched St. Augustine's 400th anniversary celebration. Robert Harper, then a youth vacationing in St. Augustine with his family and now the executive director of the Lightner Museum located in the former Hotel Alcazar, noted that the antique bedroom furniture in the suite had been replaced with contemporary 1960s chrome pieces for Johnson's visit. Presumably the hotel management wanted to appear to be fashionable.

As evidence of the modern and cosmopolitan nature of the Ponce in the 1880s, Alexander Graham Bell took the opportunity to send his wife a telegram from the hotel shortly before he completed his visit at the end of the hotel's second season. The resort hotel was designed to fulfill all guest needs, whims, and desires.[46]

The Ponce hosted special events that attracted large audiences. In 1892, a charity event chaired by Ellen Call Long, daughter of former Florida governor Richard Keith Call, raised funds for the preservation of Andrew Jackson's Tennessee home, the Hermitage, where Governor and Mrs. Call married. Holding charity events at the Ponce elevated the importance of both the event and the hotel.[47]

In 1893, Henry Flagler helped St. Augustine set the theme for a long history of Florida's participation in commemorations and celebrations. A 140' × 140' replica of Fort Marion (Castillo de San Marcos), complete with flags representing France, Spain, England, and the United States, served as

FIGURE 3.10. Henry Flagler supplied funds for construction of this replica of Fort Marion that frames the buildings on the interior of the setting, including Pennsylvania's facsimile of Independence Hall. *Florida State Building at 1893 World's Fair, The Columbian Exposition, Chicago*, published in 1893 by Laird & Lee, Illinois During the Gilded Age Project, Northern Illinois University Library, http://gildedage. lib.niu.edu/islandora/object/niu-gildedage%3A19949.

the Florida Building at the World's Columbian Exposition that opened to the public on May 1, 1893, in Chicago (fig. 3.10). The fort facsimile's patriotic theme emphasized the nation's colonial past, as did a number of other state buildings, such as Virginia's emulation of Mount Vernon and Massachusetts' representation of the John Hancock Mansion. Simultaneously, Florida's simple construction presented an image that evoked old and distinct cultural traditions, contrasting greatly with other state buildings, such as New York's elaborate Victorian-era confection and Pennsylvania's replica of Independence Hall. Florida's Fort Marion was constructed around the perimeter of a city block, literally appearing to protect other buildings including Independence Hall. Henry Flagler provided $10,000 for construction of the Florida Building. In addition, Flagler, Henry Plant, and H. Rieman Duval provided complimentary rail transportation to ship Florida's exhibits to Chicago.[48]

That same year, following the Exposition's successful promotion of Florida, Flagler had the Ponce updated. Insurance underwriters found Edison's original direct-current electrical system unacceptable in light of the advances in alternating-current technology. The entire system was replaced with twenty-nine miles of knob and tube wiring. This included more than 175,000 feet of conduit provided by Interior Conduit and Insulation Company of New York, and 100,000 feet of cable from the Okonite Company of New Jersey. (The latter company remains in business.) Underground wires set in wooden troughs ran to the lights set along the perimeter wall.[49]

The Dining Room's two-tiered circular metal chandelier had been removed by 1891. During the rewiring, supplemental lighting was provided by one hundred gilded papier-mâché lion's head lights designed by Carrère & Hastings. The plumbing was retrofitted with pipes extending through the roof for better ventilation.[50]

Flagler made these investments during a year of national financial recession. The winter of 1894–1895 brought a freeze to north Florida that destroyed citrus crops and flowering plants. The weather delivered a chilly reception to tourism in St. Augustine, too. Flagler focused on his new Florida properties farther south.[51]

Flagler's expanded railroad to Palm Beach and beyond ended St. Augustine's reign as the Winter Newport. In 1895, the Hotel Cordova facilities closed with the exception of the guest rooms. In 1903, reprogrammed as the Alcazar Annex, a concrete walkway suspended over Cordova Street, linking the two properties and enabling access to the guest rooms. Though tourism moved south, the Ponce remained dramatically impressive, and Flagler remained committed to making physical changes that would fulfill his vision for a modern tribute to the Gilded Age.[52]

In 1894, both Flagler and Rockefeller had sons in college. Each father was beyond midlife and at a stage when he considered turning over to his son major business responsibilities. Harry Harkness Flagler was a student at Columbia College (now Columbia University). John D. Rockefeller Jr. was a student at Brown University. Rockefeller was more successful, turning over Standard Oil beginning at Junior's graduation in 1897. Creation and administration of a family foundation a decade later completed the transition.[53]

Henry Flagler enlisted his son to manage the Ponce during the 1894 season. For the Ponce, the younger Flagler oversaw seasonal repairs to the hotel rooms and cottages and painting of the exterior trim. In April, after the end of the hotel's season, he returned to New York and married socialite Annie Louise Lamont. He completed his college education in 1897 and enjoyed a life immersed in the arts, particularly music. Twenty years later, the New York Symphony-Philharmonic recognized him for decades of service to that organization. His wife provided a $100,000 endowment in honor of the occasion (a $15,500,000 gift in current dollars).[54]

On February 15, 1898, the battleship U.S.S. *Maine* exploded while docked in Havana Harbor. President McKinley declared war on Spain two months later, waiting until troops could be effectively readied. The delay enabled Henry Plant's steamships docked in Havana to unload tobacco and remove all United States citizens safely from the Cuban capital. The *Olivette* returned survivors of the *Maine* to Tampa, and the *Mascotte* returned 700 evacuees to the same destination. As the nation prepared for war, Plant and Flagler each dispatched representatives to Washington to lobby for the U.S. Navy to use Tampa, St. Augustine, or Miami as the base of operations. Tampa became the location from which the war was launched, with the Tampa Bay Hotel hosting officers whose finances were sufficient to cover the tariff. Flagler settled for his Florida East Coast Railway bringing troops stationed in Jacksonville and on leave to St. Augustine to experience the city and enjoy his resorts.[55]

In 1901, Henry Flagler married North Carolina socialite Mary Lily Kenan. Shortly after, public documents verify that Flagler gave his son and his three young grandchildren, all girls, 1,000 shares of Standard Oil stock. The approximate value of the stock at that time was $2,000,000, about $48,600,000 in 2014 dollars. Harry Flagler and Thomas Edison served on the boards of directors of several major New York cultural organizations. Also, the younger Flagler maintained contact with many of his father's business colleagues, including John D. Rockefeller Sr. and his son.[56]

News accounts and correspondence of the era indicated that Henry Flagler and his son were estranged during the last two decades of the elder Flagler's life. Reportedly Henry Flagler was disappointed with his son's career as an art patron. Harry Flagler did not condone his father's marriages after the death of his mother, Mary Harkness Flagler. During the elder Flagler's marriage to Ida Alice Shourds, the time frame of much of his Florida development, his son joined the Larchmont Yacht Club to which his father belonged and which was across the harbor from the family's summer home, Lawn Beach. J. P. Morgan, Andrew Carnegie, and William K. Vanderbilt were members there as well.[57]

In 1904, Flagler appointed his thirty-one-year-old brother-in-law William Rand Kenan Jr., two years younger than Harry Flagler, to the boards of directors for the Florida East Coast Railway and hotel companies. By this time the Flagler and Kenan families had shared business interests and social circles for twenty years. Kenan, a talented chemical engineer who helped found Union Carbide, served a management role in Flagler's companies from 1904 until shortly before his death in 1965. Then his great-nephew and chosen successor Lawrence Lewis Jr. took over the role of company manager. Lewis and his sister Molly Lewis Wiley were heirs to Flagler's fortune and had spent much of their youth in St. Augustine. Their mother, Louise Wise Lewis, was Mary Lily Flagler's niece.[58]

Though Palm Beach had replaced St. Augustine as northerners' favorite winter destination, many vacationers chose to incorporate more than one resort destination in their seasonal itineraries. St. Augustine was favored in January until the chilly temperatures encouraged visitors to continue along the Florida East Coast Railway route to Palm Beach for February. Wealthy yachtsmen, including Andrew Carnegie and Frank Vanderbilt, docked at the marina adjacent to the bayfront on their treks south and again weeks later as they were heading back north to New York, Philadelphia, or New England.

European travelers, particularly royalty, drew news coverage, as did military heroes. In 1910, the Duke and Duchess of Manchester arrived for a stay at the Ponce with her parents. The Duchess was the former Helene Zimmerman, daughter of Eugene Zimmerman, president of the Cincinnati, Hamilton and Dayton Railroad (now part of CSX) and a longtime business associate with the Standard Oil partners.[59]

Socially, few changes were noticed in activities during this era. The Ponce continued to host sports, recreation, leisure, and charitable activities, annual events that had begun their traditions with the opening of the

Ponce in 1888 and maintained their audiences, even if the composition of the members changed. Though the volume of visitors had declined, the hotel maintained a steady trade. During the 1909 season, 500 people had enjoyed the hospitality of the hotel.[60]

The pomp and circumstance at the hotel continued with local dignitaries and members of the St. Augustine social set included in events throughout the years. For the January 5, 1910, seasonal opening, local newspapers predicted record registrations, the largest number of tourists since the construction of Flagler's railroads. The state had suffered a hurricane in 1909 (and would again in 1910) that prompted the positive commentary. News accounts closed out the season with the closure of the hotel's portcullis on April 5, 1910, reiterating the strong number of hotel guests.

By this time, Flagler had enjoyed his dual winter homes in St. Augustine and Palm Beach for nearly a decade. The final leg of the Key West Extension to the Florida East Coast Railway was under construction. He continued to own Lawn Beach in Mamaroneck and spend a portion of the summer season in the White Mountains.

Arguably the man who knew Flagler best came to enjoy life in Florida as well. John D. Rockefeller continued throughout his lifetime to consider Flagler his dear friend, though their personal lives differed dramatically. Rockefeller returned to Florida beginning in 1913, staying at the small coastal community of Seabreeze about sixty miles south of St. Augustine. In 1914, the year after Flagler's death, Rockefeller began annual winter stays at Flagler's Hotel Ormond near Seabreeze. Rockefeller traveled by rail requiring him to pass through St. Augustine. Perhaps he visited the Ponce on his way farther south.[61]

In 1918, five years after Flagler's death, Rockefeller purchased the Casements property immediately south across Granada Street from the Hotel Ormond. He lamented that he had waited so long to enjoy Flagler's Florida. Rockefeller stayed at the Casements over the next 22 years, enjoying golf on Flagler's course. He died at his Ormond Beach property on May 23, 1937.[62]

Rockefeller's wife, Laura Spelman Rockefeller, had been a semi-invalid since the beginning of the twentieth century. He had remained devoted to her, curbing much of his leisure travel to share in her care with his family members. Rockefeller was at the Ormond Beach Hotel in April 1915 with his son John D. Jr. and daughter-in-law Abby Aldrich Rockefeller when they received the news of his wife's death. Her deteriorating health coincided with the time of Henry Flagler's divorce and his subsequent marriage to Mary Lily Kenan. Both Rockefellers disagreed with Flagler's divorce, and Mrs. Rockefeller's health problems enabled them to distance themselves from Flagler. Possibly Rockefeller's timing in returning to Florida shortly before and his first visit to the Ormond hotel the winter after Flagler's death was more than a coincidence.[63]

The 1920s brought a brief resurgence in popularity for St. Augustine as a winter destination. On October 1, 1921, the Florida Department of Agriculture released a *Florida Tourist Quarterly Bulletin* noting that the city's hotels could accommodate 3,000 visitors with 1,500 more served in rooming houses (boarding houses or inns). Nearly 5,000 visitors could enjoy St. Augustine between October and March.[64]

A few months earlier, the Atlantic Intracoastal Waterway had opened, incorporating the Tolomato and Matanzas Rivers through St. Augustine en route to its terminus at Miami's Biscayne Bay. Along the west side of downtown, the San Sebastian River south of King Street became the home port for a segment of the former Fernandina Beach shrimping fleet. Both of these maritime elements attracted businesses and tourists.[65]

John D. Rockefeller Jr. brought his five sons to St. Augustine in the 1920s as he was beginning to make investments in Williamsburg. On January 24, 1935, his eldest son, John D. Rockefeller III, and his wife, Blanchette Ferry Rockefeller, visited the Ponce, enjoyed lunch, and toured the building and its gardens.[66]

The Great Depression dealt a devastating blow to Florida tourism, particularly to St. Augustine and the Ponce. Though the Flagler Hotel company under Kenan family management continued to operate the building, business was slow. Economic development proposals geared toward St. Augustine, including an ambitious historic preservation and heritage tourism program, provided minimal relief.

In 1931, John F. Kennedy and his family stayed at the Ponce. He was thirteen years old (fig. 3.11). The Kennedy family was en route to Palm Beach where, two years later, his father Joseph P. Kennedy Sr. bought oceanfront property that became known as the Kennedy compound. The elder Kennedy's sister, Loretta Kennedy Connelly, and her family moved

FIGURE 3.11. Joseph P. Kennedy Sr. with sons Joseph P. Kennedy Jr. (*left*) and John F. Kennedy (*right*), Palm Beach, Florida, 1931. As a youth John F. Kennedy came with his family to St. Augustine, stopping at the Ponce on their way to Palm Beach, where they would buy the property that became known as the Kennedy compound. KFC461P, E. F. Foley. Kennedy Family Collection, John F. Kennedy Presidential Library and Museum, Boston.

to St. Augustine in 1945, where they hosted her brother and his family regularly.[67]

As part of the Ponce's contribution, records dating from October 26, 1934, state that the Florida East Coast Hotel Company authorized the "Automatic" Sprinkler Corporation of America to install a fire sprinkler system, keeping pace with safety standards and requirements of the time. The installation was completed in time for the hotel's opening on December 22, recorded by the *St. Augustine Record* as the Ponce's earliest opening and a positive indication about the success of the winter season. The hotel closed for the season on April 2, 1935.[68]

Beginning in the 1930s, when she was an acclaimed athlete including an Olympic track-and-field star, baseball and tennis player, and amateur golfer, Mildred Ella "Babe" Didrikson began visiting St. Augustine. She married wrestler George Zaharias, and they both enjoyed wintering at the Ponce over the next two decades. She played golf regularly in St. Augustine and socialized throughout the town (fig. 3.12). Nancy Jo Cafaro James, daughter of St. Augustine physician Dr. Raymond Cafaro, recalled that the

FIGURE 3.12. Babe Didrikson Zaharias with her husband, George Zaharias, and dog in St. Augustine, 1947. Internationally acclaimed Olympic athlete in track and field, Babe Zaharias excelled also at golf, baseball, basketball, billiards, bowling, roller skating, and diving. This photograph was taken the year that she became a professional golfer, was first admitted to the men's league, then was a founding member of the LPGA. State Archives of Florida, *Florida Memory*, http://florida memory.com/items/show/55707.

golf champion was a patient of her father's while residing at the Ponce. In 1956, at age 45, Babe Didrikson Zaharias died of cancer.[69]

In March 1938, the Hotel Ponce de Leon hosted a grand dinner as a prelude to the upcoming opening that June of Marineland. The new entertainment and scientific enterprise was developed by Marine Studios' corporate executives Chairman of the Board Cornelius Vanderbilt (C. V.) Whitney, Vanderbilt relative and President W. Douglas Burden, Vice President Count Ilia Tolstoy, and Sherman Pratt, a grandson of Standard Oil Trust cofounder Charles Pratt. Whitney was a grandson of Cornelius Vanderbilt II. Entertainment included the Meyer Davis Orchestra that played at special events at hotels, typically in Washington, D.C., and Philadelphia. Over the years, Marineland's growth and prestige provided business for the Ponce, luring celebrities such as swimmer Johnny Weissmuller who trained at the Alcazar pool and actor Lloyd Bridges for the Marineland Circus in 1961.[70]

By the time the United States entered World War II, half a century and the Great Depression after the hotel's momentous opening, the Ponce's visitation had dwindled to 10 percent of the original numbers. William Rand Kenan Jr., brother-in-law of Henry Flagler and head of Flagler's Florida business enterprises, made the Ponce available to the United States government. The former grand hotel became the founding home of a new military unit, the Coast Guard Reserve. Between 1942 and 1945 the Ponce served as headquarters for the Coast Guard Training Center, hosting 1,500 of the 2,500 soldiers stationed in St. Augustine. The soldiers' training took between six and twelve weeks.[71]

The U.S. government made changes to the building to accommodate the trainees. The Mezzanine space became a library and chapel, and nearby balcony offices were used by the chaplains. The brig was housed in a small room on the fourth floor of the east wing immediately adjacent to the bathroom. The hallway was on the south side of the corridor and changed to the north side in the 1950s when the elevator mechanical system was modernized. Some hotel rooms became classrooms and gear storage. Fire escapes were added on the east and west sides of the Ponce. The building was kept immaculately clean.[72]

The hotel furniture was stored in the vacant Hotel Alcazar. Decorative elements in the hotel were removed or covered. Shades were attached to the frames of Tiffany's stained glass windows in the Dining Room. These shades enabled the room to be darkened so that training movies could be shown. The parade march route left the Ponce entry gate with the troops heading east on King Street, north on St. George Street, through the City Gate, to the parade field on the Fort Marion grounds.[73]

In addition to the Ponce, two other hotels were used. The Bennett and the Monson were located along the bayfront west of the Castillo de San Marcos. Women serving in the SPARS, the female component of the Coast Guard, were stationed on the bayfront at the Ocean View Hotel. The Ponce is the only one of those four buildings still standing; the other three were demolished.[74]

Socialization was important for the soldiers' morale and the community's sense of security. Sports included boat races, golf, and the most competitive and favorite activity—baseball. Dances were held regularly in the Dining Room. As was much of the nation, the military was segregated by gender and race.

In 1944, renowned African American artist Jacob Lawrence spent his first year in the Coast Guard stationed at the Ponce (fig. 3.13). Commanding officer Capt. C. S. Rosenthal knew of Lawrence's talent and encouraged the artist's efforts. Lawrence was influenced by the Harlem Renaissance and used his race as subject matter for his art. His first exhibit in New York crossed the color barrier. The show opened on December 9, 1941, two days after the Japanese bombed Pearl Harbor, initiating the United States' entry into World War II. As was the nation, the military was segregated. Lawrence's responsibility was to serve white officers their meals. None of the original works from this era are believed to have survived.[75]

The U.S. government enlisted other Flagler System hotels for the war effort: the Hotel Ormond in Ormond Beach, the Breakers in Palm Beach, and the Casa Marina Hotel in Key West. The agreement for use of the Breakers as an army hospital for nine months concluded in September 1943 and provided a $250,000 rental fee and funds to ready the hotel for that winter's season. Regardless of world events, William Kenan made certain that wealthy travelers could maintain their annual stays in Palm Beach.[76]

The physical conditions at the Ponce under military occupation were exacerbated by the 1944 Cuba-Florida Hurricane. The extraordinary storm

FIGURE 3.13. Harlem Renaissance artist Jacob Lawrence addressed race through his works. He served in the Coast Guard in World War II and was stationed for a year at the Hotel Ponce de Leon. Acme Newspictures, Inc. photo, 1945 Library of Congress, Prints and Photographs Division, Reproduction Number: LC.USZ62.129809.

that wrought damage across the state for eleven days arrived in St. Augustine on October 19. Local citizens referred to the event as the time when the rivers met.[77]

The Matanzas River was the eastern boundary of the colonial city and the natural separation of the city from its protective barrier, Anastasia Island. Also, the river was the link from the city to the Atlantic Ocean. St. Augustine's western boundary was the San Sebastian River that flowed into the Matanzas, forming the southern boundary of the city.

The hurricane unleashed winds of 130 miles per hour and rains that flooded the city. The Matanzas and the San Sebastian overflowed their banks. At least twelve inches of water ran through the streets. Coast Guard troops navigated their surfboats through the city as rescue vehicles. With the principal floors elevated, the building became a safe haven, though its carriageways were impassable and lower levels were flooded.[78]

As with the Breakers, the military use of the hotels left the buildings damaged. When the military returned the Ponce to the hotel company at the end of 1945, work was needed to return the hotel to operating condition.

A year later, Commander-in-Chief and President Harry Truman made his first of many train trips through St. Augustine en route to Key West. FEC executives notified Kenan when the president's train passed through the city. His travels through the nation's oldest city continued a longstanding presidential tradition.

Post–World War II expectations for the traveling public led to changes in hotel accommodations nationwide. The Flagler System sought to compete by updating the Ponce. In 1952, the Palm Beach engineering firm of Norman C. Schmid and Associates submitted designs for an outdoor swimming pool that would be located on the west lawn of the property. On this location a fountain marked the site of the artesian well that had powered the hotel when it opened in 1888, drawing the attention of scientific and engineering publications.[79]

Improvements through the 1950s included upgrades to elevators. As evidenced by comparing blueprints for the building to existing conditions, a change on the fourth floor to accommodate the east elevator mechanism flipped the location of the corridor and rooms. As built and used until this time, the corridor ran straight east off a short staircase from the 400 Rotunda (Solarium), with rooms located to the left or north of the corridor. Beginning with this renovation in the 1950s to the present, the corridor runs along the north side of the wing. Plaster, lathe, and stud walls exposed during 2013 renovations verified the reversal.

William Rand Kenan Jr. and his sisters Jessie Kenan Wise and Sarah Graham Kenan used the Ponce as their legal residence. The siblings each maintained a large suite on the third floor of the west wing accessed by a private elevator. The suites were large enough to entertain several dinner guests and featured a living room, two bedrooms, a bath, and a pantry from which both food and drinks could be served. Formal attire—black tie, not white tie—was required.[80]

Alyn Pope recalled that same era as a teenager working at his father's business, Neil Pope's Garage, at 58 Charlotte Street, three blocks east of the Ponce. The business served guests from the Ponce and the nearby Bennett and Monson Hotels through each hotel's bell captains. The three-story garage building accommodated about fifty cars, including those belonging

FIGURE 3.14. Group portrait at St. Augustine's Easter celebration, 1959. St. Augustine's "royal family" tradition reinforces the city's Spanish heritage and was one of the many social activities held in the Hotel Ponce de Leon. State Archives of Florida, *Florida Memory*, http://floridamemory.com/items/show/76232.

to owners of businesses with offices in the Exchange Bank Building who were primarily doctors and attorneys. Pope's father personally maintained William Kenan's 1940 black Cadillac limousine that featured gray felt interior and was driven by a chauffeur named Chappy. Pope serviced the car and kept it in running order. Louise Lewis Foster, Mrs. Wise's great-granddaughter, remembered coming to the beautiful Ponce in 1956, during spring vacation with two high school friends. Her great-grandmother toured the girls in the limousine to Weeki Wachee to see the mermaids.[81]

A cousin, Tom Kenan, reminisced that the hotel maintained a full staff, including a waiter to stand behind every chair. The food was delicious, and a small orchestra played during dinner. Gainesville attorney Roy Hunt, newly moved to Florida in 1962, verified that the hotel maintained its elegance, refinement, and a sense of grandeur. St. Augustine native and historian Michael Gannon noted that dinner dances in the Dining Room and the band music at the Gay 90s bar located beneath the Dining Room were major attractions for guests and St. Augustine residents.[82]

The Easter 1959 Royal Family event recognizing Florida's Spanish heritage was one of the many community events held at the Ponce (fig. 3.14). The Grand Parlor and Dining Room provided elegant settings for pageantry and spectacle, entertainment and dining. The dome room or 400 Rotunda, now recognized as the Solarium, hosted less dramatic activities, such as weekly bingo or card games.[83]

The Ponce played a swansong role with St. Augustine's 400th anniversary celebration, which took place between 1963 and 1965. Preparations had begun a decade earlier that brought international dignitaries to the city, and they stayed in suites at the grand hotel. On March 11, 1963, Vice President Lyndon B. Johnson led a national delegation. Senator Hubert Humphrey, who would be elected Johnson's vice president in coming months, stayed at the Ponce, as did Florida senators Bruce Smathers and Spessard Holland.[84]

On October 28, 1964, A. R. MacMannis, president of the Florida East Coast Hotel Company, announced that the Ponce would open on November 20. This schedule coincided with St. Augustine's 400th anniversary celebration. The hotel was in the process of completing major upgrades to facilities, including "an auditorium seating 200 and complete with audiovisual equipment, modernized kitchen, new telephone system, and a new room, El Toro Bravo, featuring cocktails and buffet luncheons. . . . New innovations will include refinements in the hotel's famous cuisine, a Sunday champagne brunch and a special Thanksgiving dinner to be served on Nov. 26."[85]

One contemporary entertainment that attracted visitors to the city was the television series *Route 66*, which filmed two 1964 episodes, "Dove with a Broken Wing" and "This Is Going to Hurt You More Than It Hurts Me," around town. Actors Martin Milner, George Maharis, Soupy Sales, and Lee Meriwether were featured (fig. 3.15). Scenes featured community members including St. Augustine High School student Greg Baker and a

FIGURE 3.15. Actors Martin Milner and George Maharis pose in the Hotel Ponce de Leon Lobby as part of a television episode filmed for St. Augustine's 400th anniversary and sponsored by the hotel. "This Is Going to Hurt Me More Than It Hurts You," *Route 66* television episode, Flagler College Archives.

young Len Weeks, both of whom went on to become mayors of the city. The Flagler System funded the production of the latter, with the Ponce figuring prominently in the shooting. One of the final scenes proved to be the trademark Soupy Sales routine, a cream pie fight, in this instance held in the Ponce Dining Room.[86]

The 400th anniversary programs proved to be the last major functions that the building enjoyed as a hotel. Will Kenan and his sisters, family members that were Henry Flagler's contemporaries and had sustained the hotel throughout the twentieth century, passed away in the 1960s. Lawrence Lewis Jr., Wise's grandson, assumed management of the Ponce. Discussion had been under way for some time between Kenan heirs and the Carlson family of Connecticut. The latter proposed to convert the Ponce into a four-year undergraduate women's college. As this proposal took shape, plans proceeded to conclude the building's tenure as a hotel.[87]

The Ponce's seventy-ninth and final season opened on October 28, 1966, recognized with a feature story in the *St. Augustine Record* detailing the upcoming activities that were scheduled for the building. Highlighted events were an annual Catholic priests' retreat that would use the entire hotel. Football fans in the area for the Florida-Georgia Gator Bowl would stay at the hotel, and the Woman's Exchange would hold its annual charity ball there.[88]

On April 5, 1967, the Flagler System hosted a final dinner dance that drew crowds from St. Augustine and Jacksonville to witness the end of an era. As had been the case throughout the history of the building, the final gala was held with style and attention to detail. The Bruce Thomas Orchestra played, and more than two hundred guests were invited. Elizabeth Morley Towers, Jacksonville community philanthropist with ties to St. Augustine's historic preservation program since the 1930s, brought her family to the event. Her daughter Sarah Towers Van Cleve reminisced nearly forty-five years later with her children who had enjoyed the event on the remarkable history and architecture of the Hotel Ponce de Leon. Proceeds from the event exceeded $2,500 and were earmarked to fund a scholarship for a student from St. Johns County to attend the new Flagler College.[89]

Substantial construction of the Ponce had been completed in May of 1887. The building completed its final season as a hotel eighty years later, operating continuously throughout that period with the exception of the three years between 1942 and 1945, when the building hosted the Coast Guard Reserve.

As with any luxury lodging establishment, the building was updated throughout its history. The final configuration featured 240 rooms that were rented and numerous other rooms for a sizable staff. The principal business was from conventions headquartered at the hotel. At the time of the closing, rates for the hotel ranged from a single room for one person at $10.00 to $15.00, and a double was $12.00 to $18.00. A tariff of $16.00 to $32.00 was charged for family rooms that accommodated two to four persons. A suite with a sitting room and bedroom could be reserved for $16.00 to $26.00 for a single person and $26.00 to $30.00 for two people. Each room included a private bath.[90]

With the opening of the Hotel Ponce de Leon, Henry Flagler gained international acclaim. Over the next several decades entrepreneurs had business successes capitalizing on the Flagler name and reputation. Though the following overview may seem to be a fanciful stretch in relation to the Ponce, the information illustrates the importance of the St. Augustine hotel and its reputation.

In the late nineteenth century, many of the seasonal leisure tourists, the hotel management and staff members, and artists who painted at the resorts of the North in the summers traveled each winter to the resorts of the South, especially to the Ponce. Flagler's hotels did not operate in a vacuum but were a component of a national movement encompassing travel, leisure, sports, and entertainment. In 1888, the Ponce set a high standard against which other resorts were measured for exceptional service and hospitality in an exuberant Gilded Age setting.

Those hotels and resorts that shared a relationship of staff or guests with the Ponce are discussed in the next section. Also, those hotels and resorts are mentioned that gained fame in part from their association with Henry Flagler or the Ponce, however tenuous those ties.

In 1872, in the Catskill Mountains of New York, native Carrie G. Flagler opened the Flagler House, a thirty-five-room summer hotel in (South) Fallsburg, three hours from New York City. The Flagler House thrived particularly after the *New York Times* covered activities at Henry Flagler's St. Augustine hotels. The upstate New York Flagler House appears to have enjoyed the affiliation in owners' names only. Adding to the fortunate coincidence were personal connections. Henry Flagler's sister Caroline Flagler was nicknamed Carrie, and both Presbyterian families hailed from upstate New York.[91]

In 1908, Asias Fleischer and Philip Morgenstern bought Flagler House and expanded the building in size and scope to achieve the status of a kosher hotel. By 1920, when domestic business had resumed after World War I, the renamed Flagler Hotel had attained a reputation as the most prestigious of Sullivan County's many prominent hotels. Fleischer and Morgenstern added a Sullivan County Mission style building, emulating in concept the Spanish heritage that Henry Flagler honored in St. Augustine (fig. 3.16). In 1929, the Flagler Hotel became a winter ski resort, and with major building modifications the property continued as a summer vacation destination until the 1960s.[92]

In 1898, a decade after Henry Flagler opened the Ponce, the Phelps Dodge Mining Company began construction of a hotel at Bisbee in the Arizona Territory. Completed in 1902 and named for the Copper Queen

FIGURE 3.16. The Flagler Hotel in the Catskill Mountains achieved success as a tourist attraction based on the name, though it had no relationship to Henry Flagler. Photo courtesy of Steingart Associates, South Fallsburg, New York.

mine, the hotel featured a polychromatic appearance with poured concrete walls, red brick trim, hipped-roofed corner towers, and overhanging balconies. As with the Ponce, the Copper Queen Hotel was designed by protégés of McKim, Mead & White, in this case the New York firm of Van Vleck and Goldsmith. They and their client would have been familiar with the Hotel Ponce de Leon. Interiors of the Copper Queen were reputed to have featured Italian tile, oak woodwork, and Tiffany-style glass. The building bore a strong similarity in appearance and convenience to the Ponce's guest room wings (fig. 3.17). The Copper Queen Hotel thrived as a modern hotel in the midst of the rural West. Today, the building continues its reign as the region's preeminent hotel and retains its historic appearance, albeit minus evidence of Italian tile or Tiffany-style glass.[93]

Under the presidency of New York railroad and steel executive William Earle Dodge Jr., the mining company grew exponentially. Dodge and William Rockefeller partnered in western copper mining enterprises, and their families intermarried. A namesake Dodge family member wintered at Flagler's Palm Beach hotels, traveled to the Ponce where he stayed before visiting with the Carnegie family on Cumberland Island. The New York business and social connections stretched across the nation.[94]

Flagler spent late summers in the White Mountains of New Hampshire,

FIGURE 3.17. Copper Queen Hotel in Bisbee, Arizona. Built for the Phelps Dodge Mining Company, this building shared similarities with the Hotel Ponce de Leon and reflected New York architects Van Vleek and Goldsmith's familiarity with the work of Carrère and Hastings. The building remains in use as a hotel today. Arizona State Library, Archives and Public Records, History and Archives Division, Phoenix, #94.7383.

where many of his New York business colleagues vacationed and the Ponce artists painted. About 1895, Flagler introduced native Pennsylvanian and fellow New York railroad magnate Joseph Stickney to his hotel managers John Anderson and Joseph Price who managed Flagler's Ormond Beach Hotel. Stickney hired Anderson and Price to manage his summer resort, the Mount Pleasant House in Bretton Woods.[95]

In 1896, New York architect Charles Alling Gifford designed the six-unit Sans Souci building at the Jekyl Island Club for an equal number of New York's elite and Flagler's colleagues, including Stickney and William Rockefeller. A few years later Flagler influenced Stickney to retain Gifford for the design of a new hotel near the Mount Pleasant House. Gifford's large, modern, and technologically advanced Mount Washington Hotel opened in 1902, the year after Stickney's death, and shared many similarities and conveniences with Flagler's Hotel Ponce de Leon.[96]

Gifford had designed the New Jersey state building for the World's Columbian Exposition in 1893 and, after completing the Mount Washington Hotel, went on to design the New Jersey building for the St. Louis World's Fair in 1904. Between 1899 and 1901, at the same time of the Mount Washington project, Dr. Andrew Anderson retained Gifford to redesign Markland in St. Augustine. Also, Carrère and Hastings overlapped with Gifford in the locations of their commissions, the New England mountain resorts, Long Island mansions, and properties in St. Augustine. Numerous parallels between the northern resorts and Flagler's hotels acknowledge the discerning public's demand for luxury and convenience—and Henry Flagler's role at the forefront of the trend.[97]

With construction of the Ponce, Flagler achieved artistic design, fireproof construction, and contemporary facilities. The Ponce met the needs of discerning wealthy guests, many of whom were Flagler's business colleagues and friends. Under Flagler's influence over the next quarter century, St. Augustine hosted politicians, socialites, industrialists, musicians, and athletes. The city retained its longstanding attractiveness to authors and artists. The Ponce sustained a position as the center of the region's social life, and St. Augustine continued to enjoy a reputation as a Spanish colonial city with European ambience and characteristics.

Flagler bought the Hotel Cordova (Casa Monica), 95 Cordova Street, in April of 1888, after its first season, and built or funded institutions— Grace Methodist Episcopal Church; Cathedral Basilica; Ancient City Baptist Church; a jail used today as a museum; and the *St. Augustine Record* newspaper building, now apartments. His residence Kirkside was located immediately west of Memorial Presbyterian Church. Some of his institutional buildings did not survive: Alicia Hospital on Marine Street; City Hall, 98 St. George Street; and the YMCA near Riberia and Valencia Streets. He founded the Florida East Coast Railway, headquartered on Malaga at King Streets. The General Office Buildings serve now as Flagler College residence halls, and support facilities that were located across King Street are the San Sebastian Winery.

The Hotel Ponce de Leon, a creative and exuberant reflection of the optimism and economic vitality of the Gilded Age, launched a new and lengthy chapter in Flagler's life. At the time he completed the Ponce, just 25 miles to the north Jacksonville became Florida's largest city, a status that city retained until after World War II. Jacksonville functioned as the social, economic, and political capital of Florida. Flagler continued to develop hotels, moving north and south along the east coast. Ultimately, his resort empire stretched from Jacksonville to Key West and across the water to Havana, Cuba, and Nassau, Bahamas.

Flagler developed the Florida East Coast Railway (FEC) as a means to link his resort hotels. Through the state of Florida's legal land development program, essentially a pass through of federal land, Flagler received 250,000 acres of land in North Florida, significantly more than other railroad developers. As Flagler moved down the east coast with his hotel empire, he received more than double the legally mandated number of acres for development of his rail lines. As political pressure tightened the land development process, Flagler maneuvered surreptitiously around the legal requirements, acquiring millions of acres of land in the Sunshine State.[98]

The Florida East Coast Railway's construction had reached present-day Miami by 1896, just over a decade after Henry Flagler bought his first parcel of land in St. Augustine. Flagler constructed eight hotels and acquired several more as his empire moved southward along Florida's east coast.

Also significant to Florida's development was the Plant Steamship Line that began in 1886 and operated with two ships, the *Olivette* and the *Mascotte*. The preeminent William Cramp & Sons Ship and Engine Building Company of Philadelphia built both ships. The *Mascotte* was a 215-foot-long steamer that Plant launched on October 27, 1885, with some of his PICO partners, five weeks before Henry Flagler broke ground on the Hotel Ponce de Leon. The *Olivette*, nearly 275 feet long, was ready in April 1887. The ships traveled from Port Tampa to Key West and Havana and from Miami to Nassau carrying passengers, cargo, and mail.[99]

In December of 1894, the firm of Raymond & Whitcomb, with offices in New York, Boston, and Philadelphia, promoted Raymond's Vacation Excursions. These all-expense-paid tours to Florida cities during the month of January ran along Plant's PICO rail lines or Flagler's FEC and featured Pullman cars. Guests visited St. Augustine, with an extended stay at Flagler's Ponce. From there they traveled west to the Ocklawaha and St. Johns Rivers and south to the cities of Palatka, Ormond, Rockledge, and Lake

Worth, to a lengthy stay at Flagler's Hotel Royal Poinciana in Palm Beach. The westward leg passed through Winter Park and Plant's Seminole Hotel and on to Tampa for a stay in Plant's Tampa Bay Hotel.[100]

These excursion vacations could be extended, enabling visitors to stay in Florida for five months, with the final train leaving on May 31. Also, visitors could travel to Cuba on the Plant Steamship Line, enjoying a week in Havana.[101]

Plant retained his connections to the northeastern United States. With $1,000,000 in capital, he organized the Atlantic, Canada, and Plant Steamship Line, Limited, that operated in the summers between Boston, Massachusetts, and Halifax, Nova Scotia. In 1893, Plant acquired Canada's North Atlantic Steamship Line that had operated for half a century in that country. This added routes to Cape Breton and Prince Edward Island.[102]

In 1893, Mr. and Mrs. Plant hosted Henry and Ida Alice "Alicia" Flagler for a cruise from Tampa on Plant's chartered Halifax steamship, leaving on February 16, for Nassau and Jamaica, returning ten days later. This trip was reciprocation for a recent excursion the couples shared to Flagler's properties, the Indian River and Plaza Hotels at Rockledge, Brevard County, Florida. The couples lived near each other in New York. The Flagler mansion was located at 685 Fifth Avenue at East 54th Street. The Plants lived at 586 Fifth Avenue between West 47th and West 48th Streets.[103]

Plant's steamships became significant links in the Spanish-American War. The steamships provided transportation for Teddy Roosevelt's Rough Riders to Havana and returned soldiers to the United States. The Tampa Bay Hotel served as a holding area for troops and headquarters for war correspondents, including Stephen Crane, who lived briefly in Jacksonville. Clara Barton joined the effort on behalf of the American Red Cross. Six additional Plant ships participated.[104]

In 1899, Flagler had the Colonial Hotel built on Bay Street, overlooking Nassau Harbor in the Bahamas. Canadian shipping magnate Sir Roderick Cameron and his daughters concluded their two-week visit as guests of the governor general in Nassau, arriving at the Ponce in early April. The St. Augustine hotel hosted the family and closed at a record late date of April 15, the last of the Florida hotels to conclude the winter season.[105]

At the settlement of Plant's will in 1900, Flagler acquired the Plant System's steamship lines, forging the Peninsular and Occidental Steamship

Company. Acquisition of the steamship lines worked in tandem with Flagler's efforts to extend his resort empire to the Caribbean and to complete a railroad to Key West en route to the Panama Canal. The merged line had a lengthy and distinguished career of service, long outliving its progenitors.[106]

Theodore Roosevelt, elected U.S. President in 1900, committed the United States to completing construction of the Panama Canal, which was begun as part of a French treaty twenty years earlier. Construction resumed in 1904, the year after a revolution resulted in Panama becoming a United States protectorate, and the canal was finished a decade later. Also in 1904, at the age of 74, Flagler announced that he would continue his railroad to Key West. He recognized the importance of extending his business interests beyond the borders of the continental United States and that this Overseas Extension, the "Railroad across the Sea," would accomplish that goal. Key West could provide water access closer to Panama than any other U.S. port city.

The two massive construction projects shared parallel time frames and drew comparable public attention, with "Flagler's Folly" considered as the more daunting endeavor. When the railroad terminated at Key West on January 22, 1912, twenty days after Flagler's eighty-second birthday, it was immediately acclaimed as the Eighth Wonder of the World. Riding the new rails with Henry and Mary Lily Flagler were "Assistant Secretary of War Robert Shaw Oliver and diplomats from Italy, Mexico, Portugal, Costa Rica, Ecuador, Guatemala, San Salvador and Uruguay."[107]

Over twenty-eight years Flagler's tenacity transformed St. Augustine and Florida forever. With Flagler's extensive transportation network of railroads and steamships and his participation in construction of the Atlantic Intracoastal Waterway system, Florida became a preeminent national and international vacation destination, with St. Augustine serving as the gateway.

The Hotel Ponce de Leon met Henry Flagler's expectations and those of his guests. In a 1909 interview, with construction of his overseas railway through the Florida Keys well under way, Flagler maintained that building the Ponce had been his greatest challenge.[108]

On Thursday, May 22, 1913, the undisputed Father of Modern Florida returned to St. Augustine and the Hotel Ponce de Leon one last time, where he lay in state in the Rotunda. Once again, the Ponce drew national attention. In his honor, the Florida East Coast Railway announced that on the following day, at 3:00 p.m., "every train on the Florida East Coast Railway will stand still for ten minutes. Other roads in the State will halt traffic for five minutes."[109]

The Ponce served as a luxury hotel for forty years until the Great Depression halted tourism nationally. The hotel remained open, though operating more in a community role as the favored location for the area's social events, large and small. The decade of the 1930s brought an interest in reviving heritage tourism in St. Augustine only to be stymied by the lack of a focused approach and the nation's participation in World War II. Tourism revived in the 1950s as former soldiers brought their families by auto via U.S. Route 1 to see the nation's oldest city, including new attractions and house museums. The Ponce continued as the city's grand host hotel. Under William Kenan and the Flagler System's leadership, the building offered a new audience modern amenities to the hotel property, including a swimming pool. St. Augustine's 400th anniversary preparations and celebration showcased the grand hotel one last time. This proved to be the swansong for the elder Kenans as well, as their lives paralleled the time frame of the hotel. The Ponce closed its doors on April 5, 1967.[110]

4

Historic Preservation in St. Augustine

Historic preservation has driven St. Augustine's economy for nearly 200 years. In 1821, the Spanish town became the heart of the new U.S. territory of Florida and an exotic tourism destination for northerners. Reminiscent of small European cities, this distinctiveness served as the attraction that brought Henry Flagler to St. Augustine in 1878, encouraged him to return annually beginning in 1883, and inspired him to develop the east coast of Florida until his death in 1913.

Flagler created a legacy in St. Augustine based on classical European architecture that inspired thousands of visitors to experience the unique and historic city. This legacy began with construction of the Hotel Ponce de Leon, which developed its own legacy as a luxury resort before becoming the cornerstone of a private college. The relationship between St. Augustine, the Ponce, and historic preservation in the United States is nearly inseparable. To understand fully the Ponce's transition from Gilded Age resort hotel to college campus centerpiece requires an understanding of historic preservation in St. Augustine.

Local preservation efforts can be traced to an action that took place in 1827. Lieutenant Harvey Brown, U.S. military post quartermaster at Fort Marion, halted demolition of the City Gate (fig. 4.1). In 1808, masonry columns had been constructed to identify the City Gate, the most identifiable feature from the wall that fortified the town. By the time demolition stopped, most of the bridge, sentry boxes, and abutment were disassembled, and removal of the gate posts had begun. The city planned to reuse the materials for construction of a causeway. For the next fifty-two years,

FIGURE 4.1. The Old City Gate, St. Augustine, photo taken between 1880 and 1897. Annually, millions of visitors pass between these gate posts that represent St. Augustine's era as a walled city. Photo by William H. Jackson, Library of Congress, Prints & Photographs Division, Reproduction Number: LC.DIG.det.4a03493.

throughout the Seminole Indian wars and the Civil War, the gate remained standing and continued to deteriorate. In 1879, after Reconstruction ended and as tourists returned to St. Augustine, the municipal government repaired this unique feature.[1]

In 1908, the 100th anniversary of the City Gate, the U.S. government deeded the adjacent land to the St. Johns County Board of Public Instruction for a new high school building. The dry moat was filled with earth, and demolition of the gate was proposed once again. By this time Flagler's three hotels had enjoyed twenty years of hosting some of the United States' and Europe's most glamorous and wealthiest elite. Flagler commissioned a special trophy featuring the City Gate for his Tropical Championship tennis tournament. Nationally renowned photographer William Henry Jackson included the gate in several of his works. Publications touting the heritage of the city featured the gate. Tourism had regained prominence, and the City Gate was an important component of that effort.

The year before the centennial anniversary, the National Society of The Colonial Dames of America in The State of Florida (Colonial Dames) installed a tablet describing the importance of the City Gate. The installation was undertaken with great fanfare and to draw attention to this symbol of St. Augustine's colonial past. In 1965, the Dames installed a second plaque for St. Augustine's 400th anniversary, and in 1972 a third plaque was presented in honor of the 300th anniversary of the Castillo de San Marcos.[2]

In 1912, led by Dr. DeWitt Webb, mayor of St. Augustine and a founder and president of the historical society, the city of St. Augustine obtained permission from the U.S. Army Corps of Engineers to assume responsibility for repair and maintenance of the City Gate and the adjacent property. Preservation of the gate began the following year. With establishment of Fort Marion as a national monument in 1935 under the auspices of the National Park Service, the gate, bridge, causeway, and triangular park area on which they all rested returned to federal management. A few years later, to recognize St. Augustine's Spanish heritage, the federal government reinstituted the original name Castillo de San Marcos. While threatened with destruction, neglect, and demolition for nearly two centuries, today millions of visitors appreciate the fort and cross through the passageway created in 1739 and marked originally by simple wooden guard shelters.[3]

In 1911, the St. Augustine Historical Society opened a museum on the bayfront in a long-standing building known as the Sanchez House. A few years later that building was destroyed by fire. Also in 1911, the society served as the driving force behind preserving Fort Matanzas south of St. Augustine. Two years later, led by society president New Yorker Chauncey Depew, the U.S. War Department authorized the society to develop a program of interpretation for Fort Marion, thereby institutionalizing heritage tourism for the city. In 1918, the society added reconstruction and restoration of colonial buildings to its activities. The Oldest House/Gonzalez-Alvarez House and the Tovar House were the organization's first preservation projects.[4]

Florida's fragile heritage assets were threatened by devastating storms in the 1920s and 1930s. On September 30, 1920, a tropical hurricane, described at the time as "a fierce nor'easter," came up the Gulf of Mexico and made landfall at Cedar Key before heading east across the state and into the Atlantic Ocean at St. Augustine. Property on the mainland and eastward over the barrier islands was damaged by wind and rain from the storm. With concerted physical and promotional efforts, St. Augustine recovered and hosted a celebration six months later that drew a national audience.[5]

On February 22, 1921, a crowd of thousands gathered at the fort for the George Washington birthday celebration, simultaneously the centennial anniversary of Florida becoming a U.S. territory. With President-elect and Mrs. Warren G. Harding attending and members of the Historical Society and the Colonial Dames participating, the crowd cheered the launch of new chapters in the history of Fort Marion and Fort Matanzas. The Colonial Dames presented four bronze tablets describing important eras in Florida's history. The festivities drew the largest event attendance in the city's history.[6]

About 1904, physician Luella Day McConnell developed the Fountain of Youth, about one mile north of Fort Marion, and operated it until her death in 1927. Then Walter B. Fraser bought the tourist attraction. In addition to continuing the attraction, Fraser planted orange groves and mined for titanium. In 1934, after discovery of human burials, Fraser contacted the Smithsonian Institution. Subsequently, more than one hundred burials were located. Since the 1970s, archaeologist Kathleen Deagan of the University of Florida has served as principal investigator at the property, providing the scholarly foundation for much of the interpretation of the property available for visitors and scholars today. The Fountain of Youth Archaeological Park evidences both early habitation and early tourism grounded in Florida history. The property is internationally important as part of the Menendez landing site in 1565, which extended southward to the Mission de Nombre de Dios property. Fraser's grandchildren operate the property.[7]

As Florida's role grew as an automobile tourism destination, improved transportation became necessary. In 1927, after nearly a decade of planning and construction, the federal government opened U.S. Route 1, a national road running north from Miami, Florida, up the east coast through St.

Augustine to Kent, Maine: "Connecting semi-tropical Florida with the north-temperate Maine, the road is the principal tourist route from the large eastern cities to the winter resorts of the South and the summer resorts of New England. Its strategic value as a military road in time of war is the conclusive element which stamps this road as the most important, everything considered, in the United States."[8] As U.S. 1 served as the primary north-south thoroughfare into Florida at this time, the route split south of St. Augustine, forking to provide access to the east and west coasts. With the opening of the road, travelers could arrive in St. Augustine in their personal automobiles, as well as by the long-established modes of water and rail.

One such traveler was Ernest Hemingway who commented specifically about the beauty of St. Augustine. From 1928 through at least 1941, Hemingway drove routinely between his residence in Key West and his in-laws' residence in Arkansas. When in St. Augustine he visited friends and fellow authors, including John Dos Passos, who stayed at the Ponce, and Marjorie Kinnan Rawlings who, with husband Norton Baskin, operated a small lodging establishment in the former Castle Warden.[9]

The Great Depression of the 1930s decimated Florida's tourist-driven economy, hitting St. Augustine and Key West hard. Key West, heavily in debt, with four-fifths of the population destitute, filed for bankruptcy. St. Augustine threatened to follow Key West's lead and leave financial management in the hands of the state government. Officials recognized the infeasibility of managing the operations of two municipalities, especially at opposite ends of the state and hundreds of miles from the capital at Tallahassee. Business leaders realized that Florida's ability to rebound economically hinged, in large part, on the ability to lure tourists and real estate investors back to the Sunshine State. Both groups worked with community leaders in St. Augustine to launch an alternate economic approach to bankrupty.[10]

The first public project was reconstruction of the Cubo defense line, the fortification adjacent to Fort Marion. In 1933, the National Park Service assumed management of the property. William Rand Kenan Jr., Florida East Coast Railway and Hotel Ponce de Leon chief executive, donated funds for the reconstruction of the defense line. The project was started but not completed.[11]

Henry Flagler had underwritten Florida's participation in the Columbian Exposition of 1893. In the twentieth century, through the private, non-profit corporation Florida National Exhibits (FNE), the state of Florida sponsored exhibits at special events in New York, Atlantic City, and Philadelphia. Each of these opportunities introduced northerners to the possibilities of visiting or investing in Florida, including St. Augustine. The largest audiences enjoyed Florida exhibits in 1933–1934 at the Chicago World's Fair, known as the Century of Progress, at the Great Lakes Exposition held in Cleveland in 1936–1937, and three years later at the New York World's Fair.[12]

Natural hazards threatened to sidetrack the interest in Florida generated during the Chicago World's Fair. Over Labor Day Weekend in 1935, a massive hurricane hit the Florida Keys. The storm destroyed Flagler's Overseas Railway connecting the islands to the mainland and resulted in the death of an estimated 500 people, including many out-of-work veterans sent by the federal government to construct the parallel transportation route known as the Overseas Highway.

Despite damage suffered from the hurricane, at the end of the winter tourist season a half-year later, Florida set a tourism record. Overall, Florida attracted 2,000,000 visitors, who generated $625,000,000 in income for the state. This success spurred Florida's participation in the 1939 New York World's Fair, featuring waterfront access and the largest exhibition at 118,000 square feet. The exhibit attracted an estimated 5,000,000 visitors. This pattern of Florida marketing at national events continued through the 1964 New York World's Fair, which served as a prelude to St. Augustine's Quadricentennial Anniversary the following year. Tourism sustained Florida's economy, and St. Augustine was a centerpiece of that industry.[13]

St. Augustine's assets provided the main draw for tourists. In 1933, a New Deal initiative led to establishment within the National Park Service (NPS) of the Branch of History. Verne E. Chatelain was the first chief historian. Chatelain, who possessed both a doctorate in history and a law degree, advocated an approach that reflected the continuum of a property's history when it was being incorporated under the NPS umbrella. In addition to his early efforts with national battlefields, Chatelain was instrumental in the drafting and adoption of the Historic Sites Act of 1935 that resulted in the recording of thousands of historical resources nationwide.[14]

On February 27, 1936, Fountain of Youth owner and St. Augustine mayor Walter Fraser introduced a resolution to develop a comprehensive preservation program in line with Chatelain's approach. The resolution was adopted unanimously, and Fraser appointed a citizens committee to pursue the program and develop an action plan. A major component of the plan was to establish the colonial city as a restricted area and to secure public and private funds for restoration and preservation.[15]

In March 1936, Fort Marion's superintendent Herbert Kahler led the Carnegie Institution of Washington's president John Merriam on a tour of the city's historic assets. The result was a proposal to expand preservation efforts through a federal-local partnership with National Park Service staff and the Carnegie Institution. On October 26, 1936, the National Committee for the Preservation and Restoration of Historic St. Augustine held its inaugural meeting in Washington, D.C. The list of participants is lengthy and distinguished, recognizing the importance of the program. Members included Fraser; Merriam; Kahler; Walter G. Leland, permanent secretary, American Council of Learned Societies, Washington, D.C.; Judge David R. Dunham, president, St. Augustine Historical Society; The Most Reverend Patrick Harry, bishop of the Diocese of St. Augustine; Hon. John J. Tigert, president, University of Florida; Hon. Scott Loftin, former Florida senator; Carita Doggett Corse, Florida State director, Federal Writer's Project; Honorable Wilbur C. Hall, chairman, Commission on Conservation and Development; A. V. Kidder, Division of Historical Research, Carnegie Institution; Herbert E. Bolton, professor of history, University of California–Berkeley; Honorable Harry F. Byrd, senator from Virginia; Honorable H. J. Eckenrode, director, Division of History and Archaeology, State of Virginia; Honorable Joshua C. Chase, president, Florida Historical Society; Verne Chatelain, Carnegie Institution; and John E. Pickering, editor of the *St. Augustine Observer*.[16]

Mayor Fraser's proposal was based on a historic preservation approach, preserving the nation's Spanish culture as embodied in the physical evidence remaining in the city. He presented the National Committee's plan to use restored historic buildings as a framework to interpret colonial life. In addition, financial commitments were pledged to demonstrate community support, $1,000 from the St. Augustine Historical Society and $500 from Louise Wise Lewis, Henry Flagler's niece and principal heir. The city of St. Augustine stepped up with $3,000. As a result of the meeting, Merriam pledged short-term funding contingent upon implementation of a substantive development plan. The theme illustrated St. Augustine's lengthy history and emphasized accuracy in preservation and authenticity in interpretation.[17]

The St. Augustine Historical Program was launched in two parts. One component focused on documentary research on the community, environs, and the landscape. The second segment created historic property surveys and evaluated originality of historic structures. The latter segment was led by national experts, including Leland; Bolton; Kidder; William E. Lingelbach, professor of history, University of Pennsylvania; and Matthew W. Stirling, chief, Bureau of American Ethnology, Smithsonian Institution. Merriam and Chatelain oversaw the project. Albert Manucy, a St. Augustine native and National Park Service historian, assisted in the process.[18]

The Carnegie Institution provided a $500 grant for acclaimed photographer Frances Benjamin Johnston to document St. Augustine's historic resources. Her work began in December of 1936 and supplemented architectural documentation being undertaken simultaneously as part of the Historic American Buildings Survey (HABS). The project, operating nationwide, used architects to prepare measured drawings of historic resources in a community, ultimately recording thousands of structures. In Florida, much of the HABS work focused in St. Augustine, providing a valuable record particularly of Spanish colonial buildings.[19]

Johnston took nearly 200 photographs, completing work in time for an exhibition of select photographs. In January of 1937, she previewed a Southern architecture portfolio at the Ponce before the photographs were introduced at the Smithsonian Institution in February. Johnston's work emphasized St. Augustine's Spanish colonial buildings, thereby reinforcing the Carnegie Institution's interest in fostering heritage tourism as part of the historic preservation effort. She included Flagler's Victorian-era hotels. The works were regarded as superb. The documentation was a component of the larger research project that resulted in about 7,500 negatives and formed the collection identified as the Carnegie Survey of the Architecture of the South. The project provided a record of buildings, street scenes, and landscapes under the assumption that many of the resources would be demolished in the future.[20]

In the early 1890s, Johnston had achieved fame for her photographs of the White House and of the Columbian Exposition. She demonstrated her skills with architectural photography and drew notice from the nation's architects. In 1909, Carrère & Hastings retained her to present their work in New York. Possibly this connection between the New York architects and the photographer added to her desire to include Flagler's St. Augustine hotels in the Carnegie project three decades later.[21]

In 1937, Chatelain submitted his report to the St. Augustine National Commission. The report reinforced addressing the continuum of St. Augustine's history, recognizing that the city was a changing environment in which citizens should continue to thrive. Multiple ethnicities evident in St. Augustine's history should be highlighted. Features should include walking spaces, parking areas, and a museum based in documented history. A *New York Times* article praised the recommendations in anticipation that the results would lead to efforts to showcase more than just Fort Marion. In support of this approach, articles were published in the *St. Augustine Record* featuring Flagler-era buildings. From 1938 to 1940, archaeological investigations located the former walled city's defenses. To protect these assets, the city adopted a zoning ordinance emphasizing historic landmark preservation. Although in full swing by 1940, St. Augustine's restoration was interrupted by World War II.[22]

The plan focused on properties that anchored the historic district, advocating restoration of thirty-six properties and re-creation of others based on archaeological and documentary evidence. In 1938, the Carnegie Institution bought the eighteenth-century Llambias House and transferred ownership to the city of St. Augustine. In 1955, when the post–World War II economic boom enabled a return to the preservation program, the city turned over management of the Llambias House to the St. Augustine Historical Society.[23]

Lack of financing plagued restoration attempts and threatened to dismantle the effort. The state of Florida stepped forward with an appropriation of $50,000 in 1937, scheduled for release in 1938. Unfortunately, those funds were not released until almost a decade later, after World War II. The

Carnegie Institution hesitated to commit financial resources to a multi-year program, compounding the situation. Institution president Merriam had retired in mid-1939. Before retirement he set aside funds for Chatelain to enable completion of *The Defenses of St. Augustine, 1565 to 1763*, which was released in June of 1940. Merriam's successor, noted Massachusetts Institute of Technology engineer Vannevar Bush, did not share Merriam's views and reduced financial support to a level that effectively discontinued the program.[24]

During the 1930s, private efforts in St. Augustine achieved some success. In 1931, Anna Gardener Burt offered her family's home to the city of St. Augustine as a house museum. In the eighteenth century, the royal Spanish treasurer Juan Esteban de Peña resided in the coquina stone building, and in 1837 the house was purchased by Burt's grandfather Dr. Seth Peck. The Woman's Exchange organization, of which Miss Burt was a founding member, stepped forward to partner with the city on the project. The organization rehabilitated the house and in 1932 opened it as the Peña-Peck House.[25]

Judge David Ross Dunham, president of the St. Augustine Historical Society, owned his aunt Louisa Fatio's Spanish colonial residence that had served as a boarding house throughout much of the nineteenth century (fig. 4.2). To ensure preservation of the building, he collaborated with his cousin, Mary Goff Palmer (Mrs. Richard P.) Daniel of Jacksonville, president of the Colonial Dames. The Ximenez-Fatio House, the Fatio family's only historic house in the New World, opened as a house museum in 1946, after World War II ended.[26]

Federal government initiatives through the Works Progress Administration (WPA) assisted local projects. These included the St. Augustine Civic Center (now the Visitor Information Center) west of Fort Marion. Arguably, the most dramatic project was construction in 1937 of the U.S. Custom House and Post Office on the west side of the Plaza de la Constitución. Designed by Jacksonville native and architect Mellon Greeley and referred to as the Government House, the building incorporated existing window and door openings and vestiges of wall sections from the eighteenth-century coquina stone Governor's Palace. The interior reflected twentieth-century construction techniques, building materials, and uses.[27]

In addition to tourism efforts, other historic buildings were adapted

FIGURE 4.2. Fatio House, St. Augustine, December 1936. This 1798 Spanish colonial dwelling underwent decline in the early twentieth century before being acquired and restored by the National Society of The Colonial Dames of America in The State of Florida. Photo by Frances Benjamin Johnston, Library of Congress, Prints & Photographs Division, Reproduction Number: LC.DIG. csas.00403.

for contemporary uses. In 1917, Flagler's residence Kirkside had passed to his niece by marriage, Louise Wise Lewis Francis. For the next twenty years until her death in 1937, she occupied the property seasonally with her children, Lawrence Lewis Jr. and Molly. The building sat vacant until 1942 when it opened as the administration building for a higher educa- tion consortium, the University Foundation. The unaccredited institution closed in 1949, unable to compete with four-year colleges that offered free education to veterans through the G. I. bill passed in 1944. At that time, the house was heavily termite damaged and required an estimated $20,000 in repairs, equivalent to about $200,000 today. In 1950, the house and out- buildings were demolished, and the property was subdivided into thirteen building lots. Many elements of the building were salvaged and incorpo- rated into other sites and structures throughout St. Augustine.[28]

In an article published in the *Hispanic American Historical Review* in 1944, Manucy wrote of the international role played by the city in representing Spain's important and enduring claim to settlement in the New World. He noted the difficulty of funding domestic issues in the midst of World War II, but pledged that St. Augustine's citizens would pursue their commitment to bringing their heritage to the forefront.[29]

Private initiatives resuscitated the city's tourism economy immediately after the war. In 1946, Chicago industrialist and collector Otto Lightner purchased the Hotel Alcazar, which had been vacant since 1932. In 1948, the Lightner Museum of Hobbies opened in the former casino wing of the hotel and showcased Lightner's collections. In the 1960s, for St. Augustine's 400th anniversary, the City Hall was moved into the section facing King Street and framing the courtyard.[30]

Also in 1948, George L. Potter opened the nation's first wax museum on the southwest corner of King Street and the bayfront, in a building known today as the A1A Aleworks Building. Hundreds of life-size historical and legendary wax figures, many in romantic fairytale settings, decorated the setting. One exhibit reproduced Queen Victoria holding court. Decades later, another portrayed an event that did not take place, John and Jackie Kennedy arriving for St. Augustine's Quadricentennial celebration.[31]

In the 1930s, Robert Ripley came to St. Augustine and stayed in Norton Baskin's Castle Warden. Ripley tried unsuccessfully for years to buy the property. His heirs succeeded. In 1950, they opened Ripley's Odditorium, later known as Ripley's Believe It or Not, which became the precursor of the international franchise. Although known mostly from this role as the Ripley attraction, the house of Standard Oil partner William Warden remains preserved on the exterior.[32]

In his seminal evaluation of the early historic preservation movement in the United States, historian Charles Hosmer criticized and complimented efforts in St. Augustine. He noted the importance of the public-private model that had been implemented, but chided the community on its inability to implement a unified plan.[33]

In 1944, Walter Fraser was elected to the Florida Senate. He used that statewide role to champion a reinvigorated preservation program for St. Augustine and succeeded in securing release of state funds promised before World War II. In concert with the St. Augustine Preservation and

Restoration Association, Fraser invited Kenneth Chorley to visit St. Augustine as part of a proposal for funding from John D. Rockefeller Jr. Chorley was president of Colonial Williamsburg Inc. headquartered in New York. At that time Colonial Williamsburg employed 1,000 people and operated on an annual budget of $2,000,000 from visitor receipts.[34]

Chorley and his wife came on February 23, 1947, and spent five days as guests of the Ponce. Chorley met with members of the Restoration Association, toured the historic district, spoke with about fifty tourists, and repeatedly visited all of the buildings that were open for public tours. After Chorley returned to New York, he submitted a detailed report with recommendations to Restoration Association acting president Judge David Ross Dunham and provided a copy to Senator Fraser. Chorley reported that Rockefeller had reiterated his commitment to continue exclusively with Colonial Williamsburg, a pledge he had made at the beginning of that project.[35]

Chorley echoed earlier opinions by national preservation experts that St. Augustine's success required an approach based on authenticity. This would preclude misinterpretation or confusion about the city's history. However, his recommendations emphasized St. Augustine's colonial period exclusively and contrasted with earlier recommendations that the continuum of history should be emphasized.

According to his recommendations, buildings outside the colonial era should be demolished, and colonial buildings no longer standing should be reconstructed. Settings and outbuildings should be reconstructed, including the city's colonial defense lines. All wires for utilities should be run underground. He recommended that properties and an educational program should be managed by a single organization. Commercial ventures should be separated from the interpretive program. All work should be accomplished using the highest standards.

His final recommendation addressed the political situation that had plagued the community for years: "re-examine the motivating purposes which underlie your present and future exploitation of St. Augustine's historical treasures."[36] Although failing to gain Rockefeller funding, Chorley's visit and the announcement of state funding reactivated statewide interest in St. Augustine's restoration program.

State-supported efforts to preserve Spanish colonial St. Augustine were rekindled in 1958 with a proposal authored by a Special Advisory Committee and the Florida Board of Parks and Historic Memorials. Committee members included A. Curtis Wilgus, University of Florida; Roland Dean, Winter Park; Karl A. Bickel, Sarasota; August Burghard, Fort Lauderdale; and J. D. Johnson, Pensacola. Verne Chatelain emerged from retirement to serve as executive secretary. Walter Fraser suffered a stroke and was bedridden the following year, remaining so until his death in 1972, which precluded his participation. The Parks Board chaired by St. Augustine attorney Frank D. Upchurch included John Fite Robertson, Sarasota; Howard Odom, Marianna; Kathryn Abbey Hanna, Winter Park; and John D. Pennekamp, Miami. The plan emphasized the following points: a focus on the First Spanish Period, with inclusion of the British and Second Spanish Periods, a time frame of 1565–1821; the community would continue to serve citizens; Spanish architecture, life, and culture would be reintroduced; an archival research center would be established; and property located outside St. Augustine that shared its common history would be added to the interpretation.[37]

In 1959, Governor LeRoy Collins appointed the members of the Florida Quadricentennial Commission. They represented business and community interests from throughout the state and the nation. These included H. E. Wolfe, a St. Augustine businessman as chairman; Kent McKinley, a Sarasota newspaper publisher and president of the Sarasota Foundation; Leonard Usina, vice chairman of Peoples National Bank in Miami and a St. Augustine native; William Rolleston, general manager of St. Augustine's Marineland; Mrs. Nelson (Henrietta) Poynter, founder of the *Congressional Quarterly* and wife of the publisher of the *St. Petersburg Times*; and William L. Sim II of Orlando, the retired president of Colgate-Palmolive-Peet. Saxton Lloyd, Daytona Beach, president of Daytona Motors and past president of the National Automobile Dealers' Association, succeeded Mrs. Poynter. Also, Jacksonville business leader Edward Ball participated, as did civic leader and Florida State Parks board chairman Elizabeth Morley Towers. Also that year, state senator Verle A. Pope of St. Augustine introduced legislation that established the Historical Restoration and Preservation Commission. The legislature appropriated $150,000 to protect and restore St. Augustine's Spanish colonial heritage based on the Williamsburg model. The commission's authority included a role reserved for governmental entities, the ability to acquire, manage, and sell property, including the use of condemnation. This time frame paralleled the federal policy of urban renewal.[38]

This Restoration Commission prepared a master plan, noting that St. Augustine's annual visitation of one million was projected to increase with the upcoming Quadricentennial or 400th anniversary of the city's founding in 1965. Several actions took place that assisted in meeting objectives of the master plan. City officials modified codes to eradicate blight and discourage demolition of Spanish buildings. Infill construction was encouraged as was commercial development. Features along the waterfront would be restored, enhancing the ambience of the community.[39]

With financial commitments from the state of Florida, St. Johns County, and the city of St. Augustine, the program revived goals from earlier efforts to emphasize Spanish colonial history, ensure authenticity, and attract participation by many organizations. The strong participation by international populations through the Organization of American States and the Pan American Union made the St. Augustine effort the most significant of its type ever undertaken. Participating countries included "Argentina, Brazil, Colombia, Costa Rica, Ecuador, Guatemala, Honduras, Paraguay, and the United States."[40]

The Spanish colonial city comprised five distinct zones from north to south, which showcased numerous historic and entertaining venues. Many of the city's Victorian-era buildings were derelict and, along with twentieth-century buildings located within the original town plan boundaries, were demolished to restore the Spanish theme by re-creating nearly fifty buildings.

The Mission area was the responsibility of the Diocese of St. Augustine and focused on the Mission de Nombre de Dios. The diocese built a new church of cut coquina stone after obtaining permission to reopen the historic quarry from which stone for the Castillo de San Marcos had come. Also, the diocese installed a 205-foot-tall cross to mark the site of the first Catholic Mass in the New World.[41]

Initially, the Restoration Commission's program focused on four properties in the North Restoration Area, three of which were funded through private entities. Begun in 1961, the first project funded by the state of Florida was the Arrivas House, 46 St. George Street, which served as a headquarters for the Restoration Commission. The next year, two projects were started, the Fornells House, 62 Spanish Street, sponsored by the St. Augustine Historical Society, and the Avero-Salcedo House, 42 St. George Street. A fourth project begun in 1958, the Rodriguez-Avero-Sanchez House at 52 St. George Street, was restored by Mr. and Mrs. Walter Scott Crawbuck as the Museum of Yesterday's Toys to honor their deceased son. By the time of the Quadricentennial celebration, three blocks along north St. George Street represented Spanish colonial architecture.[42]

In 1962, President Kennedy appointed a congressionally chartered federal commission and recognized the importance of St. Augustine's anniversary to the nation: "When I recall how colonial Williamsburg has served so effectively as a symbol of the bond between English speaking peoples on both sides of the Atlantic, I can see how valuable it will be to have a similar symbol of the cultural heritage which came to us from Hispanic-American sources. This can be a most important new symbolic bond with our Latin American neighbors, as well as to Spain."[43] Members included George B. Hartzog Jr., director of the National Park Service and representative of Florida, Senators Spessard Holland of Bartow and George Smathers of Miami, and Congressmen D. R. (Billy) Matthews of Gainesville and William C. Cramer of St. Petersburg. The next year President Kennedy appointed additional members: Herbert E. Wolfe, St. Augustine, chairman; Henry Ford II, Detroit; J. Peter Grace Jr., CEO of W. R. Grace & Co. Columbia, Maryland; Archbishop Joseph P. Hurley, St. Augustine; Edward Litchfield, PhD, chancellor of the University of Pittsburgh; and Charles Clark, Washington, D.C.[44]

On March 11, 1963, Vice President Lyndon B. Johnson visited St. Augustine to dedicate the city's first restored building, the Arrivas House (fig. 4.3). During Johnson's visit to St. Augustine, Father Michael V. Gannon accompanied him on a private visit to see the casket of city founder Don Pedro Menendez de Aviles at the La Leche Shrine north of downtown. According to Gannon, the vice president was humbled by the site; at the time Johnson was 55 years old, the same age Menendez was when he died. He considered the city's 400th anniversary to be symbolic of the nation's recognition of the Spanish as one of many cultures that contributed to the founding of the country.[45]

President Kennedy's announcement and Vice President Johnson's visit

FIGURE 4.3. Vice President Lyndon B. Johnson launched St. Augustine's 400th anniversary celebration on March 11, 1963. He stayed at the Hotel Ponce de Leon during his visit. LBJ at St. Augustine, 1963, St. Augustine Historical Society Research Library.

brought national attention to St. Augustine for the anniversary and as a segregated Southern city in the midst of the national Civil Rights Movement. African-Americans had been excluded from participation in the planning of the 400th anniversary activities, though they represented about one quarter of the city's population. Representatives, both black and white, interceded to rectify the situation. Following pressure from Vice President Johnson's advisors, a dinner hosted at the Hotel Ponce de Leon honoring him included two segregated tables for African-Americans.

Over the next eighteen months, both peaceful and violent demonstrations took place with national leaders, including Martin Luther King Jr., actively working in St. Augustine on behalf of civil rights. They came into direct confrontation with Ku Klux Klan members, which resulted in assaults that were broadcast by national news media. The city lost its federal appropriation for the 400th anniversary celebration, and Congress adopted the Civil Rights Act of 1964.

Dr. Michael V. Gannon grew up in St. Augustine, and earlier, as Father Gannon, he served as director of the Nombre de Dios Mission/La Leche Shrine. On November 18, 1963, he met with President John F. Kennedy in Tampa and invited the president to visit the nation's oldest city after his upcoming trip to Dallas. Kennedy died four days later. [46]

The government of Spain replaced the Weinstein Building with the Spanish Exhibition and Cultural Center or the Casa del Hidalgo located on St. George and Hypolita Street and designed as an eighteenth-century country house (fig. 4.4). The structure that served as a Spanish Tourist Information Office required an investment of about $200,000, including land, building construction, and furnishings. On September 5, 1965, Secretary of the Interior Stewart Udall, General Alonso Vega, and Secretary General Mora dedicated the Casa del Hidalgo. In the adjacent property to the north, nationally known artist Anna Hyatt Huntington's bronze statue of Queen Isabella became the focal point of the Spanish Garden.

FIGURE 4.4. The Spanish Exhibition and Cultural Center, or Casa del Hidalgo, was sponsored by the Spanish government in honor of St. Augustine's 400th anniversary. Today, the building is owned by the city of St. Augustine. Casa del Hidalgo, St. Augustine Historical Society Research Library.

Dignitaries from throughout the United States and Spain attended the festivities. In 2003, to further preservation of the building, the city of St. Augustine bought the property from the Universidad Nacional de Educación a Distancia (UNED) for about $2,600,000.[47]

Latin American participation came under the auspices of the Organization of American States. The Pan American Union (PAU) members planned exhibits to be housed in reconstructed colonial buildings.[48] Sponsors for land acquisition and reconstruction of the Florencia House to become the Centro Panamericano/Pan American Center came from American corporations with business investments in Latin America: "Ford, General Motors, Humble-Esso, Texaco, Gulf, Dupont [sic], American Tel. & Tel., W. R. Grace, American and Foreign Power, Johnson and Johnson, and others."[49] Today the building is owned by the St. Augustine Foundation.

In 1960, the state of Florida loaned $200,000 to the Restoration Commission to reconstruct the Wakeman House on King Street overlooking the Plaza. The project required demolition of the early-twentieth-century commercial Bernstein Block. Known as the Heritage House, the building housed the Florida State Exhibit Center, which interpreted the settlement of Florida from the indigenous people to the era of the Spanish conquistadors to the present. Today the Wakeman Building has a commercial use on the first floor and apartments on the second floor.[50]

As part of the state-funded project, the British era was represented by the Revolutionary War–era Watson House, a property located south of the Plaza on Charlotte Street immediately south of the Wakeman House. The building recognized carpenter William Watson's contribution to St. Augustine's history. Watson owned several buildings in that section of St. Augustine, as well as two substantial farms outside the city limits. The cost for this component was $15,000.[51]

Sections of downtown, both north and south of the central Plaza, received attention. In the oldest area of the city, more of the original building stock was intact, the area south of the Plaza; therefore, the primary focus for restoration was on the area north of the Plaza. Another advantage to an emphasis there was the proximity to the Spanish fort, the Castillo de San Marcos. Today the southern area continues to feature more historic buildings than does the area north of the Plaza.

The Castle and City Gate Area focused on the area at the north end of the colonial city. Beginning in 1952, a National Park Service (NPS) program, Mission 66, included funds to improve federal park properties—their infrastructure and interpretation—in time to celebrate the fiftieth anniversary of the National Park Service (NPS) in 1966. The initiative provided $1,000,000 (equivalent to more than $7,000,000 today) to the Castillo for physical and interpretive improvements, with an accelerated time frame to coincide with St. Augustine's 400th anniversary. NPS demolished numerous buildings, installed onsite parking, and created a new main thoroughfare to enable the visiting public to appreciate the authentic Spanish St. Augustine. NPS director Conrad Wirth served on St. Augustine's federal Quadricentennial Commission. With an annual visitation of 500,000, the Castillo provided an excellent location for interpretive expert Freeman Tilden to test his principles regarding interpretation there, including introducing cannon firing that continues to be popular today. Facilities were added to supplement the interpretation and operations. This included reconstruction or restoration of sally-port grades, drawbridges, gun carriages, and artillerymen's tools. Improved museum exhibits and public restrooms were a component of the program.[52]

To support the Mission 66 effort and St. Augustine's upcoming 400th anniversary, the Florida Department of Transportation (FDOT) proposed to widen San Marco Avenue. The road led north, past the Castillo and the Mission de Nombre de Dios site, to the outskirts of the city. The Diocese of St. Augustine planned construction of a new church on the Mission property. The plan included demolition of a house that had been owned by at least two nationally notable men, General Frederick T. Dent, commander of the St. Francis Barracks and brother-in-law of President Ulysses S. Grant, and favored Ponce artist Martin Johnson Heade. Preservationist Kenneth Dow rescued the historic house and moved it to a nearby site where it survived for a short time until it fell victim to the FDOT road widening.

Between 1963 and 1965 the National Park Service continued restoration on the Castillo de San Marcos. An administrative structure built at the north end of the property was named in honor of St. Augustine native, historian, and NPS staff member Albert Manucy. Also, the Cubo Line, part of the fortification that surrounded the town originally, was reconstructed in concrete materials to present the appearance of palm tree trunks laid horizontally and vertically. An irrigation system and foot paths were installed. A major infrastructure change was realignment of Highway A1A as it passed through downtown St. Augustine to promote easier access via the Bridge of Lions to Anastasia Island. The roadway southward from the City Gate, restored by NPS also, was widened to two lanes each way, and a parking lot was added to the south side of the Castillo grounds. These changes necessitated an appropriation of $250,000 and negotiation with landowners of properties near the City Gate, including Victor Rahner Sr. for his photography studio. The Bennett Hotel was bought from Kenneth Dow. The total expenditure for the properties was $413,000. Both properties were demolished to accomplish the roadway changes.[53]

On October 23, 1962, following the Cuban Missile Crisis, the federal government proposed a new role for the Castillo if a nuclear attack was anticipated to threaten St. Augustine. St. Johns County submitted an alternate proposal that featured the Ponce. Each building was proposed to be used as a bomb shelter. According to the county, the Ponce could hold more people and was more solidly built than the Castillo.[54]

The federal government's proposal for the colonial city established five distinct districts. Each was focused around properties that anchored that area geographically and provided an emphasis for that area's portion of the restoration.

The South Restoration Area/Calle San Francisco operated under the auspices of the St. Augustine Historical Society and included the Franciscan Convent/St. Francis Barracks. The original 1724 Franciscan Convent had been converted to the St. Francis Barracks during the American Revolution, when St. Augustine was occupied by the British. The St. Francis Barracks was used for military purposes, but the building was abandoned by the Army in 1900 and has been used by the state of Florida since 1907. In 1921, Congress donated the structure to the state of Florida. With an appropriation from the Florida legislature, St. Augustine architect Francis A. Hollingsworth orchestrated a renovation of the exterior and updated the interior of the building. Beginning in the 1950s, the building offered a home to the Florida National Guard and continues to do so today. Under the direction of Adjutant-General of the Army National Guard Henry

MacMillan, and with assistance from Air National Guard director Charles Riggle, the site was investigated for archaeological resources.[55]

The Plaza area connected the Flagler-era hotels and the St. Augustine Amphitheatre via the Bridge of Lions. In 1961, St. Johns County government joined the 400th anniversary effort by acquiring Henry Flagler's mothballed Hotel Cordova for $250,000 from William Rand Kenan Jr., president of the Florida East Coast Hotel Company. The building was converted to an administration building reflecting institutional design of the 1960s. To achieve that modernization, the 1880s elegance was eradicated. Historic photographs from the hotel era exist as the sole evidence of the building's interiors. Four decades later, Orlando hotelier Richard Kessler bought the property from the county for the same amount and re-created its Gilded Age grandeur. The Casa Monica hosted twenty-first-century dignitaries, including Spain's King Juan Carlos and Queen Sofia on April 1, 2001, and President Bill Clinton in March of 2012.[56]

The Florida National Exhibits Corporation, so critical to St. Augustine's survival during the Great Depression, grew into the nation's largest exhibit design organization. The company launched a massive and imaginative program at the 1963 New York World's Fair to celebrate that city's 325th anniversary. The state of Florida appropriated $1,000,000 to assist with Florida's participation in the World's Fair, about 20 percent of the cost. On September 9, 1964, Hurricane Dora wreaked hundreds of thousands of dollars of damage throughout northeast Florida. None of St. Augustine's restoration projects experienced damage; however, many of the city's ancient trees succumbed to the winds and rain. The area rebounded from the damage, and in 1965 more than 14,000,000 people visited Florida. Florida's closest attempt to host a World's Fair came with the 500th anniversary of Columbus' landing in the New World. Miami served as the proposed location for the October 1992 event. If the celebration had taken place in Miami, another world-renowned event, Hurricane Andrew, would have preempted the celebration by a few weeks and precluded the World's Fair.[57]

In 1957, St. Augustine revived the Easter celebrations that defined its cultural identity. The city hosted 40,000 attendants for the Easter celebration held on Sunday, April 18, 1965. Named Parada de los Caballos y Coches (Parade of Horses and Coaches), the event ran south two miles in length along San Marco Avenue through the downtown, a route still followed today. The 1972 parade was most memorable, with winter residents Cornelius Vanderbilt Whitney, cofounder and owner of Marineland, and his wife, Marylou, coming for the celebration. Whitney opened Marineland in 1938 to a crowd of 20,000. He died in 1992, shy of his ninety-third birthday. Marylou Whitney continues as honorary chair of the Whitney Lab at Marineland.[58]

The Catholic Church benefitted from significant and lasting contributions to preserve and portray religious New World history in St. Augustine. Archbishop Hurley directed renovation of the Cathedral Basilica and the building's expansion by 4,000 square feet as part of the Quadricentennial preparations and in concert with Vatican II. That effort included demolition of a block of buildings at the northeast corner of St. George and Cathedral Streets to reestablish the cathedral's original setting.[59]

On March 8, 1966, six months into the yearlong 400th anniversary celebration, St. Augustine hosted a dinner at the Ponce for His Eminence William Cardinal Conway of Ireland. The Cardinal proclaimed the importance of St. Augustine to Catholicism in the New World. Honored guests included Governors LeRoy Collins and Claude Kirk, and C. V. and Marylou Whitney.[60]

Gannon championed the restoration effort. He noted that "the church and community raised $6,000,000 for preservation of St. Augustine's colonial city, emphasizing authenticity and requiring employment of academics, one each with a doctorate in history and in archaeology. Decades later, this emphasis would translate into establishment of the Historic St. Augustine Research Institute, an academic partnership hosted by Flagler College with the University of Florida and funded by the St. Augustine Foundation Inc."[61]

Gannon verified that private individuals and organizations funded the bulk of the restoration in the colonial city. Between 1964 and 1966, private gifts of $600,000 were received, double the amount of the funds provided through the Florida Legislature. Investors included local business leaders and community residents. Leonard Tucker reconstructed the Carmona-Salcedo House for a camera shop. The Suarez-McHenry House became offices for the Thompson-Bailey Agency. On November 2, 1972, newspapers announced that St. Augustine Restoration Inc. received a gift of $50,000 from Florida senator Verle Pope for acquisition of 49–53 St. George Street. The funds enabled demolition of the Paffe building and reconstruction of the Francisco Pellicer-Jose de Burgos House.[62]

Assistance came from Jacksonville businesses and individuals with ties to St. Augustine. For example, Ring Power founder and St. Augustine resident L. C. (Lance Christian) Ringhaver restored the Oliveros House at 59 St. George Street. Following his death, his widow donated the property to the St. Augustine Foundation. Today the Flagler's Legacy Tours occupies the building. Gannon introduced Florida East Coast Railroad chairman Ed Ball to the restoration effort. Ball and his sister, philanthropist Jessie Ball (widow of Mr. Alfred I.) duPont, underwrote restoration of the Sanchez de Ortigosa House at 60 St. George Street. About 1971, civic leader, Colonial Dame, and Florida State Parks board chair Elizabeth Morley Towers became the benefactor for 57 Treasury Street. Towers contacted architect Herschel Shepard to assist her with selection and restoration of the property that, after restoration, she donated to the state of Florida, retaining a life estate.[63]

Henry Flagler's great-nephew Lawrence Lewis Jr., born at Flagler's St. Augustine home Kirkside and raised there and in Richmond, Virginia, participated with the private and public efforts to preserve St. Augustine's colonial heritage. Lewis and his sister Molly Lewis Wiley operated through their family's Flagler Foundation, assisting St. Augustine and funding some of the restoration of Flagler's Hotel Ponce de Leon as part of that building's conversion to the headquarters for Flagler College. Over the years they supported preservation at the University of Virginia. Also, in a conversation archaeologist William Kelso said he considered his friend Lewis to be the first supporter for the investigations that began in the 1980s ultimately locating Jamestown.

In 1962, Lewis and other local citizens created the St. Augustine Restoration Foundation Inc. to assist the colonial St. Augustine preservation effort. (Two decades later the foundation was renamed the St. Augustine Foundation Inc.) William Rolleston of Marineland served as the inaugural president. The foundation acquired and rehabilitated or reconstructed several properties in the city's historic business district. Five years later, the foundation and the Preservation Commission acquired a major property, the De Mesa-Sanchez House. Acquisition of properties had handicapped the Preservation Commission financially, resulting in debt of almost $300,000. With annual gifts of $150,000 from the Flagler Foundation ($1,000,000 today), the debt was paid.[64]

The Flagler Foundation underwrote the Preservation Commission's portion of the restoration program over the next several years. On October 31, 1972, the Flagler Foundation made a gift to assist with reconstruction of the Villalonga House. The community's fundraising event, Fiesta de Menendez on September 8 of that year, raised $35,000 toward the projected goal of $50,000 needed for the project. This was the first event for the Restoration Commission in its new role as the Historic St. Augustine Preservation Board, an entity of the state of Florida.[65]

Between 1968 and 1970, Lewis provided more than $150,000 for reconstruction of the east wing of the Spanish Treasurer's house. This work returned the house to its original U form from the L shape it had maintained for a century. As stated earlier, this property had been donated to the city of St. Augustine and was managed by the Woman's Exchange, a charitable organization.[66]

Lewis approached restaurant developer Cesar Gonzmart to participate in the restoration program. As a result, Gonzmart opened a Columbia Restaurant at the northwest corner of St. George and Hypolita Streets. Similar to the original in Tampa's Cuban Ybor City, St. Augustine's Columbia Restaurant anchored the center of the business district. The reconstructed Spanish colonial building replaced the Gilded Age City Hall that was constructed by Henry Flagler and demolished by the city government.[67]

In May of 1977, the St. Augustine Restoration Foundation announced an ambitious venture for which research had begun several years earlier. A $7,000,000 living history program, "1580 St. Augustine Village," was proposed to be created on fifty acres of land north of St. Augustine. The site was near the Ponce de Leon Lodge on Flagler System property inherited by Lewis and his sister. The team designing the living history program included historians Albert Manucy, Paul Hoffman, and Eugene Lyon, architect Herschel Shepard, and archaeologist Kathleen Deagan. They all worked with a California firm that planned the village.[68]

In 1974, under the directorship of John Griffin, the Historic St. Augustine Preservation Board endorsed the project during the project's research phase. Hoffman and Lyon spent the summers of 1974–1975 in the Archive of the Indies at Seville, Spain, and returned with sixteen rolls of micro-filmed records addressing sixteenth-century life in St. Augustine. Manucy provided assistance with descriptions of buildings, drawings, and inter-pretation. Deagan's archaeological investigation in 1976 indicated that the town was located south of the Plaza and bounded on the north by Artillery Lane, east by Marine Street, south by Bridge Street, and west by St. George Street. Through their collective efforts, a picture was created based on ar-chival records of the 1580 town with a wooden fort and rows of thatched houses for the estimated 250 inhabitants.[69]

Unfortunately, the nation's economic recession forced an announce-ment on January 8, 1981, of the program's postponement. Though the pro-gram was not revived, Lewis and other St. Augustine Restoration Founda-tion members channeled their energies into a project with the National Geographic Society. In 1983, the two organizations made a movie, *Struggle to Survive*, and then a second one, *Dream of Empire*, which was supple-mented by an exhibit installed in Government House. Manucy and Dea-gan served as the experts for the project. Thirty years later, Deagan served as the principal scholar for a new exhibit in Government House, "First Colony," which introduced more research on St. Augustine.[70]

One of the St. Augustine Foundation's greatest scholarly successes took place during Dr. Eugene Lyon's tenure as executive director. The project began in 1974 with a dialogue led by then-Monsignor Michael V. Gannon, director of the Institute for Early Contact Period Studies at the University of Florida. In 1987, with support from the university administration and funding from the St. Augustine Restoration Foundation, Menendez fam-ily papers were microfilmed in Spain, enabling their translation and use to advance scholarship and a greater understanding of Spanish colonial settlement.[71]

In 1984, the U.S. Department of the Interior designated the St. Augus-tine Town Plan National Historic Landmark District. During that decade, the city of St. Augustine made a significant infrastructure investment along north St. George Street, redesigning the sewer systems, installing underground utilities, converting the street to pedestrian only, redirect-ing traffic on the adjacent streets, and paving the street with coquina con-crete. Though the work increased access and convenience to the above-ground historical resources, simultaneously this project deviated from an authentic interpretation of the street's appearance and destroyed archaeological resources.[72]

In 1988, factions that had sparred for twenty years came to blows over control of the preservation program and development of the accompanying real estate. The situation reached a critical juncture when newly elected governor Bob Martinez removed Preservation Board members John D. Bailey Sr., Julio Grabiel, Roy Hunt, and Norma Lockwood. Martinez appointed William Daniell, Thomas Sliney, Jeanne Ray, Teresa Milam, Margaret Foerster, Patricia Lee, and John Sundeman. The appointments triggered the resignation of executive director Robert Gold and board members Lawrence Lewis Jr. and Michael Gannon. The September 1988 issue of *Jacksonville Today* presented evidence of Daniell's fabricated credentials and employment history.[73]

In 1989, the final chapter began in the relationship between the St. Augustine Restoration Foundation and the Preservation Board. The latter was an entity of the state of Florida, which brought a legal suit against the St. Augustine Foundation over properties on St. George Street. The Foundation's Board of Directors overlapped the Board of Trustees at Flagler College, drawing the educational institution into the political fray.

From 1974 to 1989, and with gifts provided by Molly Lewis Wiley, Flagler College rented the auditorium space in Government House for the college's drama program. The college spent more than $70,000 on maintenance of that facility and provided the space at no charge to the Preservation Board that managed the facility for the state of Florida.

Following the announcement of the Special Category grant rankings in March 1989, several of the new Preservation Board members attempted to divert Flagler College's Special Category grant into the Preservation Board's operating trust fund for use on Government House. Timothy Bradford, vice president of the Preservation Board's support organization, wrote, according to a *Florida Times-Union* article, "If state revenues are as tight as they appear to be, and the Legislature must make a choice between supporting a restoration project at a private institution that is not in danger of being destroyed or lost and a state agency restoring a building for public use, then the funds should go to the state agency."[74]

William T. Abare Jr., at that time Flagler College's assistant to the president, noted in a letter to Bradford the college's commitment to preservation of the historic campus, an investment of $12,000,000, which had been made over the previous thirteen years. He challenged the Preservation Board to make the same investment in the same number of years in the future. The college received the grant, and neither Governor Martinez nor the Florida Legislature appropriated the $250,000 that the Preservation Board had requested for Government House. The state of Florida rewarded the Preservation Board with legal purgatory.[75]

In 1994, after five years, the case was settled. Due to the nature of the court case, pertinent information relating to the decision is quoted here: "[Both parties] stipulate to the dismissal of this action with prejudice." In question was ownership of the "Acosta House, Spanish Garden, Oliveros House, Ortega House, Pan American Building, Santoya House and Villalonga House." A press release issued after the settlement stated, "The State also wishes to acknowledge specially the many contributions Mr. Lawrence Lewis Jr., a director of the Foundation, has unselfishly made and continues to make to the city of St. Augustine and the people of the state of Florida, and the key role he played in helping to settle the lawsuit." The foundation retained its position as owner of the properties, but if the foundation were dissolved, the properties would be transferred to the state of Florida.[76]

As a result of this lengthy and very public battle, the state of Florida reorganized the Preservation Boards, folding all under the authority of the Florida Secretary of State. In 1997, the state of Florida abolished the preservation boards, and the city of St. Augustine assumed management of the state properties there. After a decade, city officials approached their legislative delegation requesting assistance. On July 1, 2010, the University of Florida assumed responsibility for the properties. This transition was modeled on the partnership between the state of Florida, the University of West Florida, and West Florida Historic Preservation Inc.

Reconstructed buildings in the Spanish colonial historic district are now fifty years old, the minimum age for them to be considered for listing in the National Register of Historic Places. They could be recognized as examples of commemorative buildings. Also, they could be considered as representative illustrations of building techniques used on the eve of passage of the National Historic Preservation Act of 1966. They could be determined to have significance as evidence of an historic preservation and heritage tourism experiment between the governments of St. Augustine, the state of Florida, and the United States. In any case, the buildings assist in understanding an important chapter in the history of the nation when Spanish heritage began in 1565 in St. Augustine, half a century before the settlements at Jamestown, Virginia, in 1607, or Plymouth, Massachusetts, in 1620.

This major chapter in St. Augustine's history, in tandem with the celebration of the 400th anniversary of the city's founding in 1965, took place just over a decade before the nation celebrated its 200th or bicentennial anniversary in 1976. The new social movement, historic preservation in its fledgling institutional phase, gained momentum with the 1976 festivities and broadened the understanding of the nation's heritage.

Preservation moved beyond an appreciation of the mansions of the founding fathers. Beginning in the 1980s, entire neighborhoods and communities were designated as historic districts. Archaeological sites were recognized and many times protected in part by their locations remaining undisclosed by restricting public records. Rural historic districts and cultural landscapes added to the breadth of understanding of the country's heritage.

Recognition of these areas increased the understanding of the importance of buildings, the settings in which they are located, and the lives of the people who occupied them. The time frame of properties to be considered for preservation expanded to include settlement through the early decades of the twentieth century. A minimum of fifty years of age was required by NPS to give perspective to the evaluation of the properties.

Within the jurisdictional boundaries of St. Augustine are numerous neighborhoods with historic properties that have been identified, studied, evaluated, and protected. These are in addition to the St. Augustine Town Plan National Historic Landmark District, which comprises the platted sixteenth-century town.

Listed in the National Register of Historic Places are neighborhoods that surround the colonial downtown, reflecting late-nineteenth and early-twentieth-century growth of the city. These areas include the Model Land Company just beyond the city's original western boundary, which includes the majority of Flagler College's historic campus. Lincolnville sits west and south of the original town. Neighborhoods that flank San Marco Avenue and are north of the colonial downtown are the Abbott Tract, North City, Nelmar Terrace, and Fullerwood. East of downtown on Anastasia Island are the Davis Shores communities, identified as neighborhoods that feature mid-century modern buildings.

In all of these areas, building height limitations of 35 feet are in place, and archaeological resources are protected. Demolition of buildings is precluded without prior review by the Historic Architectural Review Board of the City of St. Augustine. Efforts are made to relocate buildings to ensure their preservation. Design guidelines are in place for many of the properties in these districts.

The state of Florida's historic preservation tax exemption works in tandem with these efforts. For properties that are rehabilitated using the Secretary of the Interior's Standards and within a prescribed time frame, property taxes on the improvements can be held in abeyance for a period of ten years. Both the city of St. Augustine and St. Johns County adopted this legislation.

The growth of historic preservation as a national movement resulted in the development of preservation techniques and materials. The use of historic preservation to regenerate urban neighborhoods and return economic viability to rural communities illustrated the adaptability of the theories. The national movement matured in the 1980s and 1990s. These national and local frameworks set the stage for the preservation of buildings from another important chapter in St. Augustine's history, those associated with Henry Flagler and the Gilded Age.

5

Rescue and Restoration

In the 1950s, Lawrence Lewis Jr. approached his uncle William Kenan about managing the Flagler System, the company that held Henry Flagler's railroads and resorts. Kenan declined the offer because he considered his nephew too inexperienced. Lewis responded by buying land in the Bahamas, not far from the site of Flagler's British Colonial hotel in Nassau, and constructing the Flagler Inn. He opened the Club Peace and Plenty at George Town on Great Exuma and bought property on Stocking Island.

In 1965, Kenan and his sisters Jessie Kenan Wise and Sarah Graham Kenan had all seen their ninetieth birthdays. Kenan, in frail health, relinquished management to his nephew. Soon after, he passed away, and in 1968 his sisters did as well. By that time, Lewis stated years later, the Ponce had lost viability as a hotel. At times, only ten guest rooms were filled, and financial losses amounted to $250,000 to $500,000 annually. The hotel had remained open to accommodate his uncle and aunts.[1]

In 1968, the Hotel Ponce de Leon assumed a contemporary role as centerpiece for the new Flagler College, named to honor the hotel's founder (fig. 5.1). The Carlson family that operated Mount Ida College, a small women's institution in Massachusetts, negotiated with Kenan and Lewis to start a sister institution in St. Augustine. The Carlsons bought the Ponce from the Flagler System for a publicly announced price of $1,500,000, with the former owner holding the note.[2]

By this point, Henry Flagler's other two St. Augustine hotels had reopened with new uses. The Lightner Museum and City Hall were located in the former Alcazar. St. Johns County purchased the Cordova for

FIGURE 5.1. The former Hotel Ponce de Leon stands majestically as the centerpiece of Flagler College. Aerial photo of Ponce de Leon Hall, Flagler College Archives.

administrative offices. Speaking on behalf of city and county government officials, Mayor John D. Bailey championed the proposed new use for the Ponce, as the educational institution would provide a viable economic use for the building and complement the historical and cultural theme being developed in St. Augustine.[3]

In contrast, the citizenry reacted to the news with mixed feelings. The community remained scarred after a contentious era as the setting for the final chapter in the Civil Rights movement, an era still fresh in the minds of residents. The community wanted out of the limelight.

A scant few years later, St. Augustine remained a reflection of the status quo in the South, a racially segregated city geographically, socially, economically, and politically. The population was three-quarters white and one-quarter African-American, with the latter concentrated in two areas near the Ponce, Lincolnville, and West Augustine.

In the late 1960s, college campuses across the nation witnessed anti–Vietnam war demonstrations, not all of which were peaceful. The demonstrations increased in 1968, the year Flagler College was founded. Property owners expressed concern for the safety of the surrounding residential neighborhood and adjacent business district. Two years later, in 1970, about 500 students at Kent State University had assembled for an anti-war protest. Ohio National Guard troops lobbed tear gas then fired shots into the crowd, killing four students. The internationally broadcast news story increased tensions locally.[4]

As with town and gown issues in many communities, resolution was temporary at best. Twenty years after the college's founding, most business owners had come to enjoy and depend upon the students as employees and customers. On the other hand, residents remained adamant about limiting students' presence on the public rights-of-way. Truces and stalemates characterized the relationship from the early days and continue to play a role nearly a half-century later.

In 1971, with the college floundering, Flagler System chairman Lewis returned to St. Augustine. He restructured the new college as a coeducational institution and retired the mortgage on the building, putting the college on a sound financial footing.[5]

When the Ponce was a hotel, the building received regular updates, as was typical with most luxury lodging establishments. Modifications included changes to room configurations, modernization of bathrooms, and incorporation of new furnishings. In contrast, the exterior of the building, original materials, floor layouts, and architectural details remained virtually unchanged over the hotel's eighty years. The exception to this situation was replacement of some windows to comply with contemporary standards but without regard to architectural accuracy, such as metal casements that had been fabricated in Jacksonville. The primary rooms, the Rotunda, Dining Room, and Grand Parlor, remained as built. Even changes made for occupancy by the Coast Guard during World War II, other than redesign of the fourth floor, were removed when the building returned to hotel use in the 1950s.[6]

At Flagler College's founding, the Hotel Ponce de Leon was renamed Ponce de Leon Hall, although it continued to be referred to as the Ponce. In contrast to the building's routine maintenance, major rehabilitation had been deferred for years. Damage from hurricanes Donna in 1960 and Dora in 1964 contributed to the deterioration. To accomplish the transition of the hotel to a higher education institution, some spaces had to be used in ways that were constrained by their architectural design and decoration.

Within a few years of the college's founding, historic preservation became a component of the institution's campus planning process. Once again, timing was important. Passed during the Johnson administration, the National Historic Preservation Act of 1966 institutionalized historic preservation. The Preservation Act brought state and local governments into the planning and implementation processes to identify and protect natural and cultural resources. The legislation grew out of Lady Bird Johnson's Keep America Beautiful program and a U.S. Conference of Mayors Special Committee on Historic Preservation. Both efforts were reactions to the demolition of thousands of buildings through the federal urban renewal and interstate highway programs implemented in the postwar Eisenhower administration of the 1950s.[7]

Flagler College's educational needs required creative treatment of spaces within the Ponce, including modifying hotel rooms for student living use. The Rotunda remained as the lobby and became the center of student activity. The former gift shop on the west side was used as an office for the academic dean's secretary, Helen Jane Matthews. Routinely, humidity in the office fogged her glasses. A new window air conditioner was justified as an expense necessary to make certain that her typing equipment functioned appropriately. The room under the dome identified as the "400 Rotunda" became the Louise Wise Francis Library, named in honor of Lewis and Wiley's mother. The Dining Room became the Dining Hall. The curved west venido was enlisted as a classroom. A small private dining room located between the marble staircase and the Dining Room was a student lounge with a television. The Artists' Studios building hosted classrooms and offices for faculty members and secretaries. The first-floor coal storerooms supported maintenance functions, and a biology lab was created on the east side of the first floor. A former Coast Guard lifesaving training facility was used minimally because of its severely deteriorated condition. The site of the present-day Kenan Plaza/Lewis Gazebo housed Art Department offices, including that of sculptor Enzo Torcoletti (fig. 5.2).[8]

FIGURE 5.2. The Coast Guard Reserve lifesaving building was appropriated for educational use by the new Flagler College. Coast Guard building on west lawn, Art Department, Flagler College Archives.

In the summer of 1971, the most creative and dramatic adaptation relocated the Louise Wise Lewis Library to the Grand Parlor. William T. Abare Jr., director of admissions, and Robert Carberry, dean of students, supervised removal of books from the top floor of the Ponce in a hand-to-hand exchange from one faculty or staff member to another, down three flights of stairs, through the Mezzanine, down the marble staircase, into the Rotunda, and through the west wing into the Grand Parlor.[9]

Flanking the Grand Parlor's eleven crystal chandeliers, fluorescent tube lights were mounted to a structural framework built from wood studs. The framework was suspended below the 23-karat-gold overlaid egg-and-dart cornice moldings that framed the Tojetti ceiling murals in the four quadrants. The marble-encased Edison electric clock set in the carved onyx mantelpiece stood as a sentinel chaperoning the coeds. They studied at round tables surrounded by significant works from Henry Flagler's art collection that had graced the walls of the room since 1888 (fig. 5.3).

The physical condition of the 400 Rotunda changed as a result of life safety codes that precluded the room's continued use as the library. In the 1970s and 1980s, the fourth floor was used for cheerleading practice, to show movies, and as headquarters for the college newspaper, *The Gargoyle*.

Later, as the college added facilities to accommodate those needs, the fourth floor functioned as a storage space. The Flagler College radio station's electronic equipment was located on the fourth floor, too.

Between 1971 and 1975, the emphasis focused on renovation of facilities for uses related to the operation of the college. The Ponce hotel's reading room at the northeast corner of the first floor became Carberry's office. He recalled A. D. Davis, owner of A. D. Davis Construction Company, coming to his office in December 1971. Davis told him that repairs taking place above his office revealed a lack of structural supports between the first and second floors. Quickly, the office was moved to the other end of the long room, and the structure was reinforced.[10]

Several alumni recalled living in the Ponce's former hotel rooms and using the hotel furniture. These alumni serve as members of the college's board of trustees today and are listed with their years at Flagler College: Viki West Freeman of Atlanta (1970–1974), Mitch Walk of Orlando (1974–1979), Richard Groux of Warrenton, Virginia (1975–1979), and Nancy Rutland of Tampa (1976–1980). Initially students lived on the lower two floors. Women lived on the west side; men resided on the east. Increased

FIGURE 5.3. Flagler College coeds study surrounded by Gilded Age art and architecture in the former Grand Parlor. Louise Wise Lewis Library in Grand Parlor, Flagler College Archives.

admissions warranted the use of additional rooms. With construction of the Lewis House in 1987, men moved to the new facility.

Women students occupied the four floors of hotel rooms in the wings that framed the central courtyard. That tradition continues today. In fact, a recent graduate was Henry Flagler's great-great granddaughter, the first member of the family to attend Flagler College. Unassumingly, she lived in the residence hall that had been her ancestor's flagship hotel.

In the 1970s, flowered wallpaper remained on the walls, and color-coordinated drapes hung at the windows. Radiators provided heat, windows were operable, and artificial air conditioning was nonexistent. Students used hotel furniture in rooms that were unchanged and included shared baths. Weekly maid service was available through Frankie, the maid in charge. The four trustees were students during the early years of the Ponce's rehabilitation. Renovations in the 1980s resulted in new housing for 200 men and 295 women students.[11]

In 1975, the Hotel Ponce de Leon was listed in the National Register of Historic Places, providing a new status for the building and enabling the property to qualify for grant funds from both public and private sources. In 1978, following the nation's bicentennial anniversary celebration, the U.S. Department of the Interior provided a grant of $68,930 from the Historic Preservation Fund to repair the building's towers. Flagler College leveraged the public award to secure a private grant of $82,967 from the Arthur Vining Davis Foundations and complete the $151,897 project. This initiative served as the college's formal introduction to historic preservation. Their efforts proved timely as President Ronald Reagan discontinued federal funding for historic preservation upon taking office three years later.[12]

Also in 1978, former Johnson White House assistant and longstanding New York Landmarks Commission member Barbaralee Diamonstein published the first major work championing adaptive use of historic buildings. In *Buildings Reborn*, she recognized the efforts to preserve the former Hotel Ponce de Leon in St. Augustine as the cornerstone of a new higher education institution, endorsing the building's transformation into a liberal arts college that was drawing students from throughout the United States.[13]

A. D. Davis Construction Company was selected as the contractor for the towers' restoration. The clay tile roofs and terra cotta details were particularly challenging. Art faculty members chairman Robert Hall and sculptor Enzo Torcoletti reproduced individual clay tiles since matching tiles were no longer available. They reproduced the terra cotta banisters on the towers with cast concrete pieces dyed to the red clay color. Thirty years later, in 2009, this treatment was used again when terra cotta details on the towers failed to retain their structural integrity and had to be recast.[14]

With completion of the towers project, the college moved forward to consider renovation of additional sections of the former hotel. A classroom building was needed as student enrollment continued to rise. Carberry characterized the Ponce as a haven for "rats, bats, roaches and termites," with the rectangular facilities building just beyond the Dining Room in the worst condition. By 1980, most of the structure had been vacated and stabilized so that in future years it could be renovated. The kitchen for the hotel remained as the kitchen for the college and was located on the second floor. Maintenance functions were housed in the basement. The college's art department used three rooms in the building. A large well-lit room with a high ceiling and tall windows in the northwest corner of the building served as a studio. Art chair Hall's office was across the corridor from that studio, and faculty member Don Martin's office was under the kitchen.[15]

According to lifelong St. Augustine resident and college trustee David Drysdale, Lewis, who had an architecture degree from the University of Virginia, planned the renovation of the building. St. Augustine architect Craig Thorn prepared the construction drawings. The building was gutted, including removal of a large central skylight and all interior walls. The work created five entirely new stories with an attic from a building that had been constructed in four stories with tall ceilings. The modern structure continued to house the college's kitchen. In addition, the 61,272-square-foot building provided a new space for the Louise Wise Lewis Library and included fifteen classrooms, thirty-nine faculty offices, six seminar rooms, science labs, and computer labs. The college's growth required these uses, and accreditation requirements mandated standards for facilities and services.[16]

The exterior of the renovated building remained true to its original appearance. Remaining was the polychromatic concrete and brick façade, a rhythm of vertically oriented windows, and a clay barrel tile roof. However, the interior design of the building reflected institutional facilities that emphasized function over aesthetics. The floor plan and architectural details were eliminated. Comments abounded from members of the community regarding the building's lack of unique character and appearance. The facility represented the standard academic college building constructed during that time. The project served as a watershed for the college in regard to facilities design and construction. Future renovations and new construction emphasized the historic character of the campus, particularly the Ponce, and incorporated design and materials that recognized the college's remarkable architecture.[17]

The $5,000,000 renovation was funded with assistance of $3,500,000 from the William R. Kenan Jr. Charitable Trust of North Carolina and $1,200,000 from the Flagler Foundation of Virginia. The Edyth Bush Foundation of Winter Park, Florida, provided funds for the college's first major computer system.[18]

Upon completion of work in 1982, the building was rededicated as Kenan Hall to honor Kenan, a renowned chemist, businessman, farmer, philanthropist, and industrialist (fig. 5.4). In addition to being Flagler's brother-in-law, Kenan served as Flagler's personal representative and oversaw management of the Ponce for sixty years. Upon Flagler's death in 1913, Kenan became president of the water companies in Miami and West Palm Beach and the Miami Electric Light and Power Company, now FP&L. A decade later Kenan became president of many of Flagler's other Florida enterprises. These included several in St. Augustine, the Model Land Company, the Golf Development Association, Florida East Coast Railway Company, and Florida East Coast Hotel Company.[19]

From 1971 to 1986, the college raised $19,500,000 for historic and new campus facilities. Much of the funding came as grants from either the William R. Kenan Jr. Charitable Trust or the Flagler Foundation, a not-for-profit corporation established by Mary Lily Kenan Flagler's heirs. Private corporations, major Florida and national foundations, and the aforementioned small federal grant accounted for the balance. Of the total, restoration activities absorbed $10,500,000, including $3,900,400 that was used

FIGURE 5.4. The former hotel service building was severely deteriorated before its conversion for use as Flagler College's first academic building and was rededicated in memory of William Rand Kenan Jr. Kenan Hall, Flagler College Archives.

to convert 245 hotel rooms to student dormitory rooms that met modern building, fire, and life safety requirements. Fireplace mantels were retained, with the chimney flues sealed. Bathrooms were updated, as had been typical throughout the building's time as a hotel. The remaining $9,000,000 was expended on property acquisition and new construction projects, including the gymnasium, tennis center, field house, athletic fields, the theatre in Government House, and classroom uses at Markland.[20]

Across the Rotunda from the former Grand Parlor, the hotel Office Floor featured a series of rooms that became the President's Wing for senior college administrators. A Telegraph Office, Ticket Office, Barber and

Manicure Rooms, and a Reading Room were on the north side of a long corridor. The south side featured a Writing Room, "Stores" (storage), and a large Smoking Room. The rooms retained original tile flooring, mantels, decorative woodwork, and tall ceilings.[21]

Glass doors were installed at the beginning of the corridor. Most rooms became executive offices, with the Reading Room converted to a Board Room. The most interesting room, the Barber Room, featured elaborate tile patterns on the walls, built-in counters and mirrors, cherub carvings, and a decorative mantel. Though the barber chairs and sink had been removed, the details depicted the original use. The room illustrated the masculine theme prevalent in other hotel spaces through the use of woodwork that was stained rather than painted white. In contrast, the former Manicure Room retained more delicate details and white woodwork. The Reading Room conversion included wood paneling, adding to the ambience. Lewis provided an $80,000 gift for the Board Room, and the college expended $42,750 for office renovations.[22]

As the Ponce approached its centennial anniversary in 1988, the Flagler Foundation provided a grant of $400,000 for restoration of the Grand Parlor. Biltmore, Campbell, Smith Restorations Inc. (BCSR) of Asheville, North Carolina, orchestrated the work, including restoration of Virgilio Tojetti's murals painted on canvas and located in the room's four quadrants. The canvas panels had delaminated and, in some areas, fallen to the floor. Those sections had been rolled and stored for more than a decade. Research was undertaken into the mural patterns, paint composition, and methods of installation. Sections of the murals were repainted and reinstalled with epoxy resin. This project's time frame overlapped the restoration of the Dining Hall, with the same techniques employed in both rooms.[23]

The Grand Parlor included furniture, decorative arts objects, and paintings that had been used in the room for a century. Many of those works were conserved, and decorative arts objects were restored. This work was accomplished by Maurine and Joseph L. Boles Sr. Original hotel furnishings were restored by conservator Edward E. Hugo Sr. of Albert Hugo Associates in Jacksonville. Custom-made reproduction carpet and drapes added to the authenticity. The room was renamed the Flagler Room and used as a living memorial honoring Henry Morrison Flagler (fig. 5.5).

FIGURE 5.5. Grand Parlor/Flagler Room, Ponce de Leon Hall. The eleven crystal chandeliers that were restored in 2012 illuminate the five salons in the Flagler Room. Reproduced with permission from Steven Brooke Studios.

As the Grand Parlor's restoration progressed, Flagler College embarked on the institution's first capital campaign. This new effort focused on the Dining Hall, described by New York architect and author George E. Kidder Smith as one of the nation's greatest rooms. The Flagler College Restoration Campaign featured a National Advisory Committee (Committee) of experts who would oversee the restoration. Committee members included some of the southeastern United States' foremost historical museum personnel and preservation architects at the time, including William A. V. Cecil, owner of the Biltmore House and president of Biltmore, Campbell, Smith Restorations (BCSR); W. Vernon Edenfield, director, Kenmore Association Inc.; Thomas A. Gray, chairman, Old Salem Restoration Committee; John E. Harbour, resident director, Mount Vernon;

Daniel P. Jordan, director of Monticello; R. Angus Murdoch, executive director, Historic Charleston Foundation; and Charles B. Simmons, director, The Henry M. Flagler Museum. Architects who participated were Kidder Smith; Nicholas A. Pappas, Colonial Williamsburg Foundation; Frederick D. Nichols, University of Virginia; and F. Blair Reeves, University of Florida. The composition of the committee provided the expertise needed to ensure authenticity and accuracy.[24]

The campaign included publication of a high-quality, full-color booklet portraying the college's history and development. A summary of completed preservation activities set the tone for the upcoming Dining Hall project. Goals for the campaign were included, and corporations responded with major gifts: Barnett [Bank] Charities, $25,000; First Union Bank, $35,000; Florida East Coast Railway, $15,000; Florida Rock Industries Inc., $5,000; Merrill-Lynch, $10,000; Nations Bank, $25,000; Northrop Grummon, $12,500; Southeast Bank, $5,000; Southern Bell, $10,000; SunTrust–Mid Atlantic, $100,000; Tree of Life, $5,000; WD (Winn-Dixie) Charities, $5,000; and Whetstone Chocolates, $5,000. Ultimately, the college secured more than $1,000,000.[25]

The oval-shaped, three-and-a-half story room featured a barrel-vaulted ceiling supported by colossal fluted columns. Each of the side walls included a clerestory with light provided through stained-glass-filled lunette windows. Carved oak and mahogany entries and balconies pierced the end walls. Oak floors were laid in a straight longitudinal pattern. Balconies projected from either end of the room. The single-story curved rooms that flanked the vaulted main hall, the venidos, contained five arches each, into which were set three double-hung stained glass windows. Each window trio measured 10' 6" in height, with the center window measuring 6' in width, and those flanking it each measuring 5' in width.[26]

With the forty windows in the Dining Hall, the triple set of stained glass windows flanking either side of the stair landing at the approach to the room, the single arched window in the porte cochère below the Dining Hall, the sets of tall windows in the rooms above the porte cochères at either end of the Dining Hall, and the circular windows flanking the building's courtyard entrance, the total collection numbers seventy-nine windows. Though important at the time, today the collection is recognized as the largest private collection of Tiffany glass in its original location in the world.[27]

George Willoughby Maynard, one of the nation's foremost muralists, created the elaborate ornamentation in the Dining Hall with assistance from fellow New York art colleague Herman Schladermundt. His emphasis in this room, as in the Rotunda, was on full-length allegorical figures. In this instance, they represented the four seasons. Spanish provincial crests and coats of arms were intermingled with colorful proverbs. Murals depicted ships similar to those of the Spanish, French, and English explorers that came to the New World. Horizontal bands with celebrating cherubs flanked the end wall entries (possibly by another though unnamed artist). Maynard had gained fame for his work on Trinity Church, Boston, before receiving his commission for the Ponce. His later works included the Metropolitan Opera House.[28]

The BCSR, chosen previously to restore the Grand Parlor (Flagler Room), would undertake restoration of the Dining Hall. The firm was most well known in the United States for work on the Biltmore House, the palatial residence of George Washington Vanderbilt II, America's largest private residence, located near Asheville, North Carolina. In addition, the firm's credits include preservation of the Pennsylvania State Capitol and the Renwick Building of the Smithsonian Institution. The architectural firm began in England in the nineteenth century, and the project list there included three internationally renowned London landmarks: Buckingham Palace, Westminster Abbey, and St. Paul's Cathedral. William Amherst Vanderbilt Cecil inherited his American mother's ancestral home, Biltmore, and honored his English father as president of the international restoration firm. BCSR worked with artisans from International Fine Art Conservation Studios Inc. (IFACS) of London, England, and Asheville.[29]

The plan for the Dining Hall involved addressing four elements. Plaster was detaching from the underlying lath, which resulted in deterioration of the artwork that was painted directly on the plaster. In the years since completion of the building's construction, virtually no repairs to these surfaces had been made. Finally, the work needed to be completed in a manner that would enable continued use by the students of the Dining Hall.

The last of the four items was easiest to resolve. The restoration program was divided into three phases, each addressing one of the three areas of the room. The other two areas remained usable, and the scaffolding was erected in a manner that enabled pedestrian access under it. The ceiling work was of primary importance, with the balance of the work on the windows, woodwork, and floors to be performed later. The BCSR firm retained experts in plaster repair and mural conservation.[30]

On October 27, 1986, the committee received an initial report on the physical investigation of the Dining Hall. The room remained as it had been built, without any major changes; however, in 1934–1935 a water-based sprinkler system had been installed in the attic. Though structurally in excellent condition, the attic floor and wood lath might have witnessed stress, though not damage, by inexperienced workmen during that instal-lation. The result was a weakening of the plaster that relied on the lath for support. Major sections of the murals painted directly onto the plaster in the curved venido rooms had fallen to the floor. Large 4' × 8' plywood sheets had been nailed to the ceiling to preclude further deterioration in the venido rooms. The massive barrel-vaulted ceiling in the main section of the room precluded that option for stabilization of that area. The exte-rior of the room was structurally sound; however, a new clay tile roof was needed as leaks were evident where the main room and the venido rooms intersected. Damage existed to the wood framing around the semicircular rooms.[31]

In regard to restoration of the ceiling and wall murals, "overpainting" was evident, the consequence of inexperienced conservators unfamiliar with their work. Also, a polyurethane varnish had been used over some of the designs in the west venido, an inappropriate treatment.[32]

Susanne Pandich of BCSR provided the initial report and produced technical data sheets illustrating her findings. She noted damage to the keyways and composition of the plaster, though more in the venido rooms than in the main hall, a total of about twenty points of separation. Little ad-ditional weight on the ceiling would take place as a result of the treatment. Because of the accelerated condition of damage in the venido rooms, the plaster would be repaired and the murals would be repainted based on photographic documentation and description. An acryloid varnish would serve as a sealant. The treatment was reversible and did not yellow as did shellac. To date, the process had been used successfully in picture restoration and monitored for about twenty years.[33]

If the restoration research was conducted today, this conservation treatment might be addressed differently from a materials standpoint. In 1980, in preparation for the American Institute for Conservation meeting, Metropolitan Museum of Art (Met) Objects Conservation Department conservator Elizabeth C. Welsh published an article attesting to the appropriateness of using Acryloid B-72 (Rohm and Haas trade name for the product). Her findings were based on its longevity and chemical properties that made it less hazardous than alternatives. The following year, Catherine Sease, in an article published in a 1981 issue of *Studies in Conservation* (International Institute for Conservation of Historic and Artistic Works, London), contradicted earlier findings, arguing that the substance failed to meet all of its desirable properties: flexibility, clear matte appearance, non-contractile, good adhesion, and water permeable. These articles addressing the controversy over the sealant were available at the time. To this day, scholars differ on whether or not this material is appropriate to use. Interestingly, by early 1982, Sease was employed by the Met as well. Today, Welsh and Sease remain colleagues and collegial. They continue to chart the future of conservation philosophy and technology.[34]

A new and untested material was available at this time and considered for use as well. BCSR was collaborating on the ceiling project with consultants retained by the Vatican for conservation of the ceiling murals created by Michelangelo in the Sistine Chapel. Those consultants were able to tell BCSR conservators in order to avoid use of the material. The Italian work included removal of this substance and re-conservation of the areas where the substance had been tried.[35]

Addressing the condition of the plaster was a significant consideration. In many areas the plaster was loose and the keys needed to be secured. The keys are areas where the plaster goes through the lath and wraps or curls around the lath, providing integral support for the plaster. BCSR firm's operations manager Steven Seebohm supervised the application of plaster resin from the attic side of the room, directly to the plaster keys. This resin held the plaster keys to the lath. After a test patch in an area of the ceiling devoid of ornamentation, and allowing for drying time, the process was applied to the 8,000 square feet of ceiling.[36]

Barney D. Lamar, director and later president of IFACS, noted that epoxy resins were used because of their strength, bonding capabilities, and lack of weight, particularly in contrast to the weight of plaster. About 1980, epoxy resin had been used successfully at Drayton Hall, a 1755 Georgian Palladian style residence outside Charleston, South Carolina, and a property of the National Trust for Historic Preservation. Regular monitoring evidenced no damage after a decade. In England, epoxy resin had been used at Fetcham Park House; Southampton University; St. Bartholomew's Hospital, London; and in the House of Lords and Peers' Lobby at the Palace of Westminster.[37]

Plaster repair included removal of earlier patches that had been completed with materials that were incompatible with the original in regard to expansion and contraction. Hemp fiber was used to strengthen areas where large cracks had resulted, and traditional plaster repair covered the surface. Cleaning was accomplished with mild detergent. In rare cases where plaster coats were separating from each other, "PVA resins were injected with a large hypodermic syringe and needle."[38] Paint analysis was undertaken to identify original colors prior to repainting. Seebohm noted that oil-based paints were used for the new work, with resins added to match the original consistency of the paint and ensure that the treatment was reversible.[39]

International artisans, including British plaster expert Peter Divers and Italian paint conservator Massimo Buschi, worked for months over the summer and fall of 1987 on the murals, woodwork, plaster moldings, and gold-leafed lions' head light fixtures, repairing, painting, re-stenciling, and reproducing the ceiling ornamentation in the Dining Hall. An eight-person team of conservators from England and Scotland worked in shifts to apply 950 books of 18- and 23-karat gold leaves at 25 leaves per book covering a total of 1,000 square feet. For these artisans accustomed to colder and drier climates than St. Augustine, another challenge was using a one-eighth-inch brush, day after day, in temperatures averaging 100 degrees and humidity close to 100 percent.[40]

At the same meeting of the committee, a report was provided on the condition of the stained glass windows. Two studios, Shenandoah Studios of Front Royal, Virginia, and Willet Studios of Philadelphia, Pennsylvania, were evaluated for the conservation of the glass. The companies verified skill level requirements of their staff and demonstrated that they possessed substantial quantities of glass, enabling replacement, where necessary, to match the original in color, texture, and composition. The Virginia firm was selected to undertake the work, submitting the lower bid by half the amount of the Pennsylvania firm.[41]

Each piece of damaged glass had a mold made and clear glass installed to verify the exactness of the mold prior to the creation of a new colored glass piece. The stained glass windows were removed and taken to the Shenandoah Studios for restoration. In their places, plywood was installed in the openings. In addition to the glass conservation, the window frames were repaired. Once restored, protective sheeting with a vapor barrier was installed on the outside of each window. The installation precluded condensation that could damage the window frames, addressed security issues, and provided protection from disasters—natural or manmade. The merits of an acrylic versus shatterproof plate glass were debated, with the latter being preferred. About every eight years, new impact-resistant polycarbonate sheets are installed, which provide protection as the ultraviolet rays from the sun yellow and cloud the surfaces.[42]

An authenticity question addressed was the presence of roller shade window fittings. In this case, research indicated and Lewis, who was in his 20s at the time, remembered that these had been installed during World War II by the Coast Guard to enable viewing of training films in the room. They were removed. Though the Coast Guard's use of the Ponce represents an important chapter in the building's history, the removal of this item from the Tiffany glass windows did not compromise the integrity of the restoration. Regardless of the decision, the fact that the question was addressed illustrates the care taken in the research and planning for the project.[43]

A compromise was made with regard to the steam radiators located symmetrically throughout the Dining Hall. Energy efficient, sustainable chillers replaced the steam-powered heating system. The radiators could be connected to the new system. After considerable discussion about their operational effectiveness, their importance to the character of the room, their safety and security with regard to students, and their adaptability as part of an alternate heating system, a decision was made to relocate the radiators only if it proved infeasible to incorporate them into the new HVAC system. They would function throughout the building cosmetically as furniture. If that proved infeasible, new unit ventilators would be installed in front of the wainscoting in a manner that would not harm the original fabric. The ventilation would enable air conditioning at occupant levels in the room. The ceilings would remain at the humidity levels comparable to their first ninety-eight years of life in the building. This latter alternative was chosen.[44]

The Restoration Campaign for the Dining Hall was anticipated to require $2,000,000 (which would be nearly $4,000,000 today). By October of 1988, Flagler College had secured total private gifts of $1,222,743 from trustees, corporations and foundations, senior administrators, alumni, students, faculty, and staff. Of the donors for the total amount raised, "Friends of Flagler" recognized individuals principally from northeast Florida. These donors made gifts totaling more than $400,000, and the college had secured a new donor pool. Also at this time, the college considered opening the grand spaces of the building for public tours on a limited basis.[45]

In 1989, the college applied to the state of Florida through the Special Category grant program. Administered through the Division of Historical Resources with peer review by the gubernatorial-appointed Historic Preservation Advisory Council, this state appropriation funding program was created in 1983 as a response to the decline in federal funding. The Florida program was the first of its kind in the nation. The college was encouraged by state officials to apply because of the national significance of the former Hotel Ponce de Leon.

The Dining Hall grant project was awarded a first-place ranking out of ninety-five applications and a recommendation for full funding of $414,712. A $150,000 challenge grant from the Kresge Foundation was more than met as well, enabling the Restoration Campaign to surpass the $2,000,000 goal. As work progressed, more damage became evident, necessitating additional funding. In 1991, the college provided verification to the state of Florida that $2,187,662 had been invested in the project.[46]

The November/December 1987 issue of the National Trust's magazine *Historic Preservation* featured an article on restoration of the former Hotel Ponce de Leon, showcasing the Dining Hall's conservation. Appropriately, the magazine was released shortly before the college celebrated the centennial anniversary of the hotel's opening on January 10, 1988, exactly one hundred years after Henry Flagler's private opening of the building. Jackson Walter, National Trust president, was one of the dignitaries present for the 1988 events, which included tours of the Dining Hall and Grand Parlor, and a formal banquet in the Dining Hall. The coverage was one of numerous stories at the time about preservation in St. Augustine. Author Thomas J. Colin stated, "part of the emerging picture of our Spanish heritage [is] being pieced together with an eye to the 1992 quincentennial celebration of Columbus's discovery of the New World."[47]

Lawrence Lewis Jr. received a prestigious National Trust for Historic Preservation Honor Award for his preservation efforts. He had supported projects in North Carolina, Virginia, and Florida, but the greatest recognition was for efforts on behalf of the Ponce. In 1995, he received the Florida Trust for Historic Preservation's highest award, the Evelyn Fortune Bartlett Award for Lifetime Achievement in Preservation Stewardship.[48]

Restoration of the Flagler College Dining Hall, including the Maynard ceiling murals, encompassed a five-year period between 1986 and 1991 (fig. 5.6). At the completion of the project, the Dining Hall restoration garnered an Outstanding Achievement Award for Restoration of a Historic Structure award from the Florida Trust for Historic Preservation, as had the Grand Parlor in 1988.

Following this extensive and expensive effort, the college initiated a more assertive effort to monitor the condition of the building to maintain the restoration effort. In 2000, Rose Leavitt was commissioned to retouch sections of the Dining Hall ceiling. She had previously worked as a conservator for BCSR, and her commissions included two projects in Palm Beach, Whitehall, Henry Flagler's winter home, and Mar-a-Lago, Marjorie Merriweather Post's former estate owned by Donald Trump. Her firm, Rose O. Leavitt Conservation of Fine Arts, spent most of the summer completing the repairs (fig. 5.7).[49]

Placing restoration of the Dining Hall into a relevant context requires stepping outside of St. Augustine. The Ponce is a one-of-a-kind building. Even with consideration of Henry Flagler's other commissions for Carrère & Hastings, the Ponce rises above the later works in architectural importance. Memorial Presbyterian Church, Flagler's final resting place, is unique among ecclesiastical buildings. Yet the sanctuary's interior, its most dramatic space, is considerably less complex architecturally and

FIGURE 5.6. Dining Hall, Ponce de Leon Hall, Flagler College. Considered one of the greatest rooms in the United States, the former Dining Room was painstakingly restored for the building's 100th anniversary in 1988. Reproduced with permission from Steven Brooke Studios.

decoratively than that of the Dining Hall, the Ponce's most remarkable room.

In Florida, several other properties come to mind that feature interiors that could be compared with regard to conservation issues to those in the Ponce: two Palm Beach properties—Whitehall (1900–1901), Flagler's winter home, and Mar-a-Lago (1927–1931), Marjorie Merriweather Post's estate. Vizcaya (1916), Charles Deering's residence on Miami's Biscayne Bay, was followed a few years later by John and Mable Ringling's Ca' d'Zan on Sarasota Bay (1924–1925). All but the last are designated as National Historic Landmarks, and, most likely, the Ringling mansion is eligible.

Historically, the properties share similar construction eras, from the

Gilded Age through the Florida Land Boom of the 1920s. Architecturally, each is unique, all of masonry construction, and each features extensive decorative arts collections. All are coastal properties with buildings and grounds that have been damaged by hurricanes and storms. Each of the properties has required research into conservation processes to enable restoration or preservation of their unique interiors. The major difference in

FIGURE 5.7. Restoration of the ceiling murals, Dining Hall, Ponce de Leon Hall, Flagler College Archives.

the conservation of the Ponce Dining Hall is that the work was undertaken in the late 1980s and early 1990s. Information, techniques, and equipment have dramatically changed in the last twenty-five years.

If undertaken today at the scale accomplished during that earlier period, restorers would use computer technology to examine plaster photographically before evaluating its composition chemically. A more comprehensive assessment of the attic space might be attainable through the use of computers instead of physical examination by people. The electronic evaluation could place less stress on fragile building components. The ceilings in the Sistine Chapel were undergoing conservation that enabled comparative analyses of materials and techniques. That the conservation and restoration firms had experience with three of England's most significant buildings lent credibility to their work on the Ponce. Artisans from Europe provided expertise that either was unavailable or was perceived to have been unavailable in the United States at the time.

The Dining Hall research effort was appropriate to the level of expertise demanded to accomplish a high-quality restoration. The process used internationally renowned experts, an advisory board of national scholars, and a procedure that was thoughtful, deliberative, and effective. Shortcomings in the process, if they exist, are not apparent either in the written record or the accomplished project.

In addition to restoration of the room, conservation of the finishes, and introduction of an HVAC system, the hotel chairs were reproduced for use by the college. Furniture company manufacturer John Foster, Lewis's son-in-law and Louise Lewis Foster's husband, had the chairs copied.[50]

In 1989, at the same time that Flagler College was in the midst of the restoration and conservation of the Dining Room, the institution began a three-phased $1,000,000 campaign to restore the Rotunda. IFACS, the firm that completed the Grand Parlor and Dining Room under the direction of BCSR, was retained to analyze the damage to the Rotunda. IFACS developed an elaborate condition assessment that addressed the space floor by floor and covered pertinent topics: plaster, decorative painting, woodwork, marble, and murals. The following summarizes information provided in the report.

Plaster damage was considerably less than that present in the Dining Hall. Cracks in the ceilings of the first and second floors resulted in paint peeling from murals that had been applied directly to plaster. Water leaks caused deterioration to plaster on the first-floor walls. Poor quality repairs that had been made over time did not correct the problem. A heavy layer of latex paint covered the principal wall along the grand staircase in an attempt to conceal plaster damage. On the Mezzanine level, in the rectangular section surrounding the Rotunda, original plaster was replaced by new plaster, or walls were covered with plaster board. Original plaster remained on the ceiling. For the third level, the plaster was attached on the underside of a circular wooden framework. That structural system supported an octagon-shaped, paneled bench seat, the top of which featured a balustrade. The recommendation was to avoid disassembly of this seating system to avoid potential for further plaster and structural damage.[51]

The report detailed damage to the walls of the Mezzanine level, which was considerably different and more challenging than the condition evident throughout the rest of the Rotunda and lobbies in the building. Vinyl wallpaper installed with a strong adhesive had been installed on the Mezzanine walls. The installation method precluded removal of the wallpaper without removing the room's original plaster and paint. The diagnosis required more substantial effort. Fortunately, this area was devoid of decorative plaster details.[52]

Decorative painting was assessed with onsite field examination. In addition, microscopic stratigraphic analysis was conducted, with the results presented through photographs. This analysis enabled determination of original and subsequent colors, and the number of times that the surfaces were painted. Paint included glazes, washes, faux graining, and similar treatments, depending upon the surface (fig. 5.8).

The first-floor lobby, grand staircase at both the lobby and Mezzanine levels, and the perimeter of the dome above the Mezzanine went through a series of color transitions. Investigation revealed that the original paint finish treatment was designed to match the pink marble wainscoting in the room. The niches, door arches, and plaster sections over the fireplace mantels had all received faux graining to imitate the oak woodwork found throughout the Rotunda and Mezzanine.[53]

Additional paint layers that were documented indicated the following order for the main floor and similar shades for the remainder of these areas: red, blue, blue, yellow, and white. The last color was on the walls at the

FIGURE 5.8. Conservation of the Maynard murals in the Rotunda. Rotunda, Ponce de Leon Hall, Flagler College Archives.

time of the restoration and obscured much of the bas relief plaster decoration on the ground floor. The ceilings' original paint color was yellow green. Plaster board replaced much of the third-floor plaster, precluding investigation into original finishes. For the areas that retained plaster, no decorative treatments were found.[54]

The report on the Rotunda dome noted that the surface featured a yellow glaze over white paint that was not adhering to the carved and decorated details. Some of the decorative elements exhibited a bronze paint that had darkened, and the figures were covered extensively with dirt and dust. Certainly this last statement could have been the result of several situations, deferred maintenance, difficulty accessing the space, difficulty cleaning the three-dimensional surfaces, or the chemistry of the paint providing a haven for dirt and dust.

The bases of wood columns had small pieces missing. The segments were created in sections that proved fragile over time. Applications such as varnishes and polishes had darkened with age and dulled surfaces, preventing display of the wood's natural grain. On the Mezzanine level a plastic coating had been applied that had dried to a brittle consistency and was chipping. Dirt and grease were present as well. The investigative report stated that the overall condition of the woodwork exhibited minor damage, including that from insect infestation, though moldings and panels exhibited significant termite infestation.[55]

The areas near the staircases exhibited the greatest concentration of damage to the woodwork and were determined to be a high priority. The bench seats that flanked the grand marble staircase displayed excessive damage, most likely from heavy use. Also, the window frames had heat, water, and vermin damage, particularly those frames that held the Bacchus themed Tiffany windows. Also, across the Rotunda at the front entrance to the building the paneling and moldings were found to be loose, damaged, or missing. In some locations, damage to moldings had been filled with plastic.

Marble was in very good condition, with grout requiring replacement in areas that received impact, such as at the base of columns. Though damage was not in evidence, the report recommended further investigation of the structural condition of the pink Numidian marble balcony at the south minstrels' gallery. The marble floors, stairs, wainscoting, and trim needed polishing.

The assessment of the murals included the structural condition of the dome on all four levels. With assistance from architect Craig Thorn, the conservation experts determined that some of the structural support in the dome had shifted over time; "transmission of weight" had caused cracking in plaster resulting in damage to the murals painted directly on that plaster. The 400 Rotunda or Solarium at the top of the building had been used since about 1980 as storage for furniture. The report recommended that the items be removed from the room as the additional weight might have exacerbated the damage.

The accepted scope of work included restoration of the mosaic tile floors, Verona and pink Numidian marble, and quarter-sawn oak wainscoting in the vestibule, lobby, and along the flanking wings; repair to the Mezzanine and grand staircase ceiling and wall plaster; restoration of decorative Turkish red glaze and stenciled friezes on plaster walls; reproduction of light fixtures; and painting ceilings Primrose yellow. At the Mezzanine level, the two Georg Schweissinger oil canvasses flanking the south minstrels' gallery were conserved. Finally, the paired oak doors, sidelights, and transom that comprised the main entrance from the courtyard into the vestibule were recommended to be reproduced (fig. 5.9).[56]

Nearly all of the work proposed for the Rotunda was completed. An exception was reestablishment of original paint colors and faux graining. Also, the door surround on the Mezzanine level that was added to meet the fire code was recommended to be removed. That was not accomplished because of code requirements.[57]

One construction and conservation team was selected to orchestrate all phases of the project. A. D. Davis Construction Company performed construction, and the Cummings Studios of North Adams, Massachusetts, restored the Tiffany windows. IFACS accomplished restoration of the plaster, decorative painting, and murals, using the same methods and techniques as had been undertaken successfully for the Dining Hall. The detailed descriptions were presented in that section and are not repeated here. The phases are outlined in the following paragraphs. When details for work items differ from those presented for the Dining Room they are described.[58]

Fundraising was a critical component of this project. As part of that effort, Flagler College applied to the state of Florida for several Special Category grants. For Phase I, a request was made for $200,000, with a match committed of $211,997. The college received an award of $92,625 in 1990 and matched the funds with more than proposed, a total of $348,917. The scope of work for this phase called for repair of the plaster cracks in the portion of the dome on which the murals and decorative paint adhered, conservation of the Maynard murals, and restoration of some of the woodwork.[59]

In 1990, Flagler College proposed Phase II, an estimated $675,000 project. The college pledged $200,000 toward this effort. The college was awarded the highest ranking for a grant of $149,888 in 1991 from the state of Florida to assist with the project. The scope of work for this segment included conservation of the Schweissinger paintings, repair and restoration of the walls, repair and cleaning of the marble walls and floors, reproduction of quarter-sawn oak paneling, restoration of decorative painting along the grand staircase, reproduction of doors and light fixtures, reconstruction of the round Tiffany window frames, and restoration of those windows.[60]

FIGURE 5.9. George Willoughby Maynard's murals adorn the ceiling of the Rotunda. The standing allegorical figures represent the Elements: Earth, Air, Fire, and Water, and the seated women depict the Exploration series: Adventure, Discovery, Conquest, and Civilization. Ponce de Leon Hall Rotunda ceiling, Flagler College Archives.

Conservation of the Schweissinger paintings included careful removal of the varnish and installation of a new lining canvas. The restoration of the dome included cleaning and repair, application of oil paint and glaze, and regilding of the Rotunda dome with 560 books of gold and 250 books of silver leaf.[61]

The scope included repairs to and restoration of the Porter's Entrance accessed from the carriageway at the rear of the hotel. The polychromatic masonry contrasted with plaster that received stencils and paint applied with designs featuring coats of armor. Conservation included removal of overpainting, determining and matching original colors, and application of protective varnish.[62]

In 1992, the college received a state of Florida grant ranking of 33 for an award of $146,220 for Phase III and provided $320,555 in matching funds. The work completed under this grant concluded the scope started in Phase II. Once work began, damage was more accurately evaluated, and additional time and funds were required. Included in Phase III was restoration of the Bacchus-themed Tiffany stained glass windows and frames on the east side of the grand staircase.[63]

As the project progressed, an additional Phase IV was needed. The college continued fundraising, and in 1993 submitted another Special Category grant application. In 1994, the state of Florida provided funding of $139,880, which the college matched dollar for dollar. The project did not receive a high ranking, coming in at 46. Multiple-phased projects tended to decline in rank as new projects stepped forward with strong needs and support.[64]

In 1996, the decade-long restoration of the Ponce was nearing completion. Dr. William L. Proctor prepared to celebrate his twenty-fifth anniversary as Flagler College's president. In a field where administrators changed institutions every few years, Proctor's tenure was rare. To honor that achievement, a newly constructed building west of the Ponce was built and dedicated as the Proctor Library. Following relocation of the library out of Kenan Hall and into the new facility, the college invested $1,035,957 to renovate the former Hotel Ponce de Leon facilities building.[65]

By this time, the major restoration efforts for the Ponce were finished, and preservation of several other historic campus buildings had been completed as well. A consulting team of engineering and environmental consultants was retained to prepare a list of additional work on the Ponce that could serve as the basis for additional preservation projects.

A low coquina-concrete wall defined the perimeter of the grounds of the Ponce. The wall featured tall concrete-capped bollards and was punctuated with inward-curving lunettes spaced at regular intervals. Heavy chains with spike mace heads hung between each bollard, emphasizing the fortress exterior of the building and precluding entry to the property. Globe fixtures provided lighting to the property. By the time that the hotel complex was nearing its century mark, the perimeter wall had suffered significant damage to all of the major components: the low wall, bollards, caps, chains, light standards, and globes. Wiring for the lights was outdated also. About half of the pieces of the metal and chain mail were missing by the time the college started the project.[66]

Although original to the Ponce property, restoration of the perimeter wall surrounding the seven-acre property was a lower priority than preservation of the five buildings that comprised the hotel complex. Abare stated that without assistance from the state, most likely the college would not have undertaken the project. Consideration was given to removing the wall for health and safety reasons.[67]

In 1998, after obtaining detailed estimates and a scope of work over several years, the college submitted an application to the state of Florida for another Special Category grant. The request was for $360,000 with a match of $408,000. The project was not funded, and grant records do not provide the reason. At this time the state of Florida set an upper limit of $350,000 on the grant awards. The college resubmitted the application the following year for funding in the 2000 state fiscal year. The project was anticipated to cost $768,000. The grant submission was for $350,000 with a match of $418,000. The college was awarded $300,000 and provided a match of $500,000.[68]

Batson-Cook Company of Jacksonville served as the general contractor for the project. The 1,600-foot wall consisted of eighty-five pillars and forty-nine light fixtures joined by sixty-four sections of spiked maces and chains. The concrete mix used for the wall repairs involved a recipe of 70 percent coquina, 20 percent cement, and 10 percent water. Seamont Ventures of St. Augustine provided the coquina. Florida Rock Industries Inc. of Jacksonville supplied the cement.

In July 2000, the consulting team identified four issues to be addressed: the portcullis or iron gate at the entrance, the loggias that flank the entrance and their light fixtures, and the concrete sidewalks in the courtyard. Specifically, over time environmental factors with assistance from airborne termites had compromised the integrity of the wood framework of the portcullis and the floor structure. The iron framework for the gate and the decorative lighting standards had suffered rust damage and corrosion. Also, the light fixtures required repair and rewiring. The concrete courtyard floor structure was cracked severely.[69]

The college applied for a state of Florida grant in the amount of $231,545 with a maximum committed match of $200,000. The project was recommended for funding for the 2001–2002 fiscal year. As work began, the college reevaluated the funds to be expended for the project. A total of $310,500 was documented as the college's participation.[70]

A. D. Davis Construction Company was selected as the construction firm, with Kenneth Smith Architects Inc. as the architectural consultant. All of the elements were repaired or replaced to match the originals in materials, techniques, design, and details. Cypress was used as the material for the portcullis structure, once again finished in iron. The terrace and steps were recreated in coquina concrete with the original coquina blocks salvaged from the Catholic church reused. The fountain with its trademark turtles and frogs was repaired, part of a regular maintenance cycle for that element.[71]

On September 15, 1999, Hurricane Floyd traveled north from the Caribbean up the Atlantic Coast, remaining just offshore from Florida and bringing wind and rain for several days. Flooding in St. Augustine reduced transportation options to canoes and kayaks. A few brave souls swam through the city's streets. In the months of August and September 2004, Florida endured four hurricanes: Charley, Frances, Ivan, and Jeanne. For both hurricanes Frances and Jeanne, mandatory evacuations required Flagler College to take students from the campus inland to safe havens. Hurricane Wilma continued the onslaught in 2005.[72]

Hurricane Floyd wrought damage to the Ponce, specifically to the clay tile roof and many of the 1,000 wood frame windows. Emergency repairs to the dormer windows and corresponding roof sections required an investment of $1,333,309. The hurricanes in 2004 and 2005 brought more damage. Those storms ranked as the greatest series of major storms in half a century.

A component of life in Florida and many other places is preparation for tropical storms and hurricanes. Property owners recognize that they must be prepared to address basic needs, evacuation, and property devastation at least, and loss of life at most. For a building such as the Ponce, the stakes are great, and preparation is dramatic in labor, materials, and cost. Time does not permit installing hurricane protection on 1,000 windows, relocating furniture, and storing irreplaceable fine and decorative arts. The Ponce must withstand environmental threats and manmade disasters. Following the early twenty-first-century hurricanes, Flagler College focused on enhanced protection for the building.

Upon the recommendation of and with assistance from the state of Florida's Northeast Florida Regional Preservation Office, the college submitted a grant request under a new federal program. Save America's Treasures had been launched during President Clinton's administration and continued through the George W. Bush administration. The initiative benefitted properties eligible for or designated as National Historic Landmarks. The program operated through the National Park Service in partnership with the National Endowment for the Humanities and the National Trust for Historic Preservation.

In 2001, Flagler College received $400,000 for repairs to more sections of the complex roof of the Ponce. The grant required an equal financial commitment from the college. This commitment was fulfilled quickly by the college and the Board of Trustees led by Chairman Randal Ringhaver. The project had a twenty-four-month time frame.[73]

In 2003, the college applied for a state of Florida grant to pursue a windows project, receiving in 2004 funds of $300,000 with $503,100 in matching funds for custom-made hurricane-resistant replacement windows in the configuration of the originals.[74]

That same year, William T. Abare Jr. succeeded William L. Proctor as president of Flagler College. Proctor became the college's chancellor, and Governor Jeb Bush chose him to be Florida's chief educational officer.

The administrative wing on the east side of the Ponce's first level underwent an update to welcome the millennium and meet Abare's needs. The scope of work included removal of the contemporary glass doors at the entry to the wing and installation of a pair of paneled wood doors. Their lion's head doorknobs provided differentiation from the original scallop shell design in use throughout the main floor. Some additional renovations provided more privacy, convenience, and security for the senior administrators. The broad hallway functioned as a reception area for visitors, and furnishings incorporated original hotel pieces, including chairs and tables.

The Grand Marnier Foundation provided a grant for conservation of the college's art collection. They numbered about forty pieces and were part of the works that Knoedler and Company secured for Henry Flagler to be exhibited in the Ponce. After conservation, the works were exhibited in the President's Wing and in the Flagler Room.

Another change made during the new millennium complemented the windows project and enabled energy conservation. With solid masonry walls precluding traditional methods of air conditioning and ventilation, introduction of a unified heat and cooling system was especially challenging. Ductwork was installed just below ceilings along the hallways outside the dorm rooms. Attic spaces were used as well for the upper floors. Chases were run at the ends of corridors where fire staircases provided open cavities. Condenser units were placed on the ground and screened with plants.

Other areas that were required to be closed for the system to operate properly were done so with framing and glass or with clear acrylic material, enabling the original openings to remain visible. Some of these compromises provided compliance with life safety codes and added temperature and humidity controls to the building.

The climate control system in the Rotunda operated similarly to the one that was installed in the Dining Hall a few years earlier. The coolest air at lowest humidity is maintained at ground level where people circulate. The plaster ornamentation, decorative woodwork, and murals on the ceilings of the first and Mezzanine floors remain unaffected by the climate control system.

The college continued to grow in the number of students admitted, faculty hired, academic programs offered, and facilities provided to meet institutional needs. The Ponce was adapted in response. The ground floor of the Dining Hall building had been updated during the hotel tenure, and the Coast Guard had modified several areas in the building during World War II. Those changed areas were ready for new uses to accommodate college requirements.

In 1955, a decade after the Coast Guard withdrew from the Ponce, William R. Kenan Jr. hired E. B. Meade and Son Construction Co. to renovate the Billiards Room and "Gay Nineties" Bar. This included installing new heating and air conditioning. The former gathering place for hotel guests continued in that role, this time for students, with the area's conversion to a student lounge and snack bar.

Thirty years later, Kenan's great-niece Molly Wiley made a gift of $263,350 to convert the space into a college snack bar. Renamed "Molly's Place" in her honor, the area retained dark woodwork and natural light from the double-hung sash windows. Another renovation in 2007, responding to new needs, converted the space to the Learning Resource Center to aid student academics.[75]

Another 1950s modification, construction of a swimming pool on the lawn west of the Ponce, benefitted from an update thirty years later. That facility and the building's landscaping were addressed with an investment of $238,650. In 2005, the college retained the landscape architecture firm of Hauber-Fowler & Associates of Longwood, Florida, to integrate the campus buildings with their settings and incorporate more outdoor gathering spaces for students.[76]

Early in the history of the college, minor modifications were made to the Artists' Studios building in order to convert the former artists' ateliers to offices for the Flagler System Inc. Contemporary modifications, including paneling, drop ceilings, and fluorescent tube lighting, replaced skylights, canvas-covered walls, and tiled fireplaces. The second floor was commissioned for classrooms, as well as one area on the first floor. Maintenance functions remained on the lower floor.[77]

In contrast to the earlier effort, a two-phased conversion of the Edison Boiler Building and Artists' Studios orchestrated by the Georgia-based firm Batson-Cook Company returned the building to art studios, offices, and a gallery. The building stood out as one of the only examples of industrial architecture from the Flagler era, adding additional importance to the undertaking. The project was supported with the state of Florida's only two back-to-back grants awarded in 2006 and 2007 at the $350,000 level, the maximum funding permitted. These public funds were matched privately almost seven times over for the $5,500,000 project (fig. 5.10).

The scope of work for the Edison Boiler Building included lifting the original roof beam structure from the boiler building and setting the beams on the west lawn in order to have these structural elements certified so that they could be reinstalled and meet hurricane standards. The beams had been an exposed construction element throughout the building's history

FIGURE 5.10. The Artists' Studios and Edison Boiler Buildings at the Hotel Ponce de Leon were creatively adapted for use as art studios and faculty offices in 2007. Molly Wiley Art Building, Flagler College Archives.

and represented a character-defining feature of this industrial building. From an interpretive standpoint, the beam structure added a unique and rare opportunity to explore preservation.

To meet fire separation requirements, yet still expose the beams on the interior, thick glass was used between rooms to enable the beam structure to remain visible and provide fire protection. The original clerestory opening (that had been covered over) was reestablished, albeit with hurricane glass.

In the Artists' Studios Building, arched openings on the first story that provided access to storage areas for coal to fuel the steam dynamos were retained and repeated in the interior. Windows and doors were repaired instead of replaced. The original palm-tree-trunk columns on the second floor of the Artists' Studios segment were certified as sound and remained. Metal reinforcing pipes inserted in the mid-twentieth century to support the balcony were removed after steel beams were concealed behind the wood horizontal floor support beam, returning the balcony to its original appearance. Fireplaces located in the studios, if remaining at the time of the restoration, were repaired. As with the hotel room areas of the Ponce, fireplace mantels and faces remain. Flues had been sealed many years earlier to meet fire code. New tiles were reproduced, and these unique elements, though nonoperational, were preserved to add interest to the building.

In addition to the $700,000 in state of Florida funding, private gifts from about forty donors assisted the effort. The principal funding came from the William R. Kenan Jr. Charitable Trust, a gift of $3,500,000 to honor Mary Lily Flagler "Molly" Lewis Wiley, Henry Flagler's great-niece and an enthusiastic supporter of Flagler College. The buildings were renamed the Molly Wiley Art Building in her honor.

When the college was preparing to celebrate the Ponce's 125th anniversary, Flagler College received a first-place-ranked state of Florida small matching grant of $50,000 for conservation of the Grand Parlor. Added to this was a prestigious $10,000 Cynthia Woods Mitchell grant from the National Trust for Historic Preservation. For this work the college retained the Atlanta firm of International Fine Arts Conservation Studio (IFACS) headed by English expert Geoffrey Steward. He and the firm had been headquartered in London when commissioned by BCSR to work on the Ponce in 1985. Today, the firm's international project list includes Buckingham Palace and St. Paul's Cathedral. El Jardin in Miami and Ca' d'Zan in Sarasota are features of their ongoing Florida repertoire.

Twenty-five years after the original effort, the damage was minimal in comparison to the conditions found in the 1980s. The four Tojetti murals were delaminating from the ceiling, but all remained in place. The synthetic laminating material had dried out in some areas. Advances in conservation materials and techniques enabled the restoration to be accomplished by using hypodermic needles to inject new laminating material along the resulting cracks and crevices, then those small areas were repainted. Woodwork was detailed, including new gold leaf applied to the egg-and-dart moldings. A glaze applied over the painted wood surfaces was reapplied also.

Based upon the consultants' investigations, the delamination appeared to be a result of fluctuations in temperature and humidity within the room, which is used heavily by the campus and community for meetings and events. Personnel in charge of the fine and decorative arts collection in the room collaborated with the campus planner and maintenance director to devise a strategy that would preclude this situation recurring in the future through a computerized temperature and humidity management system.

A dramatic change to the room took place in September of 2012 with the restoration of the eleven crystal chandeliers. The elaborate glittering lights were updated in the early twentieth century to present a more colonial appearance with electric candles installed in the sockets. Over the decades, glass pieces and prisms were damaged or removed, and the glass was cleaned with abrasive materials, clouding their surfaces. Tim Lillard, who operates through King's Chandeliers of Charleston, had restored the chandeliers in the former Hotel Alcazar a few years earlier. He was retained to accomplish similar work for the Ponce. Using William Henry Jackson's photographs, now part of the Library of Congress archives, and his on-site investigations, he rewired each light, repaired or replaced the crystal pieces, and installed new glass globes.

Though the college was committed to having the globes fabricated to match the originals, no firms were available worldwide that could accomplish the task. The global economic recession precluded custom production. Appropriate glass was not available from either China or Czechoslovakia. In 2009, Ireland's Waterford Crystal filed bankruptcy, and the production building for the 152-year-old glassmaking company was demolished in 2013. Using glass already produced, new globes were obtained for the Flagler Room that matched the original design as closely as possible.

In 2008, the state of Florida began preparations to commemorate in 2013 the 500th anniversary of Spanish explorer Juan Ponce de Leon's landing off

FIGURE 5.11. The central dome of the building is topped by a copper lantern, and the flanking roof terraces afford spectacular views of St. Augustine, the Matanzas Inlet, and Florida. The west tower is featured in the photo. Photo taken between 1880 and 1897 by William H. Jackson, Library of Congress, Prints & Photographs Division, Reproduction Number: LC.DIG.det.4a03457.

the east coast of Florida. Also in the year 2013, Flagler College planned to celebrate the 125th anniversary of the opening of the Hotel Ponce de Leon. These anniversaries renewed interest in completing restoration of the building.

At the top of the Ponce, under the central dome and between the two towers, was the last significant space in the former hotel that needed restoration (fig. 5.11). The special room identified originally as the 400 Rotunda and known contemporarily as the Solarium remained underused since 1971. In 1985, the copper lantern at the top of the dome was restored at a cost of $26,000, and tower balconies were preserved with an investment of $97,950. The college funded both.[78]

All four sides of the room feature tall, divided light windows; the southern exposure features a sliding glass wall opening onto a narrow balcony overlooking the courtyard. Square columns support vaulted walls leading to a ribbed ceiling that culminates in a circular skylight.

Side entries open from the room to the wings at the north side of the courtyard, and adjacent side entries enable access to roof terraces and the towers. When built, the center of the floor featured a large, circular opening framed by a balustrade that afforded a view downward to the narrow oculus at the top of the Rotunda and from there to the marble floor of the lobby (fig. 5.12). That opening had been closed decades earlier.

Today, the roof terraces flanking the Solarium continue to afford panoramic views to the east, views of the Castillo de San Marcos, the Matanzas River, Anastasia Island, and the Atlantic Ocean. To the west, the San Sebastian River and St. Johns County are featured. Each terrace provides a southern exposure of the Ponce courtyard, loggias, and portcullis. Beyond the immediate property, Henry Flagler's other hotels, now the Casa Monica and Lightner Building, stand majestically. Beyond the hotel buildings, a view of the Lincolnville neighborhood is framed by the confluence of the San Sebastian and Matanzas Rivers.

Historically, the Solarium served as a space where guests of the Ponce gathered for conversation, enjoyed entertainment, or watched activities taking place in town or along the bay front. Rehabilitation of the room would foster similar activities and provide an exceptional event venue. The new floor plan would accommodate a meeting room and accessible restrooms in the east wing, a catering kitchen and a storage/data room in the west wing, new mechanical systems, and an express elevator.

Original chandeliers and wall sconces were supplemented by new lighting, and audio-visual and computer technology were incorporated. The roof terraces received new decking. The most dramatic work on the terraces was rebuilding the elaborate staircases leading into the towers. Scars remaining on the tower walls provided the railing profile, and with a nineteenth-century Library of Congress photograph, accurate reconstruction

FIGURE 5.12. Between 1968 and 1971, the Louise Wise Lewis Library was located in the room under the central dome. In 2013, the beautifully restored room was re-dedicated as the Solarium, once again affording unparalleled views of St. Augustine and its environs. 400 Rotunda, Flagler College Archives.

of the stair structures was accomplished. The staircases serve as emergency egress via new metal fire-rated staircases concealed within the towers.[79]

In 2009, the college received a first-place ranking for a grant to restore the Solarium's hurricane-damaged sliding glass wall overlooking the court-yard. The decline in the global economy resulted in the Solarium rehabili-tation as the only historic preservation grant project funded by the state of Florida. Due to the significance of the resource, the project was selected to receive federal stimulus Historic Preservation Fund monies for "shovel-ready" projects. BTS Builders Inc. undertook the project with A. D. Davis Construction Company. Both local firms have extensive experience with historic preservation projects.

The glass panels were photographed. Each piece of glass was num-bered, removed, and stored. The fir framework and red oak mullions were evaluated for structural integrity. Every piece that could be reused was re-used. Each new piece was milled with the same dimensions and profile as the original. To fabricate the enormous door panels, the work had to be undertaken in the Solarium. The wall matched the original, reflecting its 1888 appearance.[80]

To maintain the momentum, the college approached Delores Lastinger, college trustee, and her husband, Allen, both of whom have a strong interest in preservation. The Lastingers provided a challenge grant of $500,000 and, in response, the college launched a program entitled "A Crowning Achievement: The Campaign for Restoration of the Solarium."

In 2012, the college achieved the fundraising goal of $2,000,000, including a second first-place-ranked state of Florida small matching grant of $50,000 to rebuild the fire stairs accessing the two towers and a Special Appropriation from the Florida Legislature of $350,000 to honor the centennial anniversary of Henry Flagler's completion of the Overseas Railway.

Flagler College completed restoration of the Solarium and fourth floor of Ponce Hall in the spring of 2013. To achieve handicapped accessibility the scope of work included cutting through the original cast coquina-concrete wall adjoining the concrete dome to the west wing. A challenging surprise in materials surfaced when the contractor encountered railroad tracks embedded in the concrete walls for stability. A small section of this concrete was retained for archival purposes. The same reinforcing technique had been used in the construction of the towers.

Flagler College graduate Natalie Karas of Philadelphia assisted the project during 2009, when she was completing a master's degree in historic preservation from the University of Pennsylvania. As a class project, she analyzed the paint and plaster from the Solarium. The main room had been a series of yellow shades in its early years. Yellow was incorporated throughout the Solarium and fourth floor (fig. 5.13).[81]

A vestige of original material was uncovered. New York's prestigious department store Arnold, Constable & Company had provided carpet padding that was found in the west wing. Most likely the padding dated from construction of the hotel or from an early renovation. That wing escaped later modifications, though it witnessed significant deterioration over the decades.[82]

In the spring of 2013, the college had the monumental Edison smokestack maintained. This functional element represents the attention to detail found throughout the building. The polychromatic construction features a rectangular concrete base, and the brick hexagonal shaft is adorned

FIGURE 5.13. The restored Solarium was rededicated in the spring of 2013 and serves Flagler College and the region as an elegant event venue with unparalleled views of the St. Augustine skyline. Solarium/400 Rotunda, Ponce de Leon Hall, Flagler College Archives.

with concrete bands and studs. The stack culminates in a corbelled band. Conservators removed dirt with gentle cleaning, and masonry was repainted to match the original mortar composition and color. This completed preservation activities for the former Boiler Building. Once again, the smokestack proudly enhances the St. Augustine skyline.[83]

Restoration and rehabilitation of the former Hotel Ponce de Leon consumed more than forty years, nearly all of the years that the building served as the centerpiece of the Flagler College campus. The most dramatic efforts began twenty-five years ago with the Dining Room, Rotunda, and Grand Parlor. The final chapter took place in 2013 with restoration of the Solarium or 400 Rotunda. The timing was particularly important as the college completed the effort for the 125th anniversary of the opening of the Hotel Ponce de Leon and the 500th anniversary of the Spanish explorer Juan Ponce de Leon's landing off the east coast of present-day Florida near St. Augustine.

Some of the early work undertaken for the 100th anniversary reflects outdated technology and conservation treatments. The college retained experts who return as part of a regular preservation, conservation, and maintenance schedule for the Ponce and the other fifteen historic campus buildings.

In addition to members of the Flagler and Kenan families on the Board of Trustees, the college added a broad range of talented people including alumni who were students early in the history of the institution. In all cases, the campus facilities rank as a critical factor for participation with the organization. Oversight for the historic campus is strong as is the demonstrated commitment to historic preservation.

6

A Most Beautiful College Campus

Flagler College's Restoration Campaign placed the academic institution and the former hotel in a national context based on the campus's architectural importance, high quality of historic preservation efforts, and attractiveness of facilities. Also, in the eyes of college administrators and trustees, the success of the capital campaign for the Ponce Dining Hall ensured that historic preservation would remain a major emphasis of the college. The Ponce's location in the heart of downtown St. Augustine and the positive response to the historic campus by parents, students, and visitors confirmed the college's decision. This reinforced the symbiotic relationship between the success of Flagler College as an educational institution and the enhancement of its reputation as an attractive campus based on historical resources.

Over the years, Flagler College grew in stature academically, attracted a stable student body of about 2,500, introduced many new programs, and bolstered the programs with facilities. The institution's adaptive use of historic buildings led to acquisitions of other properties adjacent to or near the campus. Some properties were donated; others were purchased. All possessed either a common time frame or a shared history with that of the Ponce. Some of the buildings were built in the late nineteenth century. The Flagler System had held others in its property inventory. The college campus includes fifteen historic buildings and the five-building complex constructed originally as the Hotel Ponce de Leon. These twenty historic buildings comprise about two-thirds of the college's properties used for educational purposes.

In 2006, the Department of the Interior designated the Hotel Ponce de Leon as a National Historic Landmark, the highest recognition a property in the United States can receive and a status held by approximately 2,500 properties. A few months later, *Florida Trend* magazine rated the campus as Florida's most beautiful college setting. *MSN Travel* listed Flagler College as one of the "15 Most Beautiful Campuses" for colleges that serve as tourist attractions. In 2011, *Education* ranked the campus as one of the "20 Most Gorgeous College Campuses" in the United States, and the *Princeton Review* followed, identifying the setting as one of the "20 Most Beautiful Campuses." Flagler College's beautiful campus is appreciated throughout the nation, including by prospective students and their parents.

Adding to the college's prestige was St. Augustine's national ratings that began in 2009 with *U.S. News & World Report*'s list of "10 Best Places to Live," followed in 2010 by the *Wall Street Journal*'s *SmartMoney* and *MarketWatch* lists of best cities for retirement. That ranking was echoed by *CNN Money*'s list of twenty-five best retirement locales. *Bloomberg Businessweek* emphasized the affordability of the city. In 2012, *Forbes Magazine* rated the city as one of the "10 Prettiest Towns in the U.S." *National Geographic Traveler* included St. Augustine in its twenty cities as "Best of the World 2013." *Travel and Leisure* favored the college and community in 2014 with a seventh-place ranking as one of "America's Best College Towns," noting the historic ambience, excellent bed and breakfasts, restaurants, and miles of beaches as enhancements.

Flagler College's campus has played a strong role since the Ponce opened as a hotel more than 125 years ago. In addition to the extraordinary and unique historic facilities, the campus includes the city's only auditorium, making the campus a center for events of local, state, and national importance. St. Augustine has a population of 14,000, and St. Johns County has a population of about 200,000. Yet the region supports an annual tourism base of 7,500,000 due to the recreational activities and historical resources in the area. Millions of people view or visit Henry Flagler's architectural wonder, now Ponce de Leon Hall.[1]

The Ponce is a hub for activities. On January 29, 2004, Bruce Cole, chairman of the National Endowment for the Humanities, launched the Landmarks of American History program. He made the national announcement in the former Grand Parlor, now the Flagler Room of Ponce de Leon Hall.[2]

On the weekday morning of July 18, 2011, United States Secretary of the Interior Ken Salazar addressed the inaugural meeting of the congressionally chartered St. Augustine 450th Commemoration Commission. The meeting was held in the Lewis Auditorium at Flagler College and drew federal and state dignitaries and a statewide audience of 500.[3]

On August 13, 2012, presidential candidate Mitt Romney campaigned from the west lawn in the shadow of the Ponce towers before a crowd of 4,000. Prior to the public event, he posed for a photograph in the Ponce Rotunda with Flagler College's President Abare. Making introductions was former U.S. Ambassador to the Bahamas and current Flagler College trustee John Rood.[4]

On April 2, 2013, in recognition of Spanish explorer Juan Ponce de Leon landing off the coast of La Florida, Florida Governor Rick Scott and his Cabinet held their regular monthly meeting in the Flagler Room as part of the Viva Florida 500 commemorative program. They were greeted by a standing-room-only crowd and commented with surprise on the high attendance, particularly for a weekday morning.[5]

Guests of Flagler College include dignitaries, performers, and celebrities. On February 9, 2010, civil rights leader, former mayor of Atlanta, and former United Nations ambassador Andrew Young returned to St. Augustine. At a dinner on campus honoring him, his long-time friend and 1972 presidential candidate George McGovern greeted him warmly, and they reminisced. McGovern lived six months each year in St. Augustine, where he spoke to campus and community groups regularly. Young addressed a full house of more than 800 in the auditorium. He has returned numerous times since then, most recently in May of 2014, when he served as Flagler College's commencement speaker.

Best-selling author Pat Conroy spoke to a standing-room-only crowd in the college's auditorium on January 11, 2011. After his presentation he signed books, posed for photographs, and socialized with members of the audience for nearly three hours. He professed to enjoy his inaugural visit to the city and his tour of the Ponce. Regarding the latter, he concurred with another recent visitor to the campus, folklorist Garrison Keillor, who noted that Flagler College students enjoyed the most opulent student dining environment in the nation, the former hotel's magnificent Dining Room.

St. Augustine's Spanish history and its longstanding role as a tourist attraction bring guests who would seldom visit such a small community. Each academic year, the college hosts a speaker series that is free, open to the public, and draws residents regularly from Jacksonville, Gainesville, Orlando, and Daytona Beach. The Forum on Government and Public Policy brings preeminent commentators, journalists, and television personalities. They come for the enjoyment of the community, the college's hospitality, and the beauty of the campus.

Initially, Flagler College was anticipated to operate on the seven-acre site of the former hotel; however, before the college opened in the fall of 1968, an opportunity arose to add another parcel. In January of 1968, college officials announced acquisition of the four-acre Markland property from the H. E. Wolfe family (fig. 6.1). Dr. Andrew Anderson's former estate had been sold by his daughter Clarissa Anderson Gibbs to the Wolfes three decades earlier. The former plantation house was donated to become the college president's house, and the land was sold for an undisclosed amount, though reportedly less than the appraised price of $147,000. The college added new mechanical systems and redecorated the building.[6]

The main house at Markland, constructed between 1839 and 1841, began as a two-story, coquina-stone structure with plain square columns supporting a two-story front porch. A hallway with a staircase ran the length of the west side of the house, with the rooms opening off to the right of the hallway. Clarissa Fairbanks Anderson built the structure after her husband died six weeks into the construction. In 1899, after her death, their son and Flagler's confidante Dr. Andrew Anderson II updated the house. He and his wife, Elizabeth Smethurst Anderson, retained New York architect Charles Alling Gifford to transform their simple dwelling into a Beaux Arts mansion. Most likely Flagler recommended Gifford for the project as he had been impressed with Gifford's work at several national expositions, in the White Mountains and at Jekyll Island.[7]

For the Andersons, Gifford designed a large addition of solid brick construction to the residence. This added a library and dining room, each with a fireplace. Also included were a butler's pantry, children's dining room, a

FIGURE 6.1. The Anderson family owned this property for a century before selling it to the Wolfe family. In turn, the Wolfe family sold the property and donated the house to Flagler College in 1967. Markland (Dr. Andrew Anderson House), ca. 1978, Flagler College Archives.

new rear kitchen wing with a pantry, and a bathroom. Features included stained glass windows and, in the library, a bay window with a bench seat. This arrangement enabled the hallway to run through the center of the building with the rooms flanking the hallway. A new grand staircase and a servants' staircase provided access to the upper stories. The second floor featured four principal bedrooms, a nursery, large closets, two bathrooms, and a servants' wing with bedrooms, a bath, and closets. Gifford added a shingle-covered half story with a framed attic. He completely modernized the entire interior of the building to reflect Gilded Age taste and wrapped the exterior's south and east sides with a two-story colossal Ionic-columned porch. A new Billiard Building for the gentlemen guests' entertainment was built at the back of the property. This small shingled structure mimicked the design of the main house.

For the first few years under the college's ownership, Markland House, as it was renamed, was used as guest quarters for college visitors. For three years after that time, it was used as the president's house. The college needed classrooms, and the mansion's large rooms were appropriated. Part of the former estate's setting was redeveloped for college tennis courts. The Ponce and Markland properties retained their geographical relationship to each other and served as Flagler College's two most important historical resources and physical assets. Today, they continue those roles and serve as iconic community landmarks.[8]

Between 1975 and 1989, the college repaired Markland House and its immediate environs. By 1990, Markland House was in need of a complete rehabilitation, including restoration of many features and details on the first floor. Many of the main architectural elements remained intact, but wear and tear necessitated a major effort to return those elements to their original appearance. The building was going to change use. It would become an event venue, possibly even an alumni house, with the second floor maintained as faculty and staff offices. Interiors were restored with design assistance from Robert W. Harper, executive director of the Lightner Museum. This included reproduction of curtains and architectural details.[9]

Clarissa Anderson Gibbs returned to her childhood home and provided information important for the project. Though some of those involved in the effort were skeptical, her memory for room colors proved accurate. Conservators conducted chemical analysis on the paint composition and colors, verifying her recollections. Also, she retrieved family furniture and heirlooms for the house. Restoration required an investment of more than $220,000. In addition, she established an endowment of a comparable amount for maintenance of the property, the principal of which has grown, thanks to gifts from other Anderson family members.[10]

In the mid-1980s, Flagler College needed additional facilities for students, specifically a men's residence hall. The administration proposed to build a new building on Valencia Street, directly north of the Artists' Studios building. The proposed construction required more intensive land use than was permitted by the zoning classification. In 1987, to accomplish the project, the college retained local architect Craig Thorn and applied for a Planned Unit Development (PUD). This land-use tool provides for creative use of a property, altering the parameters of building and zoning requirements to achieve a unique development.[11]

To provide a building lot of sufficient size for a new residence hall required demolition of the turn-of-the-twentieth-century McNally House located on Valencia Street. The college committed to preserving three buildings that had been constructed and used in conjunction with the Hotel Ponce de Leon. These buildings, located on the east, west, and north sides of the new building site, would serve as a buffer for the neighborhood: 20 Valencia Street, known as the Union Generals' House; 9 Carrera Street, one of the Ponce de Leon Cottages; and 6 Valencia Street, or Casa Amarylla. These three buildings and the McNally house were designated as contributing buildings in the Model Land Company Historic District, listed in the National Register of Historic Places in 1983. The $4,600,000 project included $1,400,000 for renovation of the three Flagler-era dwellings. Funds for the entire project would be provided by the William R. Kenan Jr. Charitable Trust, the Flagler Foundation, and Flagler College.[12]

After considerable negotiating between the college and the city, with significant input from community residents, the college received approval of the PUD, including removal of the McNally House. The size of the new building was reduced to two stories in height, which placed it in scale with the surrounding residential buildings. Lewis House, of brick and stucco construction, featured a symmetrical plan with open balconies and was designed in size, scale, mass, and materials to be compatible with the Artists' Studios building.[13]

Henry Flagler had several residences built near the Ponce for hotel staff or special guests. These included the residence at 20 Valencia Street (fig. 6.2). McGuire and McDonald built the house for Osborn Dunlap Seavey, manager of the Ponce. A gray concrete veneer was applied to this frame building, then the veneer was scored to appear as masonry. The trim was brick. The façade reflected the polychromatic, or many-colored, appearance of the hotel. Seavey Cottage became known as the Union Generals House in honor of two Civil War officers who retired to St. Augustine at the turn of the twentieth century and lived consecutively in the house.[14]

In 1899, John McAllister Schofield, commanding general of the United States Army and former secretary of war, moved into the cottage. Schofield graduated from the U.S. Military Academy at West Point in 1853, served in Florida during the 1850s, and was awarded the Congressional Medal of Honor for valor at the Civil War Battle of Wilson's Creek in 1861. General Schofield's "Definition of Discipline" address delivered to the corps of West Point cadets in 1879 has been memorized by generations of soldiers

FIGURE 6.2. The cottage built by Henry Flagler for his hotel manager Osborn Seavey suffered heavy termite damage. Flagler College rehabilitated the building as part of a Planned Unit Development project in the 1980s. Union Generals House, Flagler College Archives.

from that time to the present. The general died at the St. Augustine residence in 1906. Beginning a decade later, General Martin Davis Hardin occupied the house. Shortly after graduating from West Point in 1859, he served under Robert E. Lee. Hardin gained fame as a fearless field commander and was seriously wounded several times, losing an arm in 1863 in an engagement with Mosby's guerrillas. Hardin passed away in the house in 1923.[15]

In 1973, Flagler College acquired the Union Generals House. Because of its substantially deteriorated condition, the building was used sparingly. In 1985, as the need for administrative facilities grew, the college retained St. Augustine architect Craig Thorn to oversee rehabilitation of the structure with A. D. Davis Construction Company serving as the general contractor. Initially, the cost was anticipated to be $300,000, but engineering studies indicated that the cost would be $400,000. In 1986, as the project progressed, the college and trustees reevaluated the situation. The building became part of the negotiations for the Lewis House PUD. A decision was made to complete the rehabilitation. The actual cost was closer to $500,000 when the project was finished (a sum that would be significantly more than $1,000,000 today).[16]

Water channeling through a faulty built-in gutter system caused extensive damage to walls and sheathing under the concrete and brick veneer. In some areas nearly half of each structural member was destroyed. Because there was concern that the building would collapse, 2" × 10" braces were installed around the perimeter of the building. Both the roof structure and most of the veneer were removed to correct the structural deficiencies. Final damage assessments determined that 85 percent of the original materials were beyond repair. Custom-made concrete bricks, 4" high, 5" wide, and 1" thick, were fabricated by a Jacksonville firm and installed on the building. Sections of the structure had foundations insufficient to support the walls and floor loads, requiring reinforcement and reconstruction. The west wing of the building was termite eaten to the extent of being unsalvageable.[17]

In early 1987, the project was completed at a cost of $471,853. The building's new use was for the college's finance department. In addition to receiving significant local praise for the work, at the Florida Trust for Historic Preservation conference in Tampa, Governor Bob Martinez presented Flagler College with an Award of Merit for the Adaptive Use of a Historic Structure.[18]

Henry Flagler had several cottages built to accommodate winter visitors who preferred privacy over staying in the hotel. Twin residences, known as the Ponce de Leon Cottages, were built at 7 and 9 Carrera Street in the block north of the Ponce. Each was built in frame with tall, hipped roofs pierced with brick chimneys and featuring elaborate wraparound porches replete with gingerbread. An unusual feature was use of four panes of glass in each of the double hung sash windows, a pane configuration rarely used. Originally, the two houses were painted in high Victorian-era contrasting colors that showcased the elaborate trim work and architectural detailing (fig. 6.3). About 1970, the Grace United Methodist Church demolished the building at 7 Carrera Street for a surface parking lot.[19]

Guests who occupied the twin cottage at 9 Carrera Street had included Mr. and Mrs. Alexander Brinton Coxe of Pennsylvania. The Coxe Brothers

FIGURE 6.3. One of a pair of twin cottages constructed for Hotel Ponce de Leon guests who preferred more privacy than the hotel afforded. The building is used by Flagler College for academic offices and seminar rooms. Ponce de Leon Cottage/ Thompson Hall, Flagler College Archives.

and Company firm specialized in anthracite coal mining and production facilities and owned the mining lands for more than 100 years. They supported local sporting activities in St. Augustine, including golf and yachting. From 1911 to 1925, retired Union Army Captain Henry Marcotte and his wife, Anna, lived in the house. She was president of organizations that promoted medical care and municipal improvements, and she wrote the *Tatler* newspaper that commented favorably and regularly on Henry Flagler's enterprises.[20]

The house suffered deferred maintenance until incorporated into the Flagler College campus in 1971. The college undertook major capital improvements to the exterior of the structure, particularly after hurricanes, to keep the building in a usable condition. In 1987, operating under the building and life safety codes of the time, modern materials were used to convert the building to faculty office use. The building was moved forward on the lot, which enabled creation of off-street parking for the new Lewis House men's residence hall located behind the house.[21]

In 2008, the college undertook a second rehabilitation of the building. This time, the prescribed treatment met the Secretary of the Interior's Standards for Rehabilitation, restoring the historic exterior while ensuring continued functionality of the building as an educational facility. Work items included correction of termite and environmental damage, removal of drop ceilings with acoustical tiles or sprayed-on finishes, and elimination of flush doors, carpet, partition walls, and fireplace enclosures.[22]

New mechanical systems and interior finishes compatible with the original structure were introduced. Heart pine floors were sanded and refinished. Fireplace mantels were repaired, though for decorative purposes only. Hearth tiles were reproduced by a Jacksonville artist. Two original solid wood doors remained, each with seven panels. They served as a model for reproduction of the other interior doors. Ceilings, crown moldings, door and window casings, tall baseboards, and lighting fixtures added to the appearance. For aesthetics and hurricane protection, shutters were reproduced using a black and white photograph of the building taken about 1890 as a guide.[23]

The state of Florida awarded a Small Matching Grant-in-Aid of $48,000 toward the project. St. Augustine residents Pierre, Shirley, and Paul Thompson made a gift of $200,000. The building was rededicated as Thompson Hall in their honor. In addition to faculty offices, the building became home to the Upchurch Pre-Law Program.[24]

In 1898, builder James McGuire constructed a house for the Ponce hotel physician, and shortly thereafter, the house transitioned to use as a cottage for hotel guests (fig. 6.4). In 1900, Henry Flagler sold the property. New owners Mr. and Mrs. Albert Lewis of Pennsylvania updated the building, adding a large front porch, a two-story rear addition, and a cut coquina-block chimney and fireplace. They named the building Casa Amarylla, yellow house. They added electricity, with the dynamo housed in a separate coquina stone building located northwest of the main house, a Greek Revival style cottage with palm tree trunk columns and a cut coquina stone fireplace.[25]

In 1936, Louise Wise Francis, principal heir of her aunt Mary Lily Kenan (Mrs. Henry) Flagler's estate and formerly the Lewis's daughter-in-law, bought the property. She retained St. Augustine architect F. A. Hollingsworth to redesign the exterior. The updated house incorporated a

FIGURE 6.4. Casa Amarylla, or Yellow House, was built by Henry Flagler for the Hotel Ponce de Leon physician. His great-niece Mary Lily Flagler "Molly" Lewis Wiley donated the property and funds for its restoration. The building was renamed in her honor. Wiley Hall, Flagler College Archives.

Colonial Revival façade and porte cochère (carriage porch) facing Valencia Street. The east side featured a two-story sunroom wing. The interior was modified to host a nursery school and kindergarten to assist families in St. Augustine during the economic depression. In 1937, Mrs. Francis died suddenly, and the school did not open. After passing to several owners, Mrs. Francis's son Lawrence Lewis Jr. acquired the house and gave the building to Flagler College.[26]

In 1988, his sister Molly Lewis Wiley provided $709,078 for conversion of the building to offices for admissions and financial aid, working with the changes that had been completed half a century earlier with the kindergarten conversion. In January of 1989, the building was rededicated as Wiley Hall. On September 30 of that year, at Florida Southern College, Wiley Hall received an Award of Merit in the Field of Preservation from the Florida Trust.[27]

The Markland Cottage project merits mention (fig. 6.5). Almost the smallest building on the campus at 20' × 30', the cottage was constructed as a Billiard Building for Dr. Andrew Anderson II who entertained his close male friends there, including Henry Flagler. The building reflects stylistic elements and materials found in Markland House. When Clarissa Anderson Gibbs sold the Markland property to the H. E. Wolfe family, the Wolfe children used the Billiard Building for their activities.[28]

In 1967, the property passed to Flagler College as part of the transfer of the Markland estate. The college used the tiny building as a classroom. Academic standards changed, and the building was too small to meet square-foot requirements for academic purposes. For a time, the building was used as housing for a single faculty member. Then the building was relegated to a storage facility, a use it would have for more than twenty years. Throughout that time, hurricanes and storms damaged the east wall. Insects and vermin inhabited the premises. The college recognized that the

FIGURE 6.5. This tiny Billiard Building was built between 1899 and 1901 by Dr. Andrew Anderson and sits at the rear of the Markland property. In 2006, the property was meticulously restored for office use. Markland Cottage, Flagler College Archives.

National Register–listed building and local landmark needed to remain, but the college could not justify restoration of a building for which there was no use.

In 2005, Flagler College bested other northeast Florida colleges to host a charter regional center for the new state-funded Florida Public Archaeology Network (FPAN) headquartered at the University of West Florida. Flagler College committed Markland Cottage as the office headquarters for that use. The building reopened the following summer after a rehabilitation undertaken with a $48,000 State of Florida Small Matching Grant-in-Aid matched with $61,500 in funds provided by Flagler College.[29]

After competitive bidding, BTS Builders Inc. was awarded a construction contract. The small company has a big reputation for fine quality preservation work, especially when custom woodworking is required. The building was restored to its appearance of 1901, including reproducing missing details based on fragments of original materials found on the site. For example, originally the sycamore that was used in the wainscoting, columns, doors, and trim had been shipped to Florida from Pennsylvania. For the rehabilitation, new sycamore was brought south and run through a planer forty times to replicate the appearance of the original material. Every facet of the woodwork, mantel, columns, wainscoting, cornice, windows, frames, doors, shutters, latticework, and porch railing, was rebuilt exactly, including custom-milled, true-dimensioned lumber.

Where exterior shingles were damaged, others from the north side (rear) of the building became replacements. New shingles were used on the north side. The windows operate as do the louvered shutters, which serve as hurricane protection. The building retains plaster walls and canvas covered ceilings. Even the palm tree trunk column that was damaged over time was replaced with another of the same approximate age and from the same general location. Vintage flooring was located to patch damaged sections of the original pine tongue-and-groove installation. The cigar burn in the center of the floor was left intact as evidence of the building's original recreational purpose. The original marble bathroom sink was reinstalled, and a small projection that housed a shower was removed, enabling reproduction of the wall and window. New energy-efficient mechanical systems were concealed in the building. A handicapped ramp was added to the east side where it was unobtrusive. The railing matched that of the porch

FIGURE 6.6. Adjacent to Casa Amarylla is the Power House that contained the steam dynamo for the larger building. Now known as Palm Cottage, it houses college offices. Palm Cottage, Flagler College Archives.

railing, a section of which was hinged to maintain the appearance of the porch.[30]

One of the most challenging components of the project was restoration and reproduction of the small, rectangular, glazed Majolica tiles on the fireplace surround and hearth. The original materials had been impacted by wear and tear, weather, and the environment. Many of the damaged tile faces had broken loose, revealing powder-filled interiors. A Jacksonville tile artist re-created the pieces, a process that required repeated attempts over several months. The result was worth the effort, with a dramatic sycamore mantel framing the tile inset.

In 2007, the remarkably authentic and accurate effort merited an Outstanding Achievement Award from the Florida Trust at the annual conference in Pensacola and achieved accolades from the St. Augustine community and FPAN personnel. Alumni and friends, reading about the project in the *Flagler College Magazine*, were thrilled to see the tiny building returned to use.[31]

Flagler College's other tiny treasure is a charming Greek Revival style building that housed the steam dynamo, the power source for the adjacent Casa Amarylla residence (fig. 6.6). The cut coquina stone building retains

FIGURE 6.7. Dr. Robert Ellert and Dr. JoAnn Crisp-Ellert donated this Mediterranean Revival style building to Flagler College to ensure its preservation. Anderson Cottage, Flagler College Archives.

the original central entry with a stone-soldier arch and palm-tree-trunk columns supporting the gable roof with Greek broken-pediment detail. Palm-tree-trunk columns are found on other Flagler College buildings, specifically the Artists' Studios and Markland Cottage. The interior includes a finely cut coquina stone fireplace. Over time, additions enabled the building to serve as a campus guest residence before BTS Builders Inc. was retained to rehabilitate the building for office use.[32]

By 1870, widow Clarissa Fairbanks Anderson had a two-story frame guest house built on the Markland property. The house sat facing King Street east of the Anderson house. For construction of the Ponce, Henry Flagler bought a portion of the Markland property. He had the cottage moved from King Street, turned counterclockwise ninety degrees, and placed half a block farther north on the west side of Sevilla Street. Half a century later, architect Fred Henderich modified the building to reflect the architectural motif most readily associated with Florida's 1920s real estate boom, the Mediterranean Revival style (fig. 6.7).

In the 1990s, Robert Ellert and JoAnn Crisp-Ellert bought the house for their residence. They participated in arts, culture, and historic preservation activities throughout the St. Augustine community. In 2006, while in their 80s, the Ellerts participated in the Florida Trust conference hosted in St. Augustine. Shortly after that time they began dialogue with Flagler College to ensure preservation of their historic house. The Ellerts donated the property to Flagler College and retained a life estate. The Florida Trust was approached to serve an oversight role to ensure preservation of the building. Both of the Ellerts died in the next several months. The college constructed the Crisp-Ellert Art Museum to honor JoAnn Crisp-Ellert.

Anderson Cottage, the Ellerts' house, remains in good condition, though the kitchen and five bathrooms need major updating, including new mechanical systems. The house is arranged in a manner that enables common uses on the first floor, including events, and semiprivate residential suites on the second floor. In 2012, the college installed a new barrel clay tile roof on the building, matching the roof that was installed during the Mediterranean Revival conversion. Plans are under way to rehabilitate the building to its 1920s appearance.

In 2006, as Florida East Coast Industries (FECI) anticipated an international acquisition, the company approached Flagler College to assist in preserving the historically significant Florida East Coast Railway General Office Buildings (fig. 6.8). This complex of three four-story Commercial Style towers comprises nearly 60,000 square feet of space and stands as the most direct link to Henry Flagler's railroad empire. The buildings sit on the site of Flagler's original St. Augustine train station.

With assistance from a significant gift of equity by FECI, Flagler College acquired the trio, converting them to residence halls for upper-class students. The three Commercial Style towers remain much as they were constructed on the exterior. Each is identified by a first story with large plate glass storefront windows, a cornice or stringcourse separating the first from the second story, single, paired, or triple windows on the upper floors, and a substantial cornice indicating the top and flat-roofed portion of the building.

Between 1981 and 1983, the original open walkway that connected the three buildings was enclosed. In 2000, for the millennium, FECI made a major investment in the trio of buildings. The structures were in excellent condition when they were acquired by Flagler College. The floors and wainscoting were marble, as were the open staircases. Brass hardware was

FIGURE 6.8. This trio of Commercial style buildings was converted to residence hall use, retaining the marble and brass interior features. Florida East Coast Railway General Office Buildings, Flagler College Archives.

used throughout the three buildings, including the faces of the elevator doors.

The conversion from offices to upper-class student residence halls left these dramatic details in place. Room divisions were established between the triple window groupings. Doors with glass in the upper panels, heavy wood trim, and floor surfaces were changed for security reasons. Secondary fire egresses were established at the ends of the corridors. The project was recognized in 2012 with an Adaptive Use Award from the Florida Trust at its annual meeting in Gainesville.

As Flagler College continued to grow, owners of nearby properties offered them to the college for purchase. With the general decline in the national economy in 2007, this trend increased. The college added three properties to its holdings. Decades earlier, these Victorian-era residences in the St. Augustine Historic District had been converted to commercial uses. Years ago, a small frame connection joined two buildings identified under one address as 66 Cuna Street. Now they are used as faculty offices and conference rooms. WFCF 88.5 Flagler College Radio is located across the street from them in a building at 65 Cuna Street.

The city of St. Augustine maintains a strong historic preservation ordinance with rigorous design review standards based on the Secretary of the Interior's Standards for Rehabilitation. These regulations and accompanying design guidelines address rehabilitation of historic buildings and new construction in historic districts.

Flagler College has added seven new buildings to the campus that were designed to meet the guidelines in size, scale, massing, proportions, and materials: Lewis House (1987), Flagler College [now Lewis] Auditorium (1991), Proctor Library (1996), Cedar Hall (2004), Ringhaver Student Center (2007), Hanke Hall (2012), and Pollard Hall (2014). Of particular importance due to its location immediately west of the Ponce complex, Proctor Library emulates the design and materials of the Ponce, yet is new construction. The Gymnasium (1976) is compatible in size and scale, with a plaza at the street face and the main façade set back. The design and materials reflect the use, though they clearly contrast the surrounding buildings.

The ability of Flagler College to pursue historic preservation at an energetic level can be attributed, in part, to the national historic preservation movement, the inception of the state of Florida's grant programs, and the growth in heritage tourism as a vacation option. In the college's case, however, much of the success of the effort can be credited to the Flagler and Kenan families and the longstanding commitment to Flagler College by administrators and members of the board of trustees.

In 1971, when Lewis restructured the college he enlisted several distinguished community members to serve as trustees, including John D. Bailey Sr., Frank Upchurch Jr., and Howell Melton. L. C. Ringhaver had served on the board prior to 1971 and continued as a trustee. Several faculty or staff members remained, including Robert Carberry, Thomas Rahner, and Phyllis Gibbs, who added stability. In the spring of 1971, Dr. William L. Proctor and William T. Abare Jr. joined the college as president and director of admissions, respectively. They continue after more than forty years, today as chancellor and president, respectively. They introduced preservation of the Ponce into the college's mission statement, a rare pledge by a higher education institution.

Certainly one of the reasons that the Ponce remained intact can be attributed to support from the Flagler and Kenan families. Henry Flagler's third wife was North Carolina debutante Mary Lily Kenan. Her siblings had maintained legal residency at the Ponce, spending each winter there until their deaths in the mid-1960s.

Kenan created the William R. Kenan Jr. Charitable Trust. Jessie Kenan Wise's shares in Standard Oil stock established the Flagler Foundation. Her grandchildren Lawrence Lewis Jr. and Molly Lewis Wiley were entrusted with the foundation's assets and served on the Kenan Trust board. Both were involved in preservation efforts in their home state of Virginia, Lewis with Jamestown, and both with the University of Virginia. Also, both supported preservation at the University of North Carolina–Wilmington and University of North Carolina–Chapel Hill.[33]

Lewis financially supported construction of Lewis House, the college's first men's residence hall, and the Gymnasium and Auditorium. Flagler College updated the latter building in 2012, rededicating it as Lewis Auditorium in honor of Lawrence Lewis Jr. and his wife, Janet Patton Lewis. As noted previously, the rehabilitated Artists' Studios and Edison Boiler Buildings were renamed the Molly Wiley Art Building in her honor. Lewis and Wiley supported Flagler College as trustees and as donors until their deaths in 1995 and 2010, respectively.

This family association continues with their children and grandchildren. Louise Lewis Foster, eldest daughter of Lawrence and Janet Lewis, served on the Flagler College Board of Trustees for twenty-five years and her husband, John Foster, served for many years as well. The Foster Lobby in the Lewis Auditorium is one of many projects on the campus that demonstrate the family connection. Her cousin Lewis Pollard joined the Board of Trustees in 1999 and has supported the college through the Wise Foundation, named for his great-grandmother Jessie Kenan Wise. His brother Nelson Pollard provided a gift of a new academic center, designed to be compatible with the Spanish colonial architecture in the St. Augustine Historic District. Pollard Hall features classrooms, offices, and the FCTV television studio. The three-building complex opened for the 2014 academic year (fig. 6.9).

In addition, Henry Flagler's direct heirs support the institution. Though the majority of his estimated $60,000,000 estate passed to Mary Lily Flagler, his will established a trust that transferred securities to his son Harry Harkness Flagler and his granddaughters Mary Harkness Flagler, Elizabeth

FIGURE 6.9. The newest academic center at Flagler College pays homage to St. Augustine's Spanish heritage. Pollard Hall, Flagler College Archives.

Lamont Flagler, and Jean Louise Flagler. Each of the descendants inherited shares of Standard Oil stock. Currency today is valued at more than twenty-three times the amount it was a century ago. The Standard Oil Trust split by order of the U.S. Supreme Court following charges of violations of the Sherman Antitrust Act. The thirty-four successor companies include today's Chevron, ExxonMobil, and ConocoPhillips.[34]

The college's admissions and financial aid building, Hanke Hall, completed in 2012, recognizes Henry Flagler's great-grandson G. F. Robert Hanke. George Matthews, Hanke's oldest brother, supported restoration of the Dining Hall for the Ponce's Centennial anniversary in 1988. Their mother, Jean Flagler Matthews, brought the family to St. Augustine in about 1950 to see the historic city and tour the Castillo de San Marcos. She is most recognized for saving Henry and Mary Lily Flagler's Palm Beach mansion Whitehall from demolition in 1959.[35]

With regard to research on the campus buildings, Flagler College was extremely fortunate. Ownership of the Hotel Ponce de Leon transferred from Henry Flagler to a corporate holding company, the Flagler System, with his brother-in-law William Kenan as a corporate officer for sixty years. After Kenan's great-nephew Lewis became president and transferred the hotel to Flagler College, he served on the college's board of trustees from 1968 until his death in 1995.[36]

With the exception of World War II, when the Coast Guard leased the building for a training facility, for more than 100 years only three men oversaw the Ponce. During that time, the hotel rooms were updated regularly to meet the fashion of the day. In contrast and more importantly, the hotel's grand spaces, though in decline, remained unchanged from the time of completion.

The corporate and family relationships enabled the property records to remain with the building and enabled a wealth of oral history. Many of the written records remain in the Flagler College Archives. In addition, furnishings, fine and decorative arts, and many works from Henry Flagler's personal art collection, stayed with the building. Moreover, many other documents and furnishings that were removed from the Ponce are incorporated in the collection or archives at Whitehall, the Henry Morrison Flagler Museum in Palm Beach. The collaboration between the museum and the Ponce is lengthy and beneficial to both parties.

Furthermore, the Library of Congress retains in its American Memory collection dozens of black-and-white photographs of the Hotel Ponce de Leon (of the more than 260 photos of St. Augustine images). This collection includes photographs taken from the era of the hotel's construction forward through World War II. Interior photographs chronicle use through the 1960s and the hotel's closing after St. Augustine's 400th anniversary celebration. These photographs enabled accuracy in the restoration of the building's major rooms.

Many of the best quality images were made by William Henry Jackson in the 1890s. He traveled the country, frequently at the behest of the railroads, recording natural and man-made features along their routes. Jackson's photographs provide excellent representations of the interior and exterior of the Ponce in its early years, during the height of the resort era.

Archival research for the restoration of the Dining Hall, Rotunda, and Flagler Room included those primary sources. Though the research was a critical component to the restoration, it proved nearly as valuable as financing the work. Due to the deliberative nature of the project planning, the college was able to seek financial underwriting from local, state, and national foundations, corporations, and individuals.

Flagler College's commitment to scholarly research can be traced to at least 1994, as demonstrated by dialogue between the college and the University of Florida regarding an "Institute for Historic Preservation" in St. Augustine. Discussions between a variety of local officials and academics from Florida colleges and universities translated into establishment of the Historic St. Augustine Research Institute in the fall of 1999. The St. Augustine Foundation provided the financial support necessary for the institute's efforts through annual grants. From the time of its founding through today, Thomas Graham, representing Flagler College, and Kathleen Deagan, representing the University of Florida, have served as the codirectors of the institute.[37]

Flagler College's campus preservation programs illustrate the importance and benefits of public and private funding. The following summary addresses public funding within an overall framework of the state and federal grant programs for an understanding of Flagler College's role within that framework.

The college's restoration program coincided with the state of Florida's implementation of the Special Category grant program. The first state program to fund historic preservation bricks and mortar projects, this initiative grew from an initial appropriation in 1983 of $400,000 to more than $17,000,000 in 2006. Over the past thirty years of the program's existence, more than $300,000,000 has been appropriated by the state of Florida. Matching funds provided by grant applicants, including gifts from individuals, corporations, and foundations, account for more than double that amount.[38]

The peer-reviewed Special Category grant program provides funding from $50,000 to $350,000 for acquisition and development (bricks and mortar) projects, archaeological investigations, and large-scale exhibitions. In 1989, Flagler College submitted an application for funding. With inclusion of the small matching grants received and an appropriation in 2013, the college has secured a total of sixteen grants for the Hotel Ponce de Leon totaling $3,212,270 in state funds. Three other campus historic buildings have benefitted. Markland House, Markland Cottage, and Ponce de Leon Cottage/Thompson Hall shared $114,000 in state grant funds.

As noted previously, several of these grants received the highest ranking from the Historic Preservation Advisory Council reconstituted in 2002, as the Florida Historical Commission. Though state grants have benefitted hundreds of preservation projects in all of Florida's sixty-seven counties, seldom have the same applicants garnered repeated first-place postings. These rankings reflected the historic importance and architectural significance of the building, the high quality of the work proposed and accomplished, and the amount of matching funds provided.[39]

Beyond the $25,000 federal pass-through grant for the tower repairs, a second federal grant was awarded. The Save America's Treasures (SAT) grant for $400,000 assisted with window restoration. In 2010, Flagler College received a second SAT grant of nearly $49,562 for conservation of the Carrère & Hastings drawings for the hotel and the adjacent Flagler Memorial Presbyterian Church. The conservation grant was one of five awards made nationwide and the only project to receive funding outside major cities in the northeastern United States. Few projects in the country received a grant from each of the two categories.[40]

In 2013 and 2014, as part of the state's commitment to St. Augustine's 450th anniversary commemoration, the Florida Legislature provided appropriations to several St. Augustine projects. The Lightner Building/City Hall is receiving a new roof. The Ximenez-Fatio House's interior is being rehabilitated to reflect its original use as a Spanish dwelling. Renovation of the colonial properties under the management of the University of Florida will continue.

Flagler College received $2,000,000 from the Florida Legislature through the Florida Department of Education's Public Education Capital Outlay (PECO) fund. These dollars are designated for restoration on the decorative brick and terra cotta details throughout the Ponce, including the entry portcullis and loggias and in the courtyard. Windows along the front of the King Street façade will be repaired. Wood and metal trim will be repaired or reproduced. Though not a requirement of the funding, the college pledged to match the appropriation.

In 2018, Flagler College will celebrate the 50th anniversary of its founding. Both the setting and the institution have changed dramatically. The college began as a small unaccredited women's college with an enrollment of eighty on a campus with an enormous, deteriorated late-nineteenth-century hotel and an antebellum mansion. Today, Flagler College is a respected coeducational institution with an enrollment of 2,500 students from throughout the United States and the world. The campus has been recognized as one of the most beautiful in the nation, much of which is owed to the investment in historic buildings and construction of contemporary facilities that complement the former Hotel Ponce de Leon and the St. Augustine community.

7

Preserving a Legacy

Henry Flagler's legacy in Florida began with the Hotel Ponce de Leon, an architectural masterpiece and engineering wonder that embraced an era and set the tone for luxury resorts throughout the world. From there he and his northern business partners developed Florida, the southernmost frontier of the United States.

From the time of his first acquisition of Florida land in 1885, Flagler continued investing in the Sunshine State, building more than a dozen resorts linked by his Florida East Coast Railway. He financially supported and served as president of the canal company that created the Atlantic Intracoastal Waterway. His empire included the Peninsular and Occidental Steamship Company that connected his hotels in the Bahamas and Cuba to Florida.

At the turn of the twentieth century, again Flagler called on his architectural team Carrère & Hastings, by this time nationally renowned. Flagler commissioned the duo to design a marble palace in Palm Beach for his bride, Mary Lily Kenan. Today, their 125,000-square-foot Beaux Arts residence Whitehall is recognized as the Henry Morrison Flagler Museum and is preserved with assistance, in part, from Flagler and Kenan family members. The interior features and decoration illustrate the grandeur of the Gilded Age. The building design, though elegant, is a more restrained creation than the architects' first commission, their benefactor's flagship hotel in St. Augustine.

In 1912, Flagler completed the Florida East Coast Railway's extension to Key West. At the time, the Overseas Railway was touted as the "Eighth

Wonder of the World." Scarcely more than twenty years later, the railway succumbed to the ravages of the Labor Day hurricane of 1935. Bridge supports and some superstructure still stand stalwartly as artifacts of the remarkable and incomparable engineering feat that enabled a railroad to cross a sea. Similarly, the Florida East Coast Railway underwent a long chapter of economic decline before being resurrected for commercial service.

Today, nearly all of the Flagler hotels are gone. The Breakers commands the Atlantic coast on 140 acres in Palm Beach. Flagler's 1896 wood structure burned in 1903 and was rebuilt and reopened the following year. The current structure was built after a fire in 1925 and includes additions and amenities, results of a recent $100,000,000 investment. The property is owned and overseen by Kenan family members. The Casa Marina Hotel, at the terminus of Flagler's Overseas Railroad in Key West, was begun in 1914, the year after he died. The building opened in 1920 and underwent numerous transformations over the intervening decades. Today, it stands as a dramatically updated, twenty-first-century Waldorf-Astoria hotel.

Flagler's extensive landholdings continue to be transformed through the Flagler Development Company, principally for commercial business and office complexes. From Henry Flagler's millions of acres, the contemporary firm owns thousands of acres and manages millions of square feet of developed space.

In 1987, Caroline Castillo (Crimm) completed research on early preservation efforts of the Hotel Ponce de Leon. Her research was conducted before Flagler College had embarked on its multi-million-dollar restoration of the building's grand spaces, the Rotunda, Dining Room, and Grand Parlor. Even at that early stage, the importance of the historic campus to Flagler College was evident. As she noted, the campus provided an inviting setting for an independent institution focused on small teacher-student ratios.

Taking advantage of the growing popularity of preserving historic properties in the United States and St. Augustine's role in Florida's heritage tourism program, Flagler College administrators looked with new eyes at their campus centerpiece, the former Hotel Ponce de Leon. Though the building's social history was generally known in the community, the Ponce's reputation outside St. Augustine had been largely forgotten.

The college retained a number of archival documents related to the building's construction and use, transferred to the college by the Flagler System. These provided a foundation for exploring the building's importance architecturally and historically. Also, trustees were committed to preserving the building, so college policies and priorities worked toward that goal.

Early efforts emphasized reversal of deferred maintenance in the areas used most directly by the students. Hotel rooms converted to dormitory rooms had few initial aesthetic changes, but upgrades to the structure and mechanical systems began. As the college slowly grew and stabilized financially, work expanded in scope and scale. Additional portions of the Ponce were rehabilitated, and nearby historic buildings were brought into the campus.

For the building's 100th anniversary, the college embarked on its first fundraising campaign. Under the leadership of a National Advisory Committee composed of renowned preservation experts and restoration architects, the Dining Room, Grand Parlor, and Rotunda became showpieces once again. Beginning in 1987, this effort garnered significant publicity, returning the Ponce to the national spotlight, a status it held one hundred years earlier on the eve of its opening. The college's preservation program paralleled efforts taking place in Florida and at the national level.

Historic preservation as a social movement matured in tandem with Flagler College's founding and growth. The pattern of preserving buildings associated with the nation's founding fathers, which had begun in the nineteenth century, adapted to embrace community preservation during the 1930s. Identification and preservation of cultural resources became institutionalized as a component of federal policy through adoption of the National Historic Preservation Act of 1966. The elitist pattern of preservation that marked the early efforts was replaced by the 1980s with a broad and inclusive interpretation of the nation's past, recognizing the complexity and diversity of the United States.

Florida's dramatic population growth and corresponding suburban land development took place during this same period of the 1980s. To ensure that historic properties could be viable economic partners during this boom era, the state of Florida's Division of Historical Resources took a lead and partnered with the Florida Trust for Historic Preservation. Their joint emphasis resulted in a strong financial commitment by the state of Florida through an annual legislatively funded effort known as the Special Category grant program.

For twenty-five years this program was the largest and most successful of its kind in the United States in terms of funds appropriated and projects that benefitted. Private dollars invested accounted for several times those appropriated by the Florida Legislature. Historic properties with great public visibility, such as Flagler College's Ponce de Leon Hall in historic St. Augustine, were ideal candidates to benefit from this program and demonstrate the economic, cultural, and social benefits of preservation.

A little over a decade ago, the Flagler's Legacy Tour program was created as a response to public demand to see the restored former hotel. Twice daily when classes are in session and hourly in the summers, public tours are offered. These focus on the grand spaces, with trained student tour guides presenting the history and architecture of the building, leading visitors from the Courtyard, through the Rotunda, into the Grand Parlor/Flagler Room, and concluding in the Dining Hall. The tour program meets Americans with Disabilities Act (ADA) requirements. Interpretive text panels describe and illustrate the significant features of the building, enabling visitors to read each panel or to take photographs with a camera or smart phone.

Enhancing the tour program are two Flagler's Legacy shops. One is located adjacent to the Rotunda in the Ponce, and the second is in a historic building in the center of the downtown commercial district. Adapting to the twenty-first century, an online store was created. Flagler's Legacy is a successful, student-sustained business.

On January 12, 2013, ceremonies took place that honored the date on which Henry Flagler opened the hotel to the public. Bells at the Cathedral Basilica rang in celebration. The Florida East Coast Railway provided an honorific train with four cars from four significant eras in the history of the line. Twenty dignitaries traveled into St. Augustine to a stop near the historic depot site, and from there by trolley into downtown. Regional television stations covered the more than 4,000 people from throughout the southern United States who participated in the events that day. Highlights were tours of all of the major historic buildings on the campus and exhibitions featuring hotel memorabilia (fig. 7.1).

FIGURE 7.1. Hotel Ponce de Leon 125th anniversary, January 12, 2013. Opening day ceremonies, Flagler College Archives.

In preparation for the festivities, the college secured several grants. Two of them, for $25,000 each, were awarded from the state of Florida's Historic Preservation Community Education program and the St. Johns County Tourist Development Council. These funds enabled the creation and installation of a multifaceted exhibition in the west vestibule of the Rotunda and covered loggia, areas that are free and open to the public all day, every day. The Florida Humanities Council provided funds for a speaker series with national scholars presenting programs on themes revolving around the Hotel Ponce de Leon's history. The college's Community Lecture Series offered a similar focus. These programs increased both the number and cultural diversity of the visitors to the campus.

More than a quarter century after Caroline Castillo studied the college's preservation efforts on behalf of the Ponce and commented on the attractiveness of the historic campus, her assessment remains true. Flagler College's reputation as one of the top undergraduate institutions in the southeastern United States is enriched by its historic campus. Now, with twenty historic buildings in downtown St. Augustine, the college has been recognized on state and national levels as Florida's and one of the country's most beautiful campuses.

Today, the former Hotel Ponce de Leon attests to the five decades of effort that have been invested by Flagler College to return the property to a viable economic use and incorporate contemporary facilities and systems to meet academic needs. Dedication of the Solarium in the spring of 2013 completed the return of the five-building complex to active, vibrant, and compatible uses that showcase the construction, architectural details, and artistic decoration of the late nineteenth century. With recently completed construction and conservation projects, the building represents the height of the era in which it was built and serves as a testimonial to high art and architecture.

Hotel rooms have been modified to accommodate college student needs with new bathrooms and twenty-first-century technology, while retaining high ceilings, doors, woodwork, and, in some cases, fireplaces and mantels. Similarly, the facilities building identified as Kenan Hall reflects a modern interior and technologically enhanced classrooms. In both cases, those areas were updated regularly throughout the hotel era to meet the changing demands of that industry. Original fabric, if remaining at the time that preservation was initiated, continues to be part of those buildings.

The successes were showcased further in recent studies commissioned by the state of Florida and completed by the University of Florida and Rutgers University. The studies evaluated quality of life indicators and economic benefits. Flagler College was recognized for its ability to leverage private dollars to match the public funds and achieve high quality workmanship and authenticity.

The Ponce contributes greatly to the campus being recognized as one of the nation's most beautiful academic settings. The Ponce as a hotel became a destination, a location that was widely known and desirable to visit. That legacy remains. The Ponce as the centerpiece of the Flagler College campus conveys a distinct and unique sense of place.

The college serves as one of northeast Florida's strongest cultural venues for visitors, for community programs, for national and international academic conferences, and for commemorative events. Tourists visit the campus as do people who have an interest in the institution's academic programs. Adding these visitors to the Flagler's Legacy Tour participation figures, the number of visitors to the historic campus is estimated to be 100,000 annually. Flagler College is one of the region's most popular attractions in a region that has world-class historic sites, golf courses, and beaches. The attendance figures are exclusive of the approximately 1,000,000 people that view only the exterior of the building, a significant portion of St. Johns County's 7,500,000 visitors in 2013.

The St. Johns County Tourist Development Council maintains information on visitor satisfaction. Flagler College ranks consistently in the top five of the area's 69 attractions, a place it holds with the tourism barometer Trip Advisor as well. Reviewer comments regularly note that the authentic historic site is preserved accurately and interpreted effectively.

Particularly in 2013, with the college's emphasis on the 125th anniversary of the Ponce, media coverage was strong. Feature stories appeared in Atlanta, Boston, New York, and Toronto, in addition to regular coverage by Jacksonville, Orlando, and St. Augustine media. Group tours increased in number of participants, demographic diversity, and visits to the campus.

Many colleges in the United States feature historic buildings on their campuses, though most were built as part of the academic institution. Their historic and contemporary functions are similar, necessitating maintenance, but not necessarily a change in use or substantial rehabilitation of a structure.

The adaptive use of historic buildings for academic purposes has grown in popularity over the past half century, following passage of the National Historic Preservation Act. For example, Henry Plant's Tampa Bay Hotel became the cornerstone of the University of Tampa campus more than 75 years ago. The Savannah College of Art and Design (SCAD) and Roosevelt University in Chicago include buildings that originally had other purposes but were adapted to meet academic needs.

The July 2013 issue of *College Planning & Management* magazine included an article addressing the challenges faced in retrofitting historic buildings for academic purposes. The article featured buildings at Flagler College and at three Massachusetts institutions: the University of Massachusetts–Amherst, the Berklee College of Music in Boston, and Williams College in Williamstown. The article recognized Flagler College for creatively adapting former Victorian-era residences for offices, seminar uses, conference facilities, and event venues.[1]

Many families with soon-to-be college-age children vacation in St. Augustine. Typically, they spend time at the beaches and tour historic sites. These families comprise substantial numbers of the visitors who tour the campus. Repeatedly, enrolled students relay that their first experience at Flagler College was as a visitor to the Ponce. This has translated into a stable enrollment and an increasing base of support for college programs and activities.

A goal of the college's founders in 1967 was for the new educational institution to bring vitality to the Ponce, returning it to an economically viable and publicly recognizable landmark. That goal has been accomplished. Flagler College's image is inseparable from that of the Ponce. The campus has grown with historic and contemporary buildings that provide a unique architectural composition, all of which complement the former Hotel Ponce de Leon.

Arguably, the most lasting tie to Henry Flagler, the founder of modern Florida and Florida tourism, is his first Florida venture. From the time of its opening, throughout its decades as a resort, and its era as headquarters for the Coast Guard Reserve, the Hotel Ponce de Leon has served as the cultural cornerstone of the St. Augustine community and an architectural icon for Florida and the nation. Henry Flagler inspired the world with the creation of the Hotel Ponce de Leon. Today, this flagship of his resort empire enables Flagler College to inspire the world with its campus.

NOTES

Chapter 1. The Men Who Mentored a Masterpiece

1. Rockefeller, *Some Old Friends*; Chernow, *Titan*, 344–45.

2. Chernow, *Titan*, 344–45; Nevins, *Study in Power*, 94.

3. Israel, *Edison*, 231; Baldwin, *Edison*, 142–43, 456; "Edison's Electric Shark Hunt: A Great Inventor's Fun in Florida—How the Fisherman Got the Current." *The Daily Bee*, April 8, 1884. Edison Papers, Rutgers University.

4. Charles Hosmer Morse Museum of American Art, "Louis Comfort Tiffany," http://www.morsemuseum.org/louis-comfort-tiffany (accessed May 31, 2012); Libby, *Celebrating Florida*, 62–63; Vickers interview.

5. Rockefeller, *Random Reminiscences*, 10–12.

6. Collins, *Collins' Both Sides of Fifth Avenue*, 23; Flynn, *God's Gold*, 238; "Died on the Yacht: H. M. Flagler's Invalid Daughter Expires while Hurrying South," *New York Times*, March 27, 1889. http://query.nytimes.com/mem/archive-free/pdf?res=F307 1FFC395E15738DDDAE0A94DB405B8984F0D3 (accessed January 31, 2012).

7. Tarbell, *Standard Oil Company*, 276; Martin, *Flagler's Florida*, 10; "Financier's Fortune in Oil Amassed in Industrial Era of 'Rugged Individualism,'" *New York Times*, May 24, 1937. http://www.nytimes.com/learning/general/onthisday/bday/0708. html (accessed January 30, 2010); Flagler Family Genealogy, "Stephen V. Harkness." Flagler College Archives (hereafter FCA); Chernow, *Titan*, 5, 14.

8. Akin, "Southern Reflections of the Gilded Age," 12.

9. Keys, "PICO," 2; Nevins, *Study in Power*, 281; Braden, *The Architecture of Leisure*, 14.

10. The Tampa Bay Hotel became the core of the University of Tampa. Montgomery, *Georgians in Profile*, 276; Flynn, *Henry Bradley Plant*, 48–50, 162; University of Tampa, "History." http://www.ut.edu/history/ (accessed January 31, 2010); Akin, *The Sly Foxes*, 23; Rodney E. Dillon, Jr., "South Florida in 1860," *Florida Historical*

Quarterly 60:4, 440–48; "General Railroad Interests. Canada's Pacific Railway—Roads in the South," *New York Times*, November 27, 1879. http://query.nytimes.com/gst/abstract.html?res=F70913FF3D5A137B93C5AB178AD95F4D8784F9 (accessed February 9, 2011); "General Telegraph News: Workings of the Railroads," *New York Times*, February 10, 1881. http://query.nytimes.com/gst/abstract.html?res=F10611FB3E5F15738DDDA90994DA405B8184F0D3 (accessed February 9, 2011).

11. Amundson, *Sanford*, 158, 229–33; MacDonald, *Plain Talk*, 3; T. Frederick Davis, "The Disston Land Purchase," *Florida Historical Quarterly* (Gainesville: Florida Historical Society), 17:3 (January 1939), 200–210.

12. Smyth, *Henry Bradley Plant*, 162; "Benjamin Franklin Newcomer," *Biographies from Men of Mark in Maryland*. http://freepages.genealogy.rootsweb.ances try.com/~midmdroots/surnames/men/newcomerfrank.htm (accessed January 5, 2011).

13. Metropolitan Museum of Art, "Of Benefactors, Fellows and Other Members," Annual Report of the Trustees of the Metropolitan Museum of Art, 37(1906), 83. http://www.jstor.org/stable/pdfplus/40303572.pdf?acceptTC=true&jpdConfirm =true (accessed December 11, 2010). "Jesup North Pacific Expedition (1897–1902)." http://anthro.amnh.org/jesup_photos (accessed June 15, 2013); "Lynde Harrison Dead, Was a Noted Lawyer and One of Connecticut's Foremost Citizens," *New York Times*, June 9, 1906. http://query.nytimes.com/mem/archive-free/pdf?res=9F0D E0DC1231E733A2575AC0A9609C946797D6CF (accessed January 5, 2011); "H. B. Plant Estate Transfer," *New York Times*, May 4, 1902. http://query.nytimes.com/gst/abstract.html?res=9C03E4D61130E132A25757C0A9639C946397D6CF (accessed January 5, 2011).

14. J. E. Dovell, "The Railroads and the Public Lands of Florida, 1879–1905," *Florida Historical Quarterly*, 34:3(January 1955), 236.

15. "The Roads in Florida. A Reported Combination between H. M. Flagler and H. B. Plant," *New York Times*, June 22, 1892. http://query.nytimes.com/mem/archive-free/pdf?res=9E01E3D91538E233A25751C2A9609C94639ED7CF (accessed December 12, 2012).

16. Braden, *Architecture of Leisure*, 36; Seth Bramson, "A Tale of Three Henrys," *The Journal of Decorative and Propaganda Arts*, Florida Theme Issue 23 (1998), 113–43; "Henry B. Plant," *New York Times*, June 26, 1898. http://query.nytimes.com/mem/archive-free/pdf?res=9F0CE6DC1030E333A25755C2A9609C94699ED7CF (accessed January 5, 2011); "Henry B. Plant Dead, Founder of the Great Transportation System Passes Away," *New York Times*, June 24, 1899. http://query.nytimes.com/gst/abstract.html?res=9C04E0DA1430E132A25757C2A9609C94689ED7CF (accessed January 5, 2011). "H. B. Plant Company Will Dissolve," *New York Times*, March 28, 1902. http://query.nytimes.com/mem/archive-free/pdf?res=FA0B1FFF345D12738 DDDA10A94DB405B828CF1D3 (accessed December 15, 2010).

17. Denby, *Grand Hotels*, 36–38, 227–32; Tolles, *White Mountains*, 25; Tolles, *Adirondacks*, 123–24; Tolles, *Summer by the Seaside*, xxiii.

18. "Mr. Flagler Talks," *News-Herald*, June 20, 1887, photocopy, St. Augustine Historical Society Research Library (hereafter SAHSRL); Barbara A. Poleo, "James Edmundson Ingraham: Florida, Flagler, and St. Augustine," *El Escribano*; Henry Flagler: *Florida's Foremost Developer* (2003), 99; Hatton, *Tropical Splendor*, 28.

19. Martin, *Henry Flagler*, 83–86; Nevins, *Study in Power*, 393; *Amusement Bulletin*, (New York: Travelers Publishing Company, 1889), 6. http://books.google.com/books?id=R4E-AAAAYAAJ&pg=RA1-PA38&lpg=RA1-PA38&dq=The+Amusement+Bulletin,+1889&source=bl&ots=aFE3uYhAB_&sig=RZ8puFFiyREo5kgDoHnidaYBQ_E&hl=en&sa=X&ei=2cwgVNfWJIPHgwSdsIGoAg&ved=0CB4Q6AEwAg#v=onepage&q=The%20Amusement%20Bulletin%2C%201889&f=false (accessed June 19, 2012); Poultney Bigelow, et al., "The St. Johns Region in Florida," *Outing: Sport, Adventure, Travel, Fiction*, Vol. 3 (Oct 1883-March 1884), 476. http://books.google.com/books?id=JDEDAAAAYAAJ&pg=PA476&dq=isaaccrufts+hotels&hl=en&sa=X&ei= CizhT-enKIey8QTUu_WSDQ&ved=0CEAQ6AEwAA#v=onepage&q=isaaccrufts%20hotels&f=false (accessed June 19, 2012).

20. Sweetser, *The White Mountains*, 44. http://books.google.com/books?id=lsIVAAAAYAAJ&pg=PA447&dq=Palace+hotel+of+the++white+Mountai ns&hl=en&sa=X&ei=zOSmUML-I4XU9ASp30HABQ&sqi=2&ved=0CDsQ6AEwAA#v=onepage&q=Palace%20hotel%20of%20the%20%20 white%20Mountains&f=false (accessed November 16, 2012).

21. Tolles, *White Mountains*, 97, 126–27, 214–15; "Flagler Converted to Autos: His Favorite Recreation Touring in Machines He Once Abhorred," *New York Times*, October 4, 1904. http://query.nytimes.com/mem/archive-free/pdf?res=9C04EFDF123BE733A25757C0A9669D946597D6CF (accessed November 16, 2012); "White Mountains Full: All the Hotels Are Busy with Golf, Coaching Parties, and Ball Games," *New York Times*, August 16, 1908. http://query.nytimes.com/mem/archive-free/pdf?res=9F07EED81631E233A25755C1A96E9C946997D6CF (accessed November 16, 2012); "Rockefeller at Intervale: Motors to the White Mountains on His Way to Maine," *New York Times*, July 12, 1919. http://query.nytimes.com/mem/archive-free/pdf?res=9A02E1D71E3BEE3ABC4A52DFB1668382609EDE (accessed November 16, 2012).

22. Griffin, *The Impact of Tourism*, 144–45; Nevins, *John D. Rockefeller*, 3:183; White, *Railway Mail Service*, 20–21.

23. Hewitt et al., *Carrère and Hastings*, 63.

24. McCash, *The Jekyll Island Club*, 217–26; Carrere & Hastings, *Florida: The American Riviera*; Albert interview.

25. Blake, "Carrère and Hastings," 102; Kidney, *The Architecture of Choice*, 29.

26. "When Griffith Filmed in Mamaroneck," *New York Times*, December 29, 1996. http://www.nytimes.com/1996/12/29/nyregion/when-griffith-filmed-in-mamaroneck.html (accessed July 2, 2012); Martin, *Flagler's Florida*, 79; Standiford, 55–56; Laurie Ossman, "Carrère and Hastings," presentation, Flagler College, May 21, 2006; Hewitt, et al., *Carrère and Hastings*, 63.

27. Ossman and Ewing, *Carrère and Hastings*, 10, 28; "Carrère and Hastings," *New York Architecture*. http://www.nyc-architecture.com/ARCH/ARCH-CarrereHast-ings.htm (accessed June 27, 2012); Lee, *Architects to the Nation*, 174.

28. Hewitt, et al., *Carrère and Hastings* 63.

29. Carrère, *City Improvement*, 7; Gray, *Thomas Hastings*, 160.

30. Blake, *Carrère and Hastings*, 99–100.

31. "J. M. Carrère Dies of His Injuries," *New York Times*, March 2, 1911. http://query.nytimes.com/mem/archive-free/pdf?res=9F01EED6113EE233A25751C0A96 59C946096D6CF (accessed June 6, 2012).

32. "Miss Benedict Married: Becomes the Wife of Thomas Hastings at Green-wich, Conn." *New York Times*, May 1, 1900. http://query.nytimes.com/mem/archive -free/pdf?res=9C02E6DE1F3CE433A25752C0A9639C946197D6CF (accessed June 25, 2012).

33. Tolles, *White Mountains*, 97; Blake, *Carrère and Hastings*, 106.

34. Graham, *Flagler's St. Augustine Hotels*, 43–44; Appelbaum, *White City*, 62; Oss-man and Ewing, *Carrère and Hastings*, 11, 116.

35. "J. M. Carrère Dies of his Injuries," *New York Times*, March 2, 1911. http://query.nytimes.com/mem/archive-free/pdf?res=9F01EED6113EE233A25751C0A965 9C946096D6CF (accessed June 6, 2012); Todd, *Exposition*, 1:292–93; 2:20–21.

36. Morrone, *New York City*, 5.

37. Keys, *Historic Jefferson County*, 106–8; Weeter, *Louisville Landmarks*, 80–81; Campbell, *Across Fortune's Tracks*, 171–78; "Palm Beach," *Town and Country*, April 10, 1917, 72:48; Marcosson, *Marse Henry*, 141–42; Holmgren, *Modjeska*, 170; Modjeska, *Autobiography*, 363–64; "Henry Watterson Dies in Florida," *New York Times*, Decem-ber 23, 1921. http://query.nytimes.com/mem/archive-free/pdf?res=950DEFD8113 EEE3ABC4B51DFB467838A639EDE (accessed December 6, 2012); Senate Docu-ments, 67th Cong., 1st Sess., Vol. 2, 1921, "Perry's Victory Memorial," 91. http://books.google.com/books?id=uTNUAAAAIAAJ&pg=PA91&lpg=PA91&dq=henry +watterson+thomas+hastings&source=bl&ots=N8dhr_Zgv3&sig=h5lrCc6GFxSC tloLls45noWn2Vg&hl=en&sa=X&ei=POH7U_OiNYO3ogSVxYGADg&ved=0CC MQ6AEwAw#v=onepage&q=henry%20watterson%20thomas%20hastings&f=false (accessed August 25, 2014).

38. Jordy, *American Buildings*, 281.

39. Charles E. Peterson, "A Visit with Bernard Maybeck," *The Journal of the So-ciety of Architectural Historians* II: 3(October 1952), 30–31; "Frederick D. Nichols, 83, a Preservationist, Dies," *New York Times*, April 13, 1995. http://www.nytimes. com/1995/04/13/obituaries/frederick-d-nichols-83-a-preservationist-dies.html (ac-cessed October 3, 2012).

40. Laurie Ossman, "Carrère & Hastings and the Reinvention of St. Augustine," presentation, Lewis Auditorium at Flagler College, March 19, 2013; Reinhardt, "Ber-nard Maybeck," *American Heritage Magazine* 32 (August/September 1981), 5. http://www.americanheritage.com/content/bernard-maybeck (accessed June 6, 2012);

Woodbridge, *Bernard Maybeck*, 19; Akin, *Flagler*, 26; Freudenheim, *Building with Nature*, 208.

41. Andrews, *Architecture*, 198; Condit, *American Building Art*, 228.

42. Wilson, *Bernard Maybeck*, 27; Cardwell, *Bernard Maybeck*, 21–24; Bangs, *Bernard Ralph Maybeck*, 3.

43. Bangs, *Bernard Ralph Maybeck*, 79.

44. Whiffen, *American Architecture*, 152; Ossman presentation, 2013; Mary Bronson Hartt, "How to See the Pan-American Exposition," *Everybody's Magazine*, 5 (October 1901), 26. http://books.google.com/books?id=n2sXAQAAIAAJ&pg=PA488&lpg=PA488&dq=mary+hartt+everybody's+magazine&source=bl&ots=hpEDsAV-4d&sig=AE7qj4BXrfU9dExjZz6mbhKnGzk&hl=en&sa=X&ei=WjErVMCdJcq1ggSX2IG4Aw&ved=0CBQQ6AEwAA#v=onepage&q=mary%20hartt%20everybody's%20magazine&f=false (accessed September 30, 2014).

45. Francis Swales, "Master Draftsmen VII: Emmanuel Louis Masqueray 1862–1917," *Pencil Points* 5 (November 1924), 62–65; Architectural League of New York, "Carrere and Hastings: 381 Hotel Ponce de Leon, St. Augustine, Fla. Elevation, E. L. Masqueray, Draughtsman," *Year Book of the Architectural League of New York*, 19 (New York: Architectural Press, 1904), 42; Alan K. Lathrop, "A French Architect in Minnesota: Emmanuel L. Masqueray 1861–1917," *Minnesota History*, Summer 1980. http://collections.mnhs.org/MNHistoryMagazine/articles/47/v47i02p042-056.pdf (accessed June 8, 2010).

46. *Waugh's Blue Book of Leading Hotels and Resorts of the World*, (Boston: W. Wallace Waugh & Son, Publishers, 1907), 155–56; Clark, "Franklin W. Smith," 46; McDonald interview.

47. Ossman and Ewing, *Carrère and Hastings*, 28.

48. Braden, *Architecture of Leisure*, 144.

49. Florida Historical Society, "Joseph Albert McDonald," *Makers of America: An Historical and Biographical Work by an Able Corps of Writers*, Vol. 2, Florida Edition, (Atlanta: A. B. Caldwell Publishing Company, 1909), 93–94. http://books.google.com/books/about/Makers_of_America.html?id=yDo6VhLx6fEC (accessed July 2, 2012).

50. "Concrete Construction in St. Augustine, Florida," *Engineering News*, March 16, 1889, 230; "William Kennish." http://www.william-kennish.com/html/liberty.html (accessed September 16, 2012); "A Great Sulphur Spring Is Bubbling Up in the Ocean Near St. Augustine," *Daily Florida Citizen*, May 27, 1894, 2. http://ufdc.ufl.edu/UF00053708/00001/2x?vo=3 (accessed September 16, 2012).

51. Koch, *Stained Glass Decades*, 228.

52. MacKay, et al., *Long Island Country Houses*, 398; Bolger, *In Pursuit of Beauty*, 474.

53. "Buffalo's Steele MacKaye, the 'Father of Modern Acting': In an Old Buffalo Castle, Modern Acting Was Born," *Buffalo History Gazette*. http://www.buffalohistorygazette.com/2011/06/buffalos-steele-mackaye-father-of.html (accessed July 8,

2012); Koch, *Stained Glass Decades*, 120; Koch, *Tiffany: Rebel in Glass*, 70; "Lease of the Lyceum Sold," *New York Times*, August 29, 1885. http://query.nytimes.com/mem/archive-free/pdf?res=9501E0DB153FE533A2575AC2A96E9C94649FD7CF (accessed July 8, 2012).

54. Loring, *Louis Comfort Tiffany*, 241.

55. Duncan, *Tiffany Windows*, 210; Koch, *Tiffany: Rebel in Glass*, 119–20; Hatton, 25.

56. Libby, *Celebrating Florida*, 62, 20; Strock, *Trinity Episcopal Church*; Charles Hosmer Morse Museum of American Art, "Louis Comfort Tiffany and Laurelton Hall: An Artist's Country Estate," *Newsletter*, 2006.

57. Jones, *Maitland Armstrong*, 94.

58. Ibid., 206.

59. "Maitland Armstrong, Artist, Dies at 82," *New York Times*, May 27, 1918. http://query.nytimes.com/mem/archive-free/pdf?res=9902E3DE1238EE32A25754C2A96 39C946996D6CF (accessed July 8, 2012).

60. Ibid., 147, 151; Israel, *Edison*, 237.

61. Clark, "Franklin Smith," 40.

62. Baldwin, 152; "Edison and Ford Winter Estates, Guide," 4.

63. Castleden, *Ponce*, 66–67; Braden, *Architecture of Leisure*, 175; "Armington & Sims telegram to Thomas Alva Edison, September 13, 1884." Thomas Edison Papers, Rutgers University; "The Lighting of the Hotel Ponce de Leon, St. Augustine," *The Electrician*, Vol. XX, April 13, 1888. (London: George Tucker, 1888), 622. http://books.google.com/books?id=_GpNAAAAYAAJ&pg=PA622&dq=armington+a nd+sims+hotel+ponce+de+leon&hl=en&sa=X&ei=ASLGUPqKMYqo9gTRuY GQBQ&ved=0CDoQ6AEwAA#v=onepage&q=armington%20and%20sims%20 hotel%20ponce%20de%20leon&f=false (accessed December 10, 2012).

64. "William J. Hammer, Consulting Electrical Engineer," *National Encyclopedia of American Biography and the Electrical Review and Western Electrician*, pamphlet, 7–8.

65. Ibid.; Israel interview; Miner interview; Department of the Interior, National Park Service, "Hotel Ponce de Leon," National Historic Landmark Registration Form, 9.

66. Castleden, 66; *Hotel Ponce de Leon Longitudinal section through dining room*, detail drawing, Carrere & Hastings Digital Collection (hereafter CHDC). http://ufdc.ufl.edu/UF00089836/00085/1j (accessed July 25, 2012).

67. "Art Notes," *The Critic*, 9 (February 4, 1888), 59.

68. Braden, *Architecture of Leisure*, 168; Small, *Library of Congress*, 60–63; Larson, *White City*, 1; Chicago Historical Society, "Portrait of World's Columbian Exposition Planners," *Electronic Encyclopedia of Chicago*, 2005. http://www.encyclopedia.chicagohistory.org/pages/10646.html (accessed November 13, 2009). Reed and Morrone, *The New York Public Library*, 56.

69. Gray, 157; Andrew, *Otto H. Bacher*, 173.

70. Ossman and Ewing, *Carrère and Hastings*, 58–60.

71. The Hudson River Museum of Westchester, Inc. *The Artists of Bronxville: 1890–1930*. (New York, New York: The Printmore Press, 1989) 12, 16, 18. http://books.google.com/books?id=8XG69uRyTk4C&pg=PA8&lpg=PA8&dq=bron xville+art+colony&source=bl&ots=h-wo_VjwRy&sig=Six1UNpmtQgG8OFuOTSNKMTCs6s&hl=en&sa=X&ei=5jnST6i sAoOm8ASM8MmtAw&ved=0CGMQ6AEwBw#v =onepage&q=bronxville%20art%20colony&f=false (accessed June 8, 2012).

72. Braden, *Architecture of Leisure*, 170; Hailey, "San Francisco Public Library," *California Art Research*, Vol. 3, 1936. http://www.archive.org/details/californiaartre so3hail (accessed November 7, 2010). Hughes, *Artists in California*, 464–65.

73. Hughes, *Artists in California*, 464–65.

74. "Virgilio Tojetti," *Public Opinion*, 30:14 (January-June 1901), 438. http://books.google.com/books?id=idkaAAAAYAAJ&pg=PA438&lpg=PA438&dq=virgi lio+tojetti+murals+at+vanderbilt&source=bl&ots=CYCqtnXJa6&sig=V-gaHcGfn z_3uk_T9IswF1pKapQ&hl=en&sa=X&ei=UEgNUN6iNYWs8ASYsfWyC g&sqi =2&ved=0CDsQ6AEwAA#v=onepage&q=virgilio%20tojetti%20murals%20a t%20 vanderbilt&f=false (accessed November 1, 2009).

75. Hester M. Poole, "The Residence of Thomas A. Edison, Orange, N. J." *The Decorator and Furnisher* (New York: E. W. Bullinger, 1891), 19:3 (December) 95; Dickson and Dickson, *Edison*, 342; Baldwin, *Edison*, 225; DeGraaf interview.

76. Ward G. Foster, *Sunlight Pictures, Florida: Half-Tones from Photographs*, (St. Augustine: El Unica, 1895), 16–17. http://books.google.com/books?id=PO8xAQAA MAAJ&pg=PT28&lpg=PT28&dq=t ojetti+st+augustine&source=bl&ots=M1-Qgl MPBP&sig=AVAygiuXqvgY3jpdHdX2lMFsZj8&hl=en&sa=X&ei=EAnzT4q-L4 Gy8QT5zPHNCQ&ved=0CEsQ6AEwBA#v=onepage&q=tojetti%20st%20augu stine&f=false (accessed July 3, 2012).

77. Shreve, *History Worth Saving*, 11–12; Derby and White, "Auguste Pottier," 297.

78. Varner, *Bolstering a National Identity*, 12–13; Diana Strazdes, "The Millionaire's Palace: Leland Stanford's Commission for Pottier & Stymus in San Francisco," *Winterthur Portfolio* 36:4 (Winter), 218–19, 234.

79. Strazdes, "The Millionaire's Palace," 225.

80. Ibid., 229; Cardwell, *Bernard Maybeck*, 25.

Chapter 2. "The Modern Wonder of the Ancient City"

1. Castillo, "Hotels," 44.

2. Anderson Cottage stands transformed by a 1920s Mediterranean Revival modernization, facing Sevilla Street to the east of Markland. In 2007, the house was donated to Flagler College with deed restrictions to ensure its preservation.

3. Barnes, *Hurricane History*, 74–75; "Concrete Construction—Tie-Plates," *Engineering News*, March 23, 1889, 266.

4. Hewitt, et al., *Carrère and Hastings*, Vol. II, 19.

5. Castillo quoting Martin, "The Second Discovery of Florida," MA thesis, University of Georgia, 1935, 18 (thesis missing).

6. Atlas, *Concrete Country Residences*, 155; National Museum of American Illustration, "Vernon Court." http://www.americanillustration.org/history.html (accessed May 28, 2013); "Whitehall." http://flaglermuseum.us/history/whitehall (accessed May 28, 2013); "Murry & Leonie Guggenheim Cottage: A Beaux-Arts Summer Residence." http://library.monmouth.edu/about/mansion/cottage.html (accessed May 28, 2013).

7. Kenan, *Incidents*, 40; Carl W. Condit, "The Pioneer Concrete Buildings of St. Augustine," *Progressive Architecture*, 9:71, 128–33.

8. "Sarah Murray, Aged Colored Woman, Has Interesting Stories to Tell of Early Life before the 'First War,'" *St. Augustine Record*, October 21, 1934.

9. "Hotel Ponce de Leon" Registration Form; Condit, *Building Art*, 159; "Opening of Ponce Was the Event Not to Be Missed in Florida in 1888," *Supplement* to the *St. Augustine Record*, January 9, 1988, reprinted from the *Florida Times-Union*, January 12, 1888, 7, FCA.

10. "Concrete Construction," 230; "Concrete Buildings," *Engineering News*, March 9, 1889, 225; "Baetjer and Meyerstein Cement (importers of Hanover Portland Cement)," *American Architect and Building News*, XXXV, No. 836 (January-March 1892), xxii, advertisement. http://books.google.com/books?id=fvEyAQAAIAAJ&pg=PR50&lpg=PR50&dq=Baetjer+and+Meyerstein+Cement+(importers+of+Hanover+Portland+Cement)&source=bl&ots=rPmUPL2m7d&sig=YE8z7CDZ4K-ZLu8VdiZ4422-DFQ&hl=en#v=onepage&q=Baetjer%20and%20Meyerstein%20Cement%20(importers%20of%20Hanover%20Portland%20Cement)&f=false (accessed August 30, 2012).

11. Shepard interview; McKee, *Masonry*, 69.

12. "Concrete Construction," 230.

13. James Taylor, "History of Terra Cotta in New York City," *Architectural Record*, Vol. II (July 1892 to July 1893), 145; Edwin Atlee Barber, "Recent Advances in the Pottery Industry." *Popular Science Monthly*, Vol. 40 (January 1892): 317. https://books.google.com/books?id=hiADAAAAMBAJ&printsec=frontcover#v=onepage&q&f=false (accessed December 10, 2012).

14. Castillo, *Hotels*, 150.

15. Stamped imprint on clay tiles. Smith interview.

16. Walas interview.

17. Walas interview; "Concrete Construction," 230.

18. "Mr. Flagler Talks," SAHSRL; "The Great Artesian Well at St. Augustine, Florida," *Engineering News*, April 6, 1889, 300–301.

19. Graham and Keys, *Ponce*, 185.

20. Israel, *Edison*, 231, 237; "Power for Lighting from an Artesian Well," *Western Electrician*, Vol. 1–2, (Chicago, Illinois: Western Electrician Company, 1888), 177. http://books.google.com/books?id=4GJVAAAAYAAJ&pg=RA1-PA177&lpg=RA1-PA177&dq=william+kennish+ponce+de+leon&source=bl&ots=Ql4xvWf-Pc&sig=yR1xN7osGVUABuVJ4sOKonPPY-w&hl=en&ei=vXv_TaaFE6fxogHoufDdAw&sa=X&oi=book_result&ct=result&resn um=6&ved=0CCcQ6AEwBQ#v=one page&q=william%20kennish%20ponce%20de%20leon&f=false (accessed June 30, 2012).

21. Reynolds, *Tribute*.

22. Braden, *Architecture of Leisure*, 11; "Opening of Ponce."

23. Blake, *Carrère and Hastings*, 106; Nathan F. Barrett, "Fifty Years of Landscape Modeling," *Art World*, 1:3 (Dec., 1916), 184. http://www.jstor.org/stable/25587704 (accessed October 7, 2014). "The Sculpture Society," *New York Times*, May 7, 1895. http://query.nytimes.com/mem/archive-free/pdf?res=9C01E2D9133DE433A2575 4C0A9639C94649ED7CF (accessed October 7, 2014).

24. Davis interview.

25. Castleden, *Ponce*, 8.

26. Bennett, *Fort Caroline*, 65–70; Martin, *Flagler's Florida*, 119.

27. Martin, *Flagler's Florida*, 119.

28. Carrère and Hastings, *St. Augustine*, 32.

29. "Ready for Mr. Cleveland: Parlors in the Ponce de Leon Prepared for Him," *New York Times*, March 20, 1889. http://query.nytimes.com/mem/archive-free/pd f?res=F00D1EFB3D5F15738DDDA90A94DB405B8984F0D3 (accessed June 20, 2012).

30. "Written at an Inn at Henley." http://www.poemhunter.com/william-shen-stone/biography/ (accessed January 9, 2012).

31. Kjellberg, *Bronzes*, 519; Federal Writers Project, *Florida*, 160.

32. "Tiffany Windows: Flagler College Dining Hall," unpublished typescript, Flagler College Archives; McDonald interview.

33. "Tiffany Windows"; McDonald interview.

34. "Tiffany Windows."

35. "Tiffany Windows"; Hotel Ponce de Leon Registration Form.

36. "The Great Halls and Corridors of the Ponce Extend over One Mile," Special Supplement to *St. Augustine Record*, January 9, 1888, reprinted from the *Florida Times-Union*, January 12, 1988; Graham and Keys, *Hotel Ponce de Leon*, 212.

37. Max O'Rell, *Jonathan and His Continent: Rambles through American Society*. (Bristol, England: J. W. Arrowsmith, 1889), 278. http://books.google.com/books?id=4ZtWAAAAMAAJ&pg=PA280&dq=jonathan+and+his+continent+ponce+de+leon&hl=en&sa=X&ei=pXglVLaxKczDggTZn4KoCg&ved=0CBoQ6AEwAA#v=onepage&q=jonathan%20and%20his%20continent%20ponce%20de%20 leon&f=false (accessed July 9, 2012).

Chapter 3. A Spanish Renaissance Palace in a Spanish Colonial Paradise

1. Ossman and Ewing, *Carrère and Hastings* 10; Castleden, *Ponce*, 18, 34; Edwards, *Old St. Augustine*, 97.

2. Helen Love Smith, "Excerpts from a Florida Diary, St. Augustine, January 1888," *El Escribano* 2, no.1 (1965): 8; *Directory of Directors in the City of New York* (New York: Directory of Directors Company, 1914), 781. http://www.gooboogeni.com/index. php?option=com_content&view=article&id=1924:directory-of-directors-in-the-city-of-new-york-1913&catid=129:directories-gazettes-and-almanacs&Itemid=113 (accessed March 1, 2011); MacKay et al., *Long Island Country Houses*, 97–109.

3. Smith, "Excerpts," 8, 10.

4. Dunkle, *St. Augustine*, 164–72; Lee, *Tourist's Guide*, 97.

5. Lee, *Tourist's Guide*, 173–74.

6. Sanborn Map Company, Insurance Maps of St. Augustine, St. Johns County, Florida, 1910, Sheet 6, University of Florida Digital Collections (hereafter UFDC). http://ufdc.ufl.edu/UF00074227/00004 (accessed January 3, 2013).

7. Crespo, *Spanish Renaissance Revival*, 323–25.

8. Jacksonville Historic Landmarks Commission, *Jacksonville's Architectural Heritage*, 173, 206; Bean, *The First Hollywood*, 14.

9. "Letter from John Anderson to Aunt Nell dated Jan 27, 1877," John Anderson Papers Relating to Ormond Beach, UFDC. http://ufdc.ufl.edu/AA00000106/0000 1?search=anderson+=ormond (accessed October 2, 2014). http://web.uflib.ufl.edu/spec/pkyonge/andersonj.htm (accessed October 2, 2014).

10. Susan Braden, "Entrepreneurs and Empires: Henry Flagler and Henry Plant in Florida," presentation, Flagler College, St. Augustine, Florida, February 19, 2013; "Some Big Florida Hotels: Southern Palaces for Northern Millionaires," *New York Times*, April 28, 1889. http://query.nytimes.com/mem/archive-free/pdf?res=9C0 DE2D6173AEF33A2575BC2A9629C94689FD7CF (accessed June 20, 2012); Ralph, *Dixie*, 176–77; Castillo, 74; "Some Big Florida Hotels."

11. "Some Big Florida Hotels," *New York Times*, April 28, 1889.

12. "Great Halls and Corridors," *St. Augustine Record*, January 9, 1888, 8.

13. "The Architectural League." *New York Tribune*, December 19, 1887.

14. McCarthy, 74; Barbara Ball Buff, "Bronxville: The Planned Community as Art Colony," *Westchester Historian*, 66:2 (Spring) 1990, 27–34. http://www.westchester history.com/media/pdf/historian/Art.pdf (accessed June 8, 2012).

15. Favis, *Heade in Florida*, 48; Andrew, *Otto H. Bacher*, 173.

16. Favis, *Heade*, 43–45, 106–7.

17. Ibid., 56–57, 115; Graham, *Awakening*, 194–95; Roberta Favis, "Martin Johnson Heade and the Flagler Artists' Colony," unpublished typescript, 2006, 7; Martin Johnson Heade, *Giant Magnolias on a Blue Velvet Cloth*, ca. 1885–95, National Gallery of Art, Washington, D.C.; Carleton I. Calkin, "Martin Johnson Heade: Painter of Florida," *El Escribano*, 14 (1977): 37.

18. Barghini, *Flagler's Painting Collection*, 9.

19. Jackson, *Time Exposure*, 259; Hughes, *The Birth of a Century*, 202; Michael L. Carlebach, "William Henry Jackson and the Florida Landscape," *The Journal of Decorative and Propaganda Arts*. (Book 23) Florida Theme Issue. (Miami: Wolfsonian-Florida International University, 2002), 91.

20. Jackson, 186; Jones, *William Henry Jackson, Thomas Moran*, 10, 13.

21. Wilkins and Hinkley, *Thomas Moran*, 157–58.

22. The painting referred to as *Katherine* is identified in a print as *Herbst. Modjeska, Memories and Impressions*, 379–80; Holmgren, *Modjeska*, 170; "Dramatic and Musical: Helena Modjeska's Engagement," *New York Times*. February 27, 1900. http://query.nytimes.com/mem/archive-free/pdf?res=9E02E5DE1E3CE433A25751C0A9 659C946197D6CF (accessed August 12, 2012); Charles F. Lummis, ed., "Modjeska's Mountain Home," *The Land of Sunshine: A Southwestern Magazine*, Vol. VI (Los Angeles: Land of Sunshine Publishing Co., 1897), photocopy, Orange County Parks.

23. Phillips, *Abroad and at Home*, 181; Gustav Kobbe, "Mme. Sembrich at Villa Marcella," *The Delineator: An Illustrated Magazine of Literature and Fashion*, Vol. 63, No. 5, May 1904 (Paris: Butterick Publishing Co., Ltd., 1904), 845; "Jozsi Koppay Here to Paint Roosevelts," *New York Times*, October 28, 1905. http://query.nytimes.com/mem/archive-free/pdf?res=9901E7DF113AE733A2575BC2A9669D946497D 6CF (accessed August 7, 2014); "Koppay, an Admirer of American Art," *New York Times*, June 23, 1907. http://query.nytimes.com/mem/archive-free/pdf?res=9E0DE 3D9133EE033A25750C2A9609C946697D6CF (accessed August 7, 2014); "Koppay's Portraits Shown," *New York Times*, November 23, 1910. http://query.nytimes.com/ mem/archive-free/pdf?res=9E03E2DF1638E333A25750C2A9679D946196D6CF (accessed August 7, 2014).

24. Emerson and Forbes, *Journals of Ralph Waldo Emerson*, 162; Constance Fenimore Woolson, "The Ancient City," *Harper's New Monthly Magazine*, 1874–1875, 1–25; Bryant, *Letters*, 93; Lanier, *Florida*, 39–66; McCarthy, *Book Lover's Guide*, 65. Augustus Mayhew, "Oil Swells: The Standard Oil Crowd in Palm Beach," *New York Social Diary*. http://www.newyorksocialdiary.com/node/1904526/print (accessed February 24, 2013).

25. "SLC to OLC, 15 March 1902—St. Augustine, Fla., (UCCL 06301)." Catalog entry, photocopy, Mark Twain Project Online, The Bancroft Library, University of California, Berkeley (hereafter CU-MARK); "Henry M. Flagler to SLC, 4 October 1906, New York, N.Y. (UCLC 35617)." Catalog entry, photocopy (CU-MARK); Clemens, Correspondence with Henry Huttleston Rogers.

26. Kalamazoo Public Library, "Ellis L. Brooks: Bandleader and Composer," Local History, http://www.kpl.gov/local-history/music/ellis-brooks.aspx (accessed December 12, 2009).

27. Florida Division of Historical Resources, Historical Marker Program, "Surfside Dance Hall and Bath House and Vilano Beach Casino." http://www.flheritage.com/preservation/markers/markers.cfm?ID=st.%20johns (accessed December 12,

2009); Atlantic Intracoastal Waterway, "Florida Inland Navigation District: Historical Background." http://www.aicw.org/history.jsp (accessed September 29, 2014); St. Augustine Scenic Cruise, "History," http://www.scenic-cruise.com/st_augustine_scenic_cruise_history.html (accessed December 12, 2009).

28. Bean, 13–15; Mathews, *Moving Pictures*, 7.

29. "Stolen Moments." http://www.tcm.com/this-month/article.html?id=133224 |133231 (accessed January 6, 2013); "Distant Drums." http://www.tcm.com/tcmdb/title/73195/Distant-Drums/articles.html (accessed January 6, 2013); "A Fool There Was," http://www.tcm.com/tcmdb/title/482313/A-Fool-There-Was/ (accessed January 6, 2013).

30. National Park Service, "Alcazar Hotel" Registration Form; Braden, *Architecture of Leisure*, 184–87.

31. Today, of more than 300 residences, the Beckwith house is the sole surviving mansion on the row. "The St. Augustine Lawn-Tennis Tournament," *Outing* XVI no. 3 (June 1890): 180–83. http://www.la84foundation.org/SportsLibrary/Outing/Volume_16/outXVIo3/outXVIo3e.pdf (accessed December 13, 2009). "Cleveland History Lessons: The Avenue." http://www.clevelandhistorylessons.com/stories/the-avenue.html (accessed August 31, 2014); "Winter Resort Notes," *Boston Evening Transcript*, January 26, 1895, 14.

32. Drysdale interview.

33. Edward Rogers Bushnell, ed. *The History of Athletics at the University of Pennsylvania*, II, 1896–97, 1907–08 (Philadelphia: The Athletic Association of the University of Pennsylvania, 1909), 149–50. http://books.google.com/books?id=lcpMAAAAYAAJ&pg=PA150&lpg=PA150&dq=clayton+dixon+university+of+pennsylvania&source=bl&ots=wBMYkoYYi5&sig=M7pUoQ8sErPRd_w8cCQmLNxwxYo&hl=en&sa=X&ei=oqzHUJD8Dorm8gSCo4GgBg&ved=oCDIQ6AEwAQ#v=onepage&q=clayton%20dixon%20univer sity%20of%20pennsylvania&f=false (accessed December 11, 2012); "Golf at St. Augustine. George Ayrault Wins First Prize, Beating Black in Finals," *New York Times*, January 7, 1900. http://query.nytimes.com/mem/archive-free/pdf?res=940CE4DC1239E733A25754C0A9679C946197D6CF (accessed January 5, 2011); "Golf at St. Augustine; J. P. Greaves Finishes First in the New Year's Tournament," *New York Times*, January 2, 1900. http://query.nytimes.com/mem/archive-free/pdf?res=9503E2DD143DE433A25751C0A9679C946197D6CF (accessed January 5, 2011); "Golf at St. Augustine. R. C. Watson, Jr., Wins Another Cup by Beating J. P. Greaves," *New York Times*, February 4, 1900. http://query.nytimes.com/mem/archive-free/pdf?res=9A01EFD71239E733A25757C0A9649C946197D6CF (accessed January 5, 2011).

34. Browne, *Coal Barons*, 93; Heaphy, *The Negro Leagues*, 16; "Original Photo of the 1885–1886 [1890] Cuban Giants: Black Baseball's First Professional Team," The National Pastime Museum. http://www.thenationalpastimemuseum.com/article/original-photo-1885-1886-cuban-giants-black-baseballs-first-professional-team (accessed September 1, 2014).

35. Ribowsky, *Negro Leagues*, 21–23; Browne, *Coal Barons*, 66.

36. Kirwin, *Out of the Shadows*, 4–6; Bond, *Jim Crow at Play*, 101–2; Hogan, *Shades of Glory*, 35.

37. Lomax, *Black Baseball Entrepreneurs*, 95; White, *History of Colored Baseball*, 134–35; Rory Costello, S. K. Govern, "Black Baseball's Renaissance Man," http://sabr.org/bioproj/person/af52b171 (accessed September 29, 2014).

38. Busbey, *Home Life in America*, 338.

39. Graham, *Hotels*, 22; Kenan, *Incidents*, 19.

40. "Admiral Dewey and Wife. Their Approaching Visit to St. Augustine Discussed," *Tatler*, March 21, 1900; "The Charity Ball," *Tatler*, March 22, 1900; Smithsonian Institution, Book of Drawings by Anonymous Cheyenne Prisoner at Fort Marion, ca. 1875–1878. http://siris-archives.si.edu/ipac20/ipac.jsp?uri=full=310000 1~!15783!0#focus (accessed September 1, 2014).

41. The other four Cleveland visits took place in 1893, 1899, 1903, and 1905. "Ready for Mr. Cleveland: Parlors in the Ponce de Leon Prepared for Him," *New York Times*, March 20, 1889. http://query.nytimes.com/mem/archive-free/pdf?res=F00D1EFB 3D5F15738DDDA90A94DB405B8984F0D3 (accessed June 20,2012); Bramson, "A Tale of Three Henrys," 116.

42. Graham, *Mr. Flagler's St. Augustine*, 421–22.

43. "Jozsi Koppay Here to Paint Roosevelts."

44. Bramson, "A Tale of Three Henrys," 116; Theodore Roosevelt Collection. Letters to Ethel Roosevelt Derby, 1884–1919 (inclusive) 1896–1919 (bulk). MS Am 1541.2 (3–48). Letters to Kermit Roosevelt, 1890–1918. MS Am 1541 (87–138). Houghton Library, Harvard University, Cambridge, Massachusetts. "Presidential Days in the Nation's Oldest City," *St. Augustine Record*, February 15, 2010. http://staugustine.com/news/local-news/2010-02-15/presidential-days-nations-oldest-city (accessed July 23, 2010).

45. "Presidential Days."

46. Alexander Graham Bell Papers. Telegram from Alexander Graham Bell to Mabel Hubbard Bell, March 29, 1889. Series: Family Papers, Folder: Mabel Hubbard Bell, Family Correspondence, Alexander Graham Bell, 1889). http://memory.loc.gov/ammem/bellhtml/bellhome.html (accessed June 6, 2010).

47. Thomas Graham, "Flagler's Magnificent Hotel Ponce de Leon," *Florida Historical Quarterly*, LIV, July 1975, 17; Long, *Florida Breezes*, 1883.

48. Joel Hoffman, 53. Stephen Kerber, "Florida and the World's Columbian Exposition of 1893," *Florida Historical Quarterly*, 66, no. 1 (Jul., 1987):38–39; Braden, 71.

49. "The New Wiring Installation of the St. Augustine (Fla) Hotels," *Electrical World*, Vol. XXIII, January 6–June 30, 1894 (New York: W. J. Johnston Company Limited), 603. http://books.google.com/books?id=cWJNAAAAYAAJ&pg=PA603&lpg=PA603&dq=okonite+hotel+ponce+ de+leon&source=bl&ots=764ttbMTqx&sig=eQHA4BUuc Bz3-nwJzZJmqmPpEFg&hl=en&sa=X&ei=3VbFUJLuOI6G9Q

S2i4CwDg&sqi=2&ved=oCDwQ6AEwAw#v=one page&q=okonite%20hotel%20 ponce%20de%20leon&f=false (accessed December 9, 2012).

50. "Longitudinal section," CHDC; "The New Wiring Installation," 603.

51. "$80,000 for the Unemployed: Personal Offering of Citizens' Relief Committee," *New York Times*, February 18, 1894. http://query.nytimes.com/mem/archive-free/pdf?res=FA0714FA345D15738DDDA10994DA405B8485F0D3 (accessed March 13, 2011).

52. Akin, *Southern Reflections*, 41–42.

53. Akin, *Rockefeller Partner*, 130.

54. Harry Harkness Flagler left his papers to his alma mater Columbia University, including correspondence with his father's business colleagues. Ibid.; "Preparing for New York's Third Annual Music Week," *Music Trade Review*, February 18, 1922. http://mtr.arcade-museum.com/MTR-1922-74-7/MTR-1922-74-7-05.pdf (accessed December 10, 2012); "Surprise for H. H. Flagler," *New York Times*, December 9, 1914, http://query.nytimes.com/mem/archive-free/pdf?res=9C0CE5DE1438E633A2575 AC0A9649D946596D6CF(accessed December 19, 2012).

55. Abbott, *Open for the Season*, 50; Knetsch and Wynne, *Spanish-American War*, 96–97; Turner and Bramson, *The Plant System*, 29.

56. Mathematician Greg Smith prepared the financial comparison. Smith interview; "Henry M. Flagler Divorced," *New York Times*, August 15, 1901. http://query. nytimes.com/mem/archive-free/pdf?res=9A00E2DA163BE733A25756C1A96E9C 946097D6CF (accessed October 1, 2014); "Henry M. Flagler Married," *New York Times*, August 25, 1901. http://query.nytimes.com/mem/archive-free/pdf?res=980 3E2D9143FE433A25756C2A96E9C946097D6CF (October 1, 2014).

57. "Larchmont Yacht Club, 1897." http://www.worthpoint.com/worthopedia/ larchmont-yacht-club-ny-sailboat-129242981 (accessed December 20, 2013); "Flagler's Only Son Not a Business Man," *New York Sun*, May 23, 1913.

58. Campbell, *Across Fortune's Tracks*, 144.

59. "Eugene Zimmerman." http://www.scottwinslow.com/manufacturer/ZIM MERMAN_EUGENE/2359 (accessed December 23, 2013).

60. Gil Wilson, "A Short History of the Ponce de Leon Hotel, St. Augustine, Florida." http://www.drbronsontours.com/bronsonponcedeleonhotel.html?tag=infrare dheatersconsumerreports-20 (accessed December 23, 2013).

61. Ibid., 676; Chernow, *Titan*, 346, 610.

62. "John D. Rockefeller Dies at 97 in His Florida Home; Funeral to be Held Here," *New York Times*, May 24, 1937. http://www.nytimes.com/books/98/05/17/ specials/rockefeller-obit.html (accessed March 16, 2011).

63. Nevins, *Study in Power*, 435–36.

64. Florida Department of Agriculture, *Florida Tourist Quarterly Bulletin*. 1, no. 4 (October 1, 1921), Tallahassee, Florida. Limerick et al., *America's Grand Resort Hotels*, 89.

65. Dunkle, 177.

66. Dorothy Mason, "Hotel Ponce de Leon Notes," *Florida Times-Union*, n.d.; "Arthur Marsh Scrapbook D," 1289, SAHSRL.

67. Harvey Lopez, "It Could Be So," *St. Augustine Record*, March 17, 1963; "Marylou Connelly McCarthy," *St. Augustine Record*, August 5, 2009.

68. "Hotel Ponce de Leon Will Open Season on Dec. 22nd: Earliest Date Ever Set for This Hostelry," *St. Augustine Record*, October 21, 1934; "Ponce de Leon Plans Parties," *Evening Independent*, March 3, 1937.

69. Nancy Jo Cafaro James interview.

70. Messinger and McGinnis. *Images of America*, 10–13, 30, 105–6; "Ponce de Leon Plans Parties," *Evening Independent*, March 3, 1937. http://news.google.com/newspapers?nid=950&dat=19370303&id=O79RAAAAIBAJ&sjid=MlUDAAAAIBAJ&pg=4258,2332490 (accessed November 11, 2012).

71. A connection to the military chapter of the Ponce's history continued with the building's transformation as the centerpiece of Flagler College. Louis M. Thayer, a Coast Guard training instructor stationed at the Ponce, became the father-in-law of attorney and later judge Frank D. Upchurch. One of Flagler College's founding trustees, Upchurch served the institution for forty years. In 1991, his nephew Tracy, as St. Augustine's mayor, welcomed the Coast Guard Reserve for its fiftieth anniversary festivities in St. Augustine and at the Ponce. Coast Guard Reserve, "Parade Time in St. Augustine" and "St. Augustine is considered by many to be the . . . Birthplace of the CGR," *Reservist*, April 1991; Tebeau, *A History of Florida*, 320.

72. "Plans for Hotel Ponce de Leon as converted for Coast Guard Use. (United States Coast Guard Training Station, St. Augustine, Fla.)" CHDC. http://ufdc.ufl.edu/caha (accessed January 2, 2013); Rahner interview; "A Real Sacrifice," *St. Augustine Record*, August 31, 1942.

73. "Furniture," *St. Augustine Record*, August 31, 1942; Hotel Ponce de Leon National Advisory Committee for Restoration (hereafter NACR), "Minutes," October 27, 1986, 10.

74. "Furniture"; Coast Guard Reserve, "I Cover the Waterfront," *Shield*, 2:4, February 15, 1943, JMP; Coast Guard Reserve, "First SPARS Appear at Ponce," *Shield*, 2:5, March 1, 1943, JMP; Coast Guard Reserve, "The St. Augustine Coast Guard Training Facility," *Shield*, 2:10, May 15, 1943, JMP; Coast Guard Reserve, "At SPARS' First Anniversary Dance," *Shield*, 2:23, December 1, 1943, JMP; Coast Guard Reserve, "Parade Time in St. Augustine," *Reservist*, April 1991, JMP; *St. Augustine Record*, St. Augustine Remembers, 2006.

75. U.S. Coast Guard, "Jacob Lawrence." http://www.uscg.mil/history/faqs/Jacob_Lawrence.asp (accessed January 10, 2013).

76. Campbell, 289.

77. Rahner interview.

78. Rahner interview.

79. "Proposed Swimming Pool for Hotel Ponce De Leon, St. Augustine, Fla,

Mechanical and Plumbing Details," CHDC. http://ufdc.ufl.edu/UF00089836/001 72?search=plumbing (accessed January 20, 2013).

80. Williams interview; Kenan interview.

81. The garage was demolished for a Spanish colonial building reconstruction that houses La Pentola Restaurant today. Pope interview; Foster interview.

82. Kenan interview; Hunt interview; Gannon interview.

83. Williams interview.

84. "He Rubbed Back of Johnson," news clipping, n.d., COSA.

85. "Hotel Ponce de Leon Will Open Early for St. Augustine Event," *Florida Times-Union*, October 29, 1964.

86. Baker interview; "This Will Hurt Me More Than It Hurts You" *Route 66* television episode, FCA.

87. The Kenan heirs split the Flagler System. Lawrence Lewis Jr. retained ownership of the Ponce. His cousins, led by Frank H. Kenan, held The Breakers Hotel in Palm Beach and continue to do so. Versaggi interview.

88. "Ponce De Leon Hotel Will Open 79th Season Friday," *St. Augustine Record*, October 23, 1966, 1-B. Flagler College Archives.

89. "Plans Finalized for Ponce de Leon Ball," *St. Augustine Record*, March 31, 1967, FCA; "Doors of Old City Hotel Are Closed," *Florida Times-Union*, April 6, 1967; "Ball Ushers in New Era for Hotel Ponce de Leon," *St. Augustine Record*, April 6, 1967, FCA.

90. "Hotel Is City Landmark," *St. Augustine Record*, January 18, 1967, Flagler College Archives; "Hotel Ponce de Leon, St. Augustine, Florida, Flagler System, Schedule of Rates," advertising brochure insert, 1964, FCA.

91. In 1889, Flagler House owner Carrie Flagler became Mrs. Myron Angel. The couple split time between her New York business and San Luis Obispo, where he helped found the California Polytechnic School; Myron Angel, *History of the California Polytechnic School at San Luis Obispo*, San Luis Obispo, Tribune Print, 1908, 13–14. https://archive.org/stream/historyofcaliforooange#page/12/mode/1up (accessed September 29, 2014); Conway, *Sullivan County Catskills*, 85; Brown, *Catskill Culture*, 62–63.

92. John Conway, "Retrospect: New Uses for Old Hotels," December 2, 2011, http://sullivanretrospect.com/ (accessed September 29, 2014); Brown University, the Catskills Institute, "Hotels and Bungalows," http://catskills.brown.edu/hotels-bungalows.shtml (accessed November 26, 2012).

93. Nicholl Boyd, *Bisbee, Arizona, Then and Now* (Phoenix: Cowboy Miner Productions, 2003), 39. http://books.google.com/books?hl=en&lr=&id=RLzEVN5k oWkC&oi=fnd&pg=PA6&dq=%22copper+queen+hotel%22&ots=qjYzwJbKUe& sig=qIgYJz6JscSTPsf2KrKd9dVDC3k#v=onepage&q=%22copper%20queen%20 hotel%22&f=false (accessed November 10, 2012).

94. "A Good Life-Work Ended: The Career of William E. Dodge Suddenly Closed," *New York Times*, February 10, 1883. http://query.nytimes.com/gst/abstract

.html?res=9D04E1DF1731E433A25753C1A9649C94629FD7CF (accessed November 10, 2012); "Society at the Winter Resorts, Palm Beach" *New York Times*, March 24, 1912. http://query.nytimes.com/mem/archive-free/pdf?res=9502E3DC133AE633A 25756C2A9649C946396D6CF (accessed December 3, 2012).

95. "Mount Pleasant House." http://whitemountainhistory.org/Mt._Pleasant_ House.html (accessed November 10, 2012); "White Mountains. Summer Guests Looking Forward to the Golf and Tennis Tournaments," *New York Times*, June 26, 1910. http://query.nytimes.com/mem/archive-free/pdf?res=F10716FC395417738D DDAF0A94DE405B808DF1D3 (accessed June 10, 2012); "Flagler Converted to Autos;" "Rockefeller at Intervale;" Tolles, *White Mountains*, 214.

96. Tolles, *White Mountains*, 214–15; "History of the Mount Washington Hotel." http://www.whitemountainhistory.org/Mount_Washington_Hotel.html (accessed September 29, 2014).

97. McCash and McCash, 102; "Yachts Reported," *New York Times*, June 23, 1894. http://query.nytimes.com/mem/archive-free/pdf?res=9800E0DB1730E033A25750 C2A96E9C94659ED7CF (accessed July 7, 2012).

98. Akin, *The Sly Foxes*, 22–36.

99. Credit is given to Mrs. Plant who appreciated opera. *Olivette* and *Mascotte* were comedic operas performed by the French Opera Company for the first time in New York, Boston, and Philadelphia over the winter of 1881–82; "Amusements. Musical Notes," *New York Times*, July 21, 1881. http://query.nytimes.com/mem/ar-chive-free/pdf?res=9804E5DC133EE433A25752C2A9619C94609FD7CF (accessed February 26, 2011); Montgomery, 275; J[efferson Beale] Browne, *Key West: The Old and the New* (St. Augustine: The Record Company, 1912), 81, John Luther Ringwalt, *Development of Transportation Systems in the United States* (Philadelphia: Railway World Office, 1888), 291. http://books.google.com/books/about/Development_ of_Transportation_Systems_in.html?id=tkcKAAAAIAAJ (accessed September 29, 2014); James W. Covington, "The Tampa Bay Hotel," *Tequesta*, Number 26 (1966): 4. http://digitalcollections.fiu.edu/tequesta/files/1966/66_1_01.pdf (accessed February 24, 2011).

100. Lyman Abbott, Hamilton Wright Mabie and Ernest Hamblin Abbott, *The Outlook: A Family Paper*, 50 no. 2 (December 1, 1894): 946. http://books.google. com/books?id=vosAAAAAYAAJ&pg=PA946&lpg=PA946&dq=plant+steamsh ip+line&source=bl&ots=coQALDoNQF&sig=YAkKFK6g5cDh51PdDAMJeiSx a1g&hl=en&ei=V_puTai-KdSEtgfDydyADw&sa=X&oi=book_result&ct=resul t&resnum=2&ved=0CBkQ6AEwATgK#v=onepage&q=plant%20steamship%20 line&f=false (accessed March 2, 2011).

101. Abbott, 946.

102. "Nova Scotia Transportation. Two Steamship Lines Form a Combination," *New York Times*, February 7, 1893. http://query.nytimes.com/mem/archive-free/pd f?res=9400E7DC1731E033A2575BC0A9649C94629ED7CF (accessed February 26, 2011).

103. Turner and Bramson, 29; "Died on the Yacht: H. M. Flagler's Invalid Daughter Expires While Hurrying South," *New York Times*, March 27, 1889. http://query.nytimes.com/mem/archive-free/pdf?res=9C0DEEDD123AE033A25754C2A9659C94689FD7CF (accessed January 31, 2012); Jesus Mendez, "Henry Flagler: Florida Wizard and Bahamian Magician," Florida Historical Society Annual Conference, May 24, 2013.

104. Turner and Bramson, *The Plant System*, 29–34.

105. "What Is Doing in Society," *New York Times*, January 12, 1899. http://query.nytimes.com/mem/archive-free/pdf?res=9B01EED71730E132A25756C1A9629C94689ED7CF (accessed July 7, 2012).

106. Ibid., 38; Mendez presentation; "Fighting for Plant Estate. Application for Removal of Executors Now Ready for Judicial Decision," *New York Times*, September 3, 1903. http://query.nytimes.com/mem/archive-free/pdf?res=9E05EFDD173AE733A25750C0A96F9C946297D6CF (accessed January 5, 2011); Edward A. Mueller, "The Florida East Coast Steamship Company," *Tequesta*, 36:43–53 http://digitalcollections.fiu.edu/tequesta/files/1976/76_1_03.pdf (accessed October 1, 2014); "Nova Scotia Transportation, Two Steamship Lines Form a Combination," *New York Times*, February 7, 1893. http://query.nytimes.com/mem/archive-free/pdf?res=9400E7DC1731E033A2575BC0A9649C94629ED7CF (accessed February 26, 2011).

107. On the centennial anniversary of this event, the state of Florida and media outlets throughout the Sunshine State reaffirmed the importance of Henry Flagler's contributions.

108. Edwin Lefevre, "Flagler and Florida," *Everybody's Magazine* (February, 1910), 182.

109. "Flagler's Only Son Not a Business Man," *New York Sun*, May 23, 1913. http://fultonhistory.com/newspaper%209/New%20York%20NY%20Sun/New%20York%20NY%20Sun%201913%20%20Grayscale/New%20York%20NY%20Sun%201913%20%20Grayscale%20-%203618.pdf (accessed December 19, 2012).

110. "Doors of Old City Hotel Are Closed," *Florida Times-Union*, April 6, 1967.

Chapter 4. Historic Preservation in St. Augustine

1. Albert Manucy, "The City Gate at St. Augustine," *El Escribano* 10:1 (January 1973), 1–6.

2. Dena Snodgrass, "The City Gate Tablet," *El Escribano* 10:1 (January 1973), 14–18.

3. Ibid., 7; "Castillo de San Marcos Tricentennial, 1672–1972," *El Escribano* 9:1 (January 1972), 1–19.

4. Today, the site is occupied by the Hilton St. Augustine Historic Bayfront. Lawson, *The Saint Augustine Historical Society*, 1; Shaughnessy, "Crises of Authenticity," 32; St. Augustine Historical Society, "About the St. Augustine Historical Society." http://www.staugustinehistoricalsociety.org/about.html (accessed December 8, 2009).

5. "The History of the St. Augustine Alligator Farm and Zoological Park." https://alligatorfarm.com/history.html (accessed February 18, 2013); Barnes, *Florida's Hurricane History*, 162–63; "Hurricanes: Science and Society: 1926-Great Miami Hurricane." http://www.hurricanescience.org/history/storms/1920s/GreatMiami/ (accessed February 18, 2013).

6. "History News," *El Escribano* 10:1 (1973), 20; "Triple Celebration at St. Augustine Was Patriotic and Inspiring, With President-Elect Harding at Old Fort," *Florida Times-Union*, February 23, 1921, National Society of The Colonial Dames of America in the state of Florida Archives, Jacksonville (hereafter NSCDAFL).

7. Fraser interview; Florida Division of Historical Resources, "The Great Floridians 2000." http://dos.myflorida.com/historical/preservation/great-floridians-program/great-floridians-2000/ (accessed September 30, 2014); Kathleen Deagan, "Colonial St. Augustine," *Discover First America: Legacies of La Florida*, public presentation, November 23, 2009; Florida Museum of Natural History, "The Nombre de Dios Mission Sites." http://www.flmnh.ufl.edu/histarch/ndd_mission_sites.htm (accessed February 5, 2013).

8. U.S. Department of Agriculture, Office of Information, Press Service, "United States Route No. 1 is a Highway of History," October 9, 1927. http://www.fhwa.dot.gov/highwayhistory/us1pr.cfm (accessed December 1, 2009); Henry Alverson Franck, *Roaming through the West Indies*, (New York: Blue Ribbon Books, 1920), 3. http://books.google.com/books?hl=en&lr=&id=O-AoAAAAYAAJ&oi=fnd&pg=PA3&dq=1920+hurricane+st+augustine&ots=tpvRTn_6WE&sig=j27iVmEesqVMdxvwKP7RkNxoGhI#v=onepage&q&f=false.

9. McCarthy, *A Book Lover's Guide*, 9–10, 63–131; Hawkins interview; Ernest Hemingway, letter to his mother-in-law Mrs. Mary Pfeiffer dated December 13, 1928, Patrick Hemingway Papers (C0066), Manuscripts Division, Firestone Library, Princeton University; Hemingway-Pfeiffer Museum and Educational Center, Hemingway-Pfeiffer Time Line. http://hemingway.astate.edu/timeline/ (accessed December 1, 2009); "Castle Warden," Florida Site File Form, typescript copy, COSA.

10. Garry Boulard, "'State of Emergency': Key West in the Great Depression," *Florida Historical Quarterly* 67:2 (October 1988), 166.

11. Kenan, *Incidents by the Way*, 102; Beeson, 110.

12. Paul E. Hoffman, "St. Augustine 1580, The Research Project," *El Escribano* 14 (1977), 58.

13. Ibid., 68–72; Standiford, *Last Train to Paradise*, 7, 247.

14. Chatelain taught at the University of Maryland from 1945 to 1965 and died in 1991 at 97 years old. National Park Service, "Interpretation in the National Park Service: A Historical Perspective." http://www.nps.gov/parkhistory/online_books/mackintosh2/branching_inagurating.htm (accessed June 5, 2015); Historic Sites Act of 1935, 16 USC 461–67.

15. Walter B. Fraser Papers.

16. "Restoration Summary Giving Definite Steps in Historic Movement," *St. Augustine Record*, July 30, 1936.

17. Shaughnessy, 32; "St Augustine timeline between Oct. 1936 and May 1944," Charles Bridgham Hosmer, Jr., Series 2, box 6, folder 6, Special Collections, University of Maryland Libraries, College Park.

18. Eleanor Beeson, "The St. Augustine Historical Restoration," *Florida Historical Quarterly* 16:2 (October 1937), 110–18; V. E. Chatelain, "Reports of Sub-Committees of the National Committee for the Survey and the Development of the Historical Resources of St. Augustine, Florida," St. Augustine, March 1937, Historic St. Augustine Preservation Board Archives (hereafter HSAPB).

19. Library of Congress, "Frances Benjamin Johnston—Biographical Overview and Chronology." http://www.loc.gov/rr/print/coll/fbjchron.html (accessed December 3, 2012); Library of Congress, "Carnegie Survey of the American South." http://www.loc.gov/pictures/collection/csas/background.html (accessed December 3, 2012).

20. Woods, *Beyond the Architect's Eye*, 150; Berch, *The Women behind the Lens*, 108–9, 122–23; Ausherman, *Frances Benjamin Johnston*, 149.

21. Watters, *Gardens for a Beautiful America*, 18–19.

22. Bradley G. Brewer, "A Synopsis of Restoration," *El Escribano* 7 (1970), 62–73; "Flagler Hotels Here Are Veritable Olden Spanish Palaces," *St. Augustine Record*, July 1, 1937; "Florida's Railroad History Should Be Carefully Preserved," *St. Augustine Record*, July 4, 1937.

23. Brewer, "A Synopsis of Restoration," *El Escribano* 7 (1970), 66; Hosmer, *Preservation Comes of Age*, vol. 2, 318.

24. Hosmer, *Preservation Comes of Age*, Vol. 1, 318–21; Chatelain, *The Defenses of St. Augustine, 1565–1763*. Washington, D.C.: Carnegie Institution of Washington, Publication 511, 1941, HSAPB. Vannevar Bush is noted for leading a team at MIT in the 1930s that developed the first analog computer. Hosmer papers give dates as 1939 appropriation for release in 1940. Beeson, "The St. Augustine Historical Restoration," *Florida Historical Quarterly* 16:2 (October 1937), 110; Albert Manucy, "A review of the St. Augustine Historical Program," *Hispanic American Historical Review* 24:2 (May 1944), 352–56.

25. Waterbury, *The Treasurer's House*, 200–205; Rajtar and Goodman, *Historic St. Augustine*, 73.

26. Ximenez-Fatio House Museum, "Ximenez-Fatio House Timeline," NSCDAFL.

27. F. Blair Reeves, "The Architecture of Historic St. Augustine: A Photographic Essay," *Florida Historical Quarterly* 44 (1965), 96; "St. Augustine Civic Center," National Register Form.

28. Lumadue, "The University Foundation," 5, 21, 141–42, 150–51.

29. Manucy, "Review," 352–56.

30. "Alcazar Hotel," National Register Form; Kiley Mallard, "The Lightner Museum: A Collector's Dream," *Florida History and the Arts*, Winter 2006; Bowen and the St. Augustine Historical Society, *St. Augustine in the Gilded Age*, 15.

31. Mark M. Nelson, "Wax Museum Stays Alive While Others Melt Away," *St. Petersburg Times*, May 30, 1985.

32. Florida Division of Historical Resources, Historical Marker Program, "Warden Winter Home." http://www.flheritage.com/preservation/markers/markers.cfm?ID=st.%20johns (accessed December 12, 2009); "Castle Warden" Florida Site File Form.

33. Hosmer, *Preservation Comes of Age*, Vol. I, 319–20.

34. Fraser Papers.

35. Kenneth Chorley, president, Colonial Williamsburg Inc., Letter to Judge David R. Dunham, Acting President. St. Augustine Historical Preservation and Restoration Association, March 17, 1947, Fraser Papers; "Williamsburg Head Visits Here, Confers With Local Citizens," *St. Augustine Record*, February 28, 1947.

36. *St. Augustine Record*, February 28, 1947.

37. Fraser interview, February 4, 2013; The St. Augustine Restoration Plan, St. Augustine Foundation, Inc., Archives (hereafter SAF); "St. Augustine has Unique Restoration Commission," *St. Augustine Record*, September 8, 1965, 7B.

38. Ibid.; "San Augustin Antiguo: The Restoration of Old St. Augustine, 1960–66," typescript copy, SAHRPC, COSA; "Restoration in St. Augustine: An International Project," *History News*, 21:7 (July 1966), 142–43; John Schnaffner, "St. Augustine Busy Dressing for 400th Birthday Party," *Evening Independent*, November 22, 1963.

39. Master Plan, preface, unpublished typescript, 1960, SAHRPC, COSA; Schnaffner, 142–43; Rick Bothwell, "Florida Will Show a Colorful Past to Visitors Beginning Next Year," *St. Petersburg Times*, December 20, 1958.

40. Master Plan; "San Agustin Antiguo," SAHRPC, COSA; *History News*.

41. *St. Augustine Record*, September 8, 1965, 7B.

42. Master Plan, preface; Bothwell, "Florida Will Show a Colorful Past;" *History News*, 21:7(July, 1966), 142.

43. "Cultural Bridge within the Hemisphere: Pan American Center, San Agustin Antiguo: The Restoration of Old St. Augustine, 1960–1966," SAHRPC.

44. Schnaffner, "St. Augustine Quadricentennial Slated," *St. Petersburg Times*, April 10, 1964.

45. "Restoration Program Is Underway: Spain, Latin Americans Are Participating," *Saint Augustine and St. Johns County Explorer*, Fall-Winter 1965.

46. Gannon interview.

47. San Augustin Antiguo, COSA.

48. San Augustin Antiguo, COSA.

49. "General Motors Gives $10,000 to Restoration, Spain Expands Project," *St. Augustine Record*, June 19, 1964.

50. St. Augustine Restoration Commission, "Exhibit Centers," HSAPB; "H. E. Wolfe to Be Honored at Dinner: Governor to Lay Cornerstone for Florida Center Tomorrow," *St. Augustine Record*, November 22, 1964; "Governor Lays Cornerstone for State Exhibition Building Here," *St. Augustine Record*, November 24, 1964; "Purchase of Two Properties for Restoration Announced," *St. Augustine Record*, April 29, 1964, HSAPB.

51. Carling, February 17–18, 1968, HSAPB.

52. National Park Service, "Mission 66 for Castillo de San Marcos National Monument," Timucuan Ecological & Historic Preserve Archives; "Freeman Tilden," The National Park Service: The First 75 Years, Biographical Vignettes. http://www.nps.gov/parkhistory/online_books/sontag/tilden.htm (accessed October 1, 2014); Tilden, *Interpreting Our Heritage*; "Festivals and Special Events: Quadricentenial" folder, Minutes of the December 5, 1963 meeting, SAHSRL.

53. B. C. Roberts letter to Thad T. Behm, May 17, 1965, HSAPB.

54. "Ancient City Will Use Old Fort as A-Shelter," *St. Augustine Record*, October 24, 1962.

55. "Florida Military Headquarters Building Was Once Franciscan Monastery, Convent," *St. Augustine Record*, September 8, 1965, 4B; "8SJ10 St. Francis Barracks," Florida Site File Form, COSA.

56. "Actions Speak Louder Than Words," *St. Augustine Record*, November 5, 1961, 8A.

57. Hoffman, "St. Augustine 1580," *El Escribano* 14 (1977), 77–86; Charles Stafford, "Sliced by Summer's Storms," *Gainesville Sun*, September 13, 1964; F. Blair Reeves, "The National Quadricentennial Celebration: St. Augustine, Florida," *Florida Architect*, June 14–22, 1965, COSA; "Drama Tells St. Augustine Story: Paul Green's 'Cross and Sword' Being Presented in Amphitheatre," *St. Augustine and St. Johns County Explorer*, Summer 1965, COSA; "St. Augustine 400 Years Old," *St. Augustine and St. Johns County Explorer*, Fall-Winter 1965, COSA.

58. Griffin, "The Impact of Tourism," 145; "Easter Festival Parade Is Hailed as Biggest, Best Ever," *St. Augustine Record*, April 19, 1965, 1, COSA; "How About St. Augustine Easter Parade?" *Palm Beach Daily News*, April 2, 1972, 4.

59. San Agustin Antiguo; "Catholic Diocese of St. Augustine builds, beautified and celebrates its 400th Anniversary," SAHRPC.

60. "Completion of Cathedral Restoration Climaxes Centuries of Struggle: City Greets His Eminence William Cardinal Conway, Church Officials, Priests," "Jacksonville Symphony to Play for Mass," and "Ancient Mission Bells to Ring Out Once Again at Restored Cathedral," *St. Augustine Record*, March 8, 1966; Bailey interview.

61. Gannon interview.

62. Folk artist Earl Cunningham's OverFork Gallery occupied part of the Paffe building. "Earl Cunningham: Artist Was Particular about Sharing His Work," *Florida Times-Union*, October 26, 1986; San Agustin Antiguo; Gannon interview; "History News," *El Escribano* 10:1 (1973), 19.

63. Master Plan; Shepard interview; "400th Anniversary Inc. Responsible for Planning Anniversary Celebration," *St. Augustine Record*, September 8, 1965, 3B; Bothwell, "Florida Will Show a Colorful Past," *St. Petersburg Times*, December 29, 1958.

64. Lawrence Lewis, Jr., "An Open Letter to the Citizens of St. Augustine and St. Johns County," *St. Augustine Record*, July 12, 1988, 10A.

65. "History News," *El Escribano* 10:1 (1973), 19; Lewis Letter.

66. Lewis Letter.

67. Bailey interview.

68. Waterbury, 210–12; Shepard interview.

69. Albert Manucy, "Toward Recreation of 16th Century St. Augustine," *El Escribano*, 14 (1977), 1–4; Eugene Lyon, "St. Augustine 1580: The Living Community," *El Escribano*, 14 (1977), 21; "Construction of 1580 St. Augustine Postponed," press release, January 8, 1981, SAF; Hoffman, "St. Augustine 1580," *El Escribano* 14 (1977), 14–16.

70. Lawrence Lewis Jr., letter to Dennis B. Kane, February 7, 1983, SAF.

71. St. Augustine, miscellaneous correspondence, SAF.

72. "SJ10 St. Augustine Historic District."

73. Member File, HSAPB; Leggitt and Hammer, *Times-Union*, A-10; Michael Reynolds, "The Cast of Characters Grows in the St. Augustine Horror Show: 'A Nightmare on St. George Street,'" *Jacksonville Today*, September 1988, 44.

74. Advancement, Grant Records, FCA; "Flagler College Wins Battle with Historic Board over Grant," *Florida Times-Union*, June 10, 1989.

75. "Flagler College Wins Battle with Historic Board over Grant;" Jim Smith, Florida Secretary of State, Grant award letter to Dr. Beverly Copeland, Director of Development, Flagler College, July 27, 1989, Advancement, Grant Records, FCA.

76. "State of Florida Successor to the Historic St. Augustine Preservation Board v. St. Augustine Foundation Inc." Case No.: 89-1820-CA, Division: F, June 23, 1994, Circuit Court, Seventh Judicial Circuit, St. Johns County, Florida.

Chapter 5. Rescue and Restoration

1. Ossman and Ewing, *Carrère and Hastings,* 31; Lewis interview; Thomas J. Colin, "Lush Legacy of a Robber Baron: A Gilded Era Landmark in St. Augustine Nears the End of Remarkable Transformation," *Historic Preservation*, November/December (Washington, D.C.: National Trust for Historic Preservation, 1987), cut sheet overrun, FCA; "Flagler College" files, SAF.

2. "Hotel Ponce de Leon Is Sold," *St. Augustine Record*, January 18, 1967; "Dr. Carlson Outlines Plans for Flagler College," *St. Augustine Record*, January 19, 1967.

3. Anne Carling, "Flagler College Seen As Great Cultural, Economic Asset Here," *St. Augustine Record*, January 19, 1967.

4. Carling, "Flagler College Seen," January 19, 1967; Castillo, 183; Abare interview.

5. A. H. Tebault, "Reorganization Set At Flagler College," *St. Augustine Record*, [1971], FCA. Beverly Copeland, letter to David Ferro, August 18, 1989, FCA; St. Johns County Public Records, "Release and Satisfaction of Mortgage," Book 197, Page 364, FCA; "Ringhaver, Auchter Are Named Trustees of Flagler College," *St. Augustine Record*, January 29–30, 1969, FCA.

6. Colin; Abare interview; Campbell, 289; Castillo, 156.

7. Rains and Henderson, *With Heritage So Rich*, 11.

8. Carberry interview; Martin interview; Leon Shimer, "St. Augustine to See Pace at Hotel Change," *Florida Times-Union*, September 17, 1967.

9. Abare interview; Carberry interview; Flagler College, *Desiderata*, yearbook, 1972, 104.

10. Carberry interview.

11. Freeman interview; Rutland interview; Groux interview; Walk interview; Castillo, 199.

12. Craig Thorn Papers, SAHSRL.

13. Diamonstein, *Buildings Reborn*, 198.

14. Thorn Papers, FCA; "The Flagler College Restoration Campaign" booklet, FCA; Martin interview; Castillo, 149.

15. Carberry interview.

16. Drysdale interview; Carberry interview; Castillo, 195; Kenan Hall booklet and grant records, FCA; Thorn Papers, FCA.

17. Castillo, 192.

18. Kenan Hall booklet, FCA.

19. Restoration Campaign booklet, FCA; Kenan Hall booklet, FCA.

20. Restoration Campaign booklet, FCA.

21. Restoration Campaign booklet, FCA; "Office Floor, Hotel Ponce de Leon," CHDA. http://ufdc.ufl.edu/UF00089836/00141/1x?vo=31&vp=3830,0 (accessed April 6, 2013).

22. Restoration Campaign booklet, FCA.

23. Dining Hall Grant Records, FCA.

24. Restoration Campaign booklet, FCA.

25. Office of Institutional Advancement, "Gift Detail Report," 2002, FCA.

26. McDonald interview.

27. Ruggiero interview; McDonald interview.

28. Small, *Handbook of the New Library of Congress in Washington*, 60–63.

29. "Flagler's Ponce at 100," *Special Supplement* to the *St. Augustine Record*, January 9, 1988, 2.

30. Biltmore, Campbell, Smith Restorations, Inc. *Conservator*, newsletter 1:2, n.d. [ca. 1987].

31. Abare interview; Castillo, 160; NACR, Minutes of the Meeting, October 27, 1986, St. Augustine, 4–5, FCA; *Conservator*.

32. *Conservator.*

33. NACR Minutes, October 27, 1986, 4–5.

34. "Soluble Nylon Reevaluated," *Abbey Newsletter*, 6, no.1 (February 1982): 1–2. http://cool.conservation-us.org/byorg/abbey/an/an06/an06-1/an06-101.html (accessed December 25, 2011); Elizabeth C. Welsh, Catherine Sease, Basil Rhodes, Steven C. Brown, and Miriam Clavir, "Multicultural Participation in Conservation Decision-Making," WAAC Annual Meeting, Seattle, September 30, 1991. http://cool. conservation-us.org/waac/wn/wn14/wn14-1/wn14-105.html (accessed December 25, 2011).

35. Abare interview; Martin interview.

36. *Conservator.*

37. Barney D. Lamar, Director, IFACS, letter to Robert Honiker, Director of Campus Planning, Flagler College, March 14, 1990, FCA.

38. *Conservator,* FCA.

39. *Conservator,* FCA.

40. "College's grand dining hall being renovated," *Florida Times-Union*, October 6, 1987; "Craftsmen restoring Ponce Hall dining area to former glory days," *St. Augustine Record*, October 3, 1987; Abare interview; *Conservator,* FCA; Colin, Historic Preservation, FCA.

41. Proctor interview; "Flagler College Spruces up Dining Room, Lobby," *Florida Times-Union*, October 6, 1967.

42. NACR, Minutes, October 27, 1986, 6; Drysdale interview.

43. NACR, Minutes, October 27, 1986, 10.

44. NACR, Minutes, October 27, 1986, 9–10.

45. Institutional Advancement, Grant Records, FCA; Historic Preservation & Development, Inc., "Proposal for Public Visitation of the Grand Parlors, Flagler College, Saint Augustine, Florida," unpublished typescript, March 28, 1988, FCA.

46. Advancement, Grant Records, FCA.

47. Colin, *Historic Preservation,* FCA.

48. Business Services Records, FCA.

49. Institutional Advancement, Grant Records, FCA. "Restoring a Relic: Rose Leavitt and Crew are Returning the Splendor to Flagler College's Dining Hall One Spot at a Time, *St. Augustine Record,* July 7, 2000, FCA.

50. Foster interview.

51. IFACS, "Analysis of Decorative Finishes and Proposal for Restoration and Decoration to the Rotunda, Flagler College, St. Augustine, Florida." unpublished typescript, 1990, FCA.

52. IFACS, Rotunda report, FCA.

53. IFACS, Rotunda report, FCA.

54. IFACS, Rotunda report, FCA.

55. IFACS, Rotunda report, FCA.

56. Institutional Advancement, Grant Records; "Flagler College Rotunda Restoration Project," Historic Preservation Grants-in-Aid, Special Category Application Form, 1989–1990, FCA.

57. IFACS Rotunda report, FCA.

58. Institutional Advancement, Grant Records, "Rotunda," 1989–1990, FCA.

59. Institutional Advancement, Grant Records, "Rotunda," 1989–1990, FCA.

60. Institutional Advancement, Grant Records, "Rotunda," 1989–1990, FCA.

61. Institutional Advancement, Grant Records, "Rotunda," 1989–1990, FCA.

62. Institutional Advancement, Grant Records, "Rotunda," 1989–1990, FCA.

63. Institutional Advancement, Grant Records, "Rotunda," 1989–1990, FCA.

64. Institutional Advancement, Grant Records, "Rotunda," 1989–1990, FCA.

65. Business Services Records, FCA.

66. Institutional Advancement, Grant Records, "Flagler College Perimeter Wall," FCA; Groux interview.

67. Abare interview.

68. Grant Records, "Perimeter Wall," FCA.

69. Grant Records, "Courtyard," FCA.

70. Philip Wisley, letter from Nicole Donnelly, August 28, 2001, Advancement, Grant Records, FCA.

71. Grant Records, "Courtyard," FCA.

72. National Hurricane Center, "Preliminary Report: Hurricane Floyd, November 18, 1999."

73. Advancement Grant Records, FCA.

74. Advancement Grant Records, FCA.

75. Restoration Campaign booklet; CHDA, "Additions & Repairs to Billiards Room and Gay Nineties Bar (for Ponce de Leon Hotel)," CHDA. http://ufdc.ufl.edu/UF00089836/00022/1x?vo=12&vp=5791,1376 (accessed April 6, 2013).

76. "Proposed Swimming Pool for Hotel Ponce De Leon, St. Augustine, Fla, Concrete & Reinforcing Details," CHDA. http://ufdc.ufl.edu/UF00089836/00173 (accessed April 6, 2013).

77. Castillo, 187.

78. Restoration Campaign booklet, FCA.

79. Institutional Advancement, Grant Records, 2012–2013, FCA.

80. Institutional Advancement, Grant Records, 2009–2010, FCA.

81. Karas, "Ponce de Leon Hotel," 2008.

82. Lehman Brothers Collection-Contemporary Business Archives, "Arnold Constable Corporation," Baker Library Historical Collections, Harvard Business School.

83. Lawrence Biemiller, "Flagler College Restores an Architectural Treasure," *Chronicle of Higher Education*, March 2, 1988, B7, FCA.

Chapter 6. A Most Beautiful College Campus

1. Carling, "Landmark," January 18, 1967; "Doors of Old Hotel Are Closed," *Florida Times-Union*, April 6, 1967, FCA.

2. National Endowment for the Humanities, "NEH Chairman Bruce Cole Also Announces 1st Quarter 2004 We the People Grants," press release, January 29, 2004.

3. Rachel Leitao, "Salazar Attends Inaugural Meeting of St. Augustine Commission." http://staugustine.firstcoastnews.com/news/politics/salazar-attends-inaugural-meeting-st-augustine-commission/56943 (accessed September 24, 2014).

4. "Romney Coming to St. Augustine on Monday," *St. Augustine Record*, July 31, 2012.

5. Tiffanie Reynolds, "Gov. Scott Marks Future with the Past at Flagler College," *Gargoyle*. http://gargoyle.flagler.edu/2013/04/gov-scott-marks-future-with-the-past-at-flagler-college/ (accessed April 6, 2013).

6. Tom King, "Flagler College Purchases Historic King Street Home," *St. Augustine Record*, January 25, 1968, FCA; "Old Home Bought by Flagler College," *Florida Times-Union*, January 26, 1968, FCA.

7. "Markland House" file, FCA.

8. Carberry interview.

9. "Markland House" file, FCA.

10. "Markland House" file, FCA.

11. Baker interview.

12. Williams interview; "Model Land Company Historic District, 8SJ2462," National Register Form, 1983.

13. Jackie Feagin, "College Completes Historic Seavey Cottage Restoration," *St. Augustine Record*, April 24, 1987, FCA.

14. "20 Valencia Street" file, FCA.

15. "20 Valencia Street" file, FCA.

16. Feagin, "Seavey Cottage Restoration," FCA.

17. "20 Valencia Street" file, FCA; Feagin, "Seavey Cottage Restoration," FCA.

18. Jackie Feagin, "Home to Generals Receives $500,000 New Lease on Life," *St. Augustine Record*, April 25, 1987, FCA; Feagin, "Seavey Cottage Restoration."

19. "Ponce de Leon Cottage/Thompson Hall," Grant Records, FCA.

20. Advancement, Grant Records, FCA.

21. Feagin, "Seavey Cottage Restoration"; Advancement, Grant Records, FCA.

22. Advancement, Grant Records, FCA.

23. Advancement, Grant Records, FCA.

24. Advancement, Grant Records, FCA.

25. Flagler College Grant Records. "Casa Amarylla SJ2293" Florida Site File, FCA.

26. "Casa Amarylla" file, FCA.

27. Restoration Campaign Booklet, FCA; "Dedication of College Hall Set Friday," *St. Augustine Record,* January 26, 1989, FCA; "Wiley Hall Wins Award for Flagler," *St. Augustine Record,* September 30, 1989, FCA.

28. "Billiard Building/Markland Cottage" file, FCA.

29. Advancement, Grant Records, FCA.

30. Advancement, Grant Records, FCA.

31. Advancement, Grant Records, FCA.

32. "Power House/Palm Cottage" and "Wiley Hall" files, FCA.

33. Campbell, 329; Foster interview.

34. Cornell University Law School, Legal Information Institute, "Cary v. Commissioner of Internal Revenue Flagler v. Same, Flagler's Estate v. Same, Matthews v. Same." 313 U.S. 441 (61 S.Ct. 978, 85 L.Ed. 1446). http://www.law.cornell.edu/supremecourt/text/313/441#fn1 (accessed December 16, 2012); "Jean Flagler Matthews (formerly Jean Flagler Mook, Formerly Jean Flagler Gonzales, Formerly Jean Flagler Defina), Individually, and As Executrix of the Estate of Ricardo C. Gonzales, Deceased v. the United States," 425 F.2d 738, April 17, 1970. http://law.justia.com/cases/federal/appellate-courts/F2/425/738/175303/ (accessed December 16, 2012).

35. "Hanke Hall" file, FCA.

36. Kenan Trust, Annual Report; Campbell, *Across Fortune's Tracks,* 329–32.

37. "Historic Studies in St. Augustine: Flagler College Sets Up Institute," *Florida Times-Union,* September 25, 1999, B-3, FCA; "College Founds Research Institute," *Gargoyle,* September 27, 1999, FCA.

38. Center for Governmental Responsibility, University of Florida Levin College of Law, Economic Impacts of Historic Preservation in Florida: Executive Summary, 2003, 7.

39. Advancement, Grant Records, FCA.

40. Advancement, Grant Records, FCA.

Chapter 7. Preserving a Legacy

1. Mark Rowh, "Renovation vs. Historic Preservation," *College Planning & Management,* 16:7 (July 2013), 18–21.

BIBLIOGRAPHY

Primary Sources

1959 Fla. Laws 1758. (Fla. Stat. as amended, Ch. 266), 1997.

1967 Fla. Laws 116. (Fla. Stat. Ch. 267), 1997.

1985 Fla. Laws 207. (Fla. Stat. 163.3161–163.3211), 1997.

Abandoned Shipwreck Act of 1987 (ASA), 43 USC 2101–2106.

Abare, William T., Jr. Interview with the author, May 25, 2012.

A B C Pathfinder Shipping and Mailing Guide. Boston: New England Railway Publishing Company, 1899.

Albert, Tonya. Interview with the author, July 20, 2010.

Anderson, John. Papers Relating to Ormond Beach. University of Florida, George A. Smathers Libraries, Gainesville, Florida.

Anonymous. Interview with the author, July 20, 2010.

Antiquities Act of 1906 (16 USC 421–433).

Archaeological and Historic Preservation Act of 1974, 16 USC 469.

Archaeological Resources Protection Act of 1979, 16 USC 470.

Arizona State Library, Archives and Public Records, History and Archives Division, Phoenix.

Bailey, John D. Sr. Interview with the author, November 28, 2012.

Baker, Greg. Interview with the author, December 14, 2012.

Bell, Alexander Graham. Papers. Series: Family Papers, Folder: Mabel Hubbard Bell, Family Correspondence, Alexander Graham Bell, Library of Congress, Washington, D.C.

Carberry, Robert. Interview with the author, February 8, 2013.

Carrère and Hastings Digital Archives, George A. Smathers Libraries, University of Florida, Gainesville.

City of St. Augustine. Archaeological Preservation Ordinance. (Code 1964, Section 5 1/2–1).

City of St. Augustine Records, St. Augustine.

City of St. Augustine, Historic Architectural Review Board Records, St. Augustine.

Conway, John. Interview with the author, January 31, 2012.

Davis, Mike. Interview with the author, June 3, 2013.

DeGraaf, Leonard. Interview with the author, October 20, 2010.

Department of Transportation Act. 49 USC Section 202 and 23 USC Section 138, 1966.

Drysdale, David. Interview with the author, February 6, 2013.

Edison, Thomas A. Papers, Rutgers University, Piscataway.

Executive Order 11593. "Protection and Enhancement of the Cultural Environment." 1971. 36 FR 8921, 3 CFR, 1971–1975 Comp.

Flagler College Archives, Proctor Library, St. Augustine.

Flagler College Files, St. Augustine Foundation.

Flagler County Public Records.

Florida Attorney General Advisory Legal Opinion–Historic Preservation Boards. Number: AGO 81-67, September 16, 1981.

Foster, Louise Lewis. Interview with the author, February 15, 2013.

Fraser, John. Interview with the author, February 4, 2013.

Fraser, Walter B. Papers, Fraser Family, St. Augustine.

Freeman, Viki West. Interview with the author, February 20, 2015.

Gannon, Michael. Interview with the author, January 23, 2013.

Graham, Roy. Interview with the author, February 11, 2013.

Groux, Richard. Interview with the author, February 1, 2013.

Hawkins, Ruth. Interview with the author, April 7, 2006.

Heade, Martin Johnson. *Giant Magnolias on a Blue Velvet Cloth*, ca. 1885–95. National Gallery of Art, Washington, D.C.

Hemingway, Patrick. Patrick Hemingway Papers (C0066), Manuscripts Division, Firestone Library, Princeton University, Princeton.

Historic St. Augustine Preservation Board Archives.

Hosmer, Charles Bridgham, Jr., Special Collections, Hornbake Library, University of Maryland Libraries, College Park.

Hunt, E. L. Interview with the author, January 23, 2013.

Israel, Paul. Interview with the author, June 6, 2005.

James, Nancy Jo Cafaro. Interview with the author, February 20, 2013.

Kelso, William. Interview with the author, May 27, 2008.

Kenan, Thomas. Interview with the author, January 27, 2013.

Lehman Brothers Collection–Contemporary Business Archives. "Arnold Constable Corporation," Baker Library Historical Collections, Harvard Business School, Boston.

Lewis, Lawrence, Jr. Interview with Robert Neeland, October 31, 1985. St. Augustine Historical Society Research Library, St. Augustine.

Lewis, Lawrence, Jr. Letter to Dennis B. Kane, National Geographic Society, February 7, 1983. St. Augustine Foundation Inc., St. Augustine.

Library of Congress, Prints & Photographs Division.

Marsh, Arthur. Scrapbook D, 1289, St. Augustine Historical Society Research Library.

Martin, Donald. Interview with the author, February 22, 2013.

McDonald, Thomas. Interview with the author, August 13, 2007.

Miner, Pam. Interview with the author, May 14, 2005.

Modjeska, Helena. *Memories and Impressions of Helena Modjeska: An Autobiography.* New York: MacMillan & Co., 1910.

"National Historic Preservation Act of 1966." Public Law 89–665; 16 USC 470 et seq.

National Society of the Colonial Dames of America in the State of Florida Archives, Jacksonville.

National Trust for Historic Preservation. "Heritage Tourism Assessment & Recommendations for St. Augustine, Florida." 2003.

Nichols, Frederick D. Papers. 1940s–1990s, Accession # 12798, Albert and Shirley Small Special Collections, University of Virginia Library, Charlottesville, Virginia.

Penn Central Transportation Company v. City of New York. 438 U.S. 104, 1978.

Pope, Alyn. Interview with the author, July 30, 2012.

Proctor, William L. Interview with the author, November 12, 2012.

Rahner, Margaret Eberhart. Interview with the author, September 19, 2014.

Roosevelt, Theodore. Collection. Letters to Ethel Roosevelt Derby, 1884–1919 (inclusive) 1896–1919 (bulk). MS Am 1541.2 (3–48). Letters to Kermit Roosevelt, 1890–1918. MS Am 1541 (87–138). Houghton Library, Harvard University, Cambridge.

Ruggiero, Laurence. Interview with the author, November 5, 2009.

Rutland, Nancy. Interview with the author, January 25, 2013.

San Agustin Antiguo: The Restoration of Old St. Augustine, 1960–1966, SAHRPC.

Shepard, Herschel. Interview with the author, December 18, 2012.

Smith, Kenneth. Interview with the author, January 31, 2013.

St. Augustine Code of Ordinances.

St. Augustine Foundation Inc. Archives, St. Augustine.

St. Augustine Historical Restoration and Preservation Commission, a Florida State Commission. City of St. Augustine Records. *Hotel Ponce de Leon, construction of corner towers, HS4680.* Undated photograph, St. Augustine Historical Society Research Library, St. Augustine.

St. Augustine Historical Society Research Library. "Festivals and Special Events: Quadricentennial" folder, Minutes of the December 5, 1963 meeting.

St. Johns County Public Records.

State Archives of Florida.

State of Florida. William D. Hall Jr., Assistant Attorney General to George Firestone, Secretary of State, Advisory Legal Opinion 81–67, September 16, 1981.

"State of Florida Successor to the Historic St. Augustine Preservation Board v. St. Augustine Foundation Inc." Case No.: 89-1820-CA, Division: F, June 23, 1994, Circuit Court, Seventh Judicial Circuit, St. Johns County, Florida.

Storhaug, Arthur N., Faribault, Minnesota, Letter to postcard donor, from Jacqueline Fretwell, Librarian. "Festivals: Ponce de Leon Celebration." Correspondence and Clippings Files, St. Augustine Historical Society Research Library, St. Augustine.

Tax Reform Act of 1976, HR 10612, 94th Congress, Public Law 94-455.

Tax Reform Act of 1986, H.R. 3838, 99th Congress, Public Law 99-514.

Thorn, Craig. Craig Thorn Papers. St. Augustine Historical Society Research Library, St. Augustine.

Twain, Mark. Mark Twain Papers and Project. Bancroft Library, University of California, Berkeley.

"Unearthing St. Augustine's Colonial Heritage: An Interactive Digital Collection for the Nation's Oldest City." George A. Smathers Libraries, University of Florida, Gainesville.

U.S. Coast Guard Reserve Records.

U.S. Department of the Interior, National Park Service. "Alcazar Hotel," National Register of Historic Places Registration Form, 1971.

———. "Forest of Arden," National Register of Historic Places Registration Form, 1986.

———. "Glenview Historic District." National Register of Historic Places Registration Form, 1983.

———. "Hotel Ponce de Leon." National Historic Landmark Registration Form, 2005.

———. "Model Land Company Historic District, 8SJ2462." National Register of Historic Places Registration Form, 1983.

———. "SJ10 St. Augustine Historic District." National Historic Landmark Registration Form, 1986.

———. "St. Augustine Civic Center (Visitor Information Center)." National Register of Historic Places Registration Form, 2002.

———. Technical Preservation Services, "Historic Preservation Tax Incentives," 2009.

———. Timucuan Ecological & Historic Preserve Archives, Jacksonville.

———. "Whitehall." National Historic Landmark Registration Form, 1999.

Versaggi, Pamela Morris. Interview with the author, June 20, 2013.

Vickers, Sam, and Robbie Vickers. Interview with the author. September 25, 2009.

Walas, Jim. Interview with the author, December 7, 2012.

Walk, Mitchell. Interview with the author, February 21, 2013.

Williams, Janis Versaggi. Interview with the author, February 5, 2013.

Secondary Sources

Abbott, Karl P. *Open for the Season*. Garden City: Country Life Press, 1950.

Akin, Edward N. *Flagler: Rockefeller Partner and Florida Baron*. Gainesville: University Press of Florida, 1988.

———. "The Sly Foxes: Henry Flagler, George Miles, and Florida's Public Domain." *Florida Historical Quarterly*, 58, no. 1 (July), 22-26.

———. "Southern Reflection of the Gilded Age: Henry M. Flagler's System, 1885–1913." PhD diss., University of Florida, 1975.

Amundson, Richard J. "The American Life of Henry Shelton Sanford." PhD diss., Florida State University, 1963.

Andrew, William. *Otto H. Bacher*. Madison: Education Industries Inc., 1981.

Andrews, Wayne. *Architecture, Ambition and Americans: A Social History of American Architecture*. New York: Harper and Brothers, 1947.

Appelbaum, Stanley. *Spectacle in the White City: The Chicago 1893 World's Fair*. Mineola: Calla Editions, 2009.

Armstrong, Maitland, and Margaret Armstrong, eds. *Day Before Yesterday: Reminiscences of a Varied Life*. New York: Charles Scribner's Sons, 1920.

Armstrong, Matthew. "Bernard Maybeck: Examining the Architect through His Berkeley Cottage." Unpublished typescript, Flagler College, 2008.

Atlas Portland Cement Company. *Concrete Country Residences: Photographs and Floor Plans of Turn-of-the-Century Homes*. Mineola: Dover Publications Inc., 2003.

Ausherman, Maria Elizabeth. *The Photographic Legacy of Frances Benjamin Johnston*. Gainesville: University Press of Florida, 2009.

Baldwin, Neil. *Edison: Inventing the Century*. New York: Hyperion, 1995.

Bangs, J. M. "Bernard Ralph Maybeck, Architect, Comes Into His Own." *Architectural Record* 103 (January 1948): 72–79.

Barbour, George M. *Florida for Tourists, Invalids and Settlers. 1882*. Facsimile edition. Gainesville: University Press of Florida, 1964.

Barghini, Sandra. *A Society of Painters: Flagler's St. Augustine Art Colony*. Palm Beach: Flagler Museum, 1998.

———. *Henry M. Flagler's Painting Collection: The Taste of a Gilded Age Collector*. Palm Beach: Flagler Museum, 2002.

Barnes, Jay. *Florida's Hurricane History*. Chapel Hill: University of North Carolina Press, 1998.

Bean, Shawn C. *The First Hollywood: Florida and the Golden Age of Silent Filmmaking*. Gainesville: University Press of Florida, 2008.

Bennett, Charles E. *Laudonniere & Fort Caroline: History and Documents*. Tuscaloosa: University of Alabama Press, 1964.

Berch, Bettina. *The Woman Behind the Lens: The Life and Work of Frances Benjamin Johnston, 1864–1952*. Charlottesville: The University Press of Virginia, 2000.

Bill, Ledyard. *A Winter in Florida*. New York: Wood and Holbrook, 1869.

Blackburn, Winfrey P., Jr., and R. Scott Gill. *Country Houses of Louisville: 1899–1939*. Louisville: Butler Books, 2011.

Blake, Curtis Channing. "The Architecture of Carrère and Hastings." PhD diss., Columbia University, 1976.

Bolger, Doreen. *In Pursuit of Beauty: Americans and the Aesthetic Movement*. New York: The Metropolitan Museum of Art and Rizzoli, 1987.

Bond, Gregory. "Jim Crow at Play: Race, Manliness, and the Color Line in American Sports." PhD diss, University of Wisconsin–Madison, 2008.

Bowen, Beth Rogero, and the St. Augustine Historical Society. *St. Augustine in the Gilded Age*. Charleston: Arcadia Publishing, 2008.

Boykin Hayter, Kennette. "The 'Ultimate' in Spa Resorts: The Renaissance of the Alcazar, St. Augustine." MArch thesis, University of Florida, 1988.

Braden, Susan. *The Architecture of Leisure: The Florida Resort Hotels of Henry Flagler and Henry Plant*. Gainesville: University Press of Florida, 2002.

———. "Entrepreneurs and Empires: Henry Flagler and Henry Plant in Florida." Presentation, Lewis Auditorium at Flagler College, February 19, 2013.

Bramson, Seth. *The Greatest Railroad Story Ever Told: Henry Flagler and the Florida East Coast Railway's Key West Extension*. Charleston: The History Press, 2011.

———. *Images of Rail: Florida East Coast Railway*. Charleston: Arcadia Publishing, 2006.

———. *Speedway to Sunshine: The Story of the Florida East Coast Railway*. Boston: Boston Mills Press, 1984.

Branch, Taylor. *Pillar of Fire: America in the King Years 1963–65*. New York: Simon & Schuster, 1988.

Brinton, Daniel G. *A Guide-Book of Florida and the South for Tourists, Invalids and Emigrants*. 1869. Facsimile edition. Gainesville: University Presses of Florida, 1978.

Brooks, Abbie T. *Petals Plucked from Sunny Climes*. 1880. Facsimile edition. Gainesville: University Presses of Florida, 1976.

Brown, Phil. *Catskill Culture: A Mountain Rat's Memories of the Great Jewish Resort Area*. Philadelphia: Temple University, 1998.

Browne, Jefferson Beale. *Key West: The Old and the New*. St. Augustine: The Record Company, 1912.

Browne, Paul. *The Coal Barons Played Cuban Giants: A History of Early Professional Baseball in Pennsylvania, 1886–1896*. Jefferson: McFarland & Company Inc. Publishers, 2013.

Bryant, William Cullen. *Letters of a Traveler, 1843*. New York: G. P. Putnam, 1850.

Burg, David. *Chicago's White City of 1893*. Lexington: University Press of Kentucky, 1976.

Busbey, Katherine Graves. *Home Life in America*. London: Methuen & Co., Ltd., 1910.

Campbell, Walter E. *Across Fortune's Tracks: A Biography of William Rand Kenan, Jr.* Chapel Hill: University of North Carolina Press, 1996.

Cardwell, Kenneth H. *Bernard Maybeck: Artisan, Architect, Artist.* Santa Barbara: Peregrine Smith Inc., 1977.

Carr, E. S. *Saint Augustine, Florida.* New York: G. P. Putnam and Son, 1869.

Carrère, John M. *City Improvement.* Hartford: Municipal Art Society, 1908.

Carrère, John M., and Thomas Hastings. *Florida: The American Riviera; St. Augustine: The Winter Newport.* New York: Gilliss Brothers & Turnure, 1887.

"Casa Amarylla SJ2293." Florida Site File Form, 1985. Flagler College Archives.

Castillo, Ana Caroline. "Two Gilded Age Hotels: The History, Restoration and Adaptive Use of the Tampa Bay and Ponce de Leon Hotels in Florida." MA thesis, Texas Tech University, 1987.

Castleden, Louise Decatur. *The Early Years of the Ponce de Leon: Clippings from an Old Scrap Book of Those Days Kept by the First Manager of This 'Prince of Hotels.'* n.p., 1958.

"Castle Warden." Florida Site File Form, 1985, City of St. Augustine Planning and Building Department.

Center for Governmental Responsibility, University of Florida Levin College of Law. "Contributions of Historic Preservation to the Quality of Life in Florida," 2006.

———. "Economic Impacts of Historic Preservation in Florida." Executive Summary, 2003.

———. "Economic Impacts of Historic Preservation in Florida." Executive Summary, Update, 2010.

Chandler, David Leon. *Henry Flagler: The Astonishing Life and Times of the Visionary Robber Baron Who Founded Florida.* New York: Macmillan Publishing Company, 1986.

Chernow, Ron. *Titan: The Life of John D. Rockefeller, Sr.* New York: Vintage, 1998.

Clark, Susan L. "Franklin W. Smith: St. Augustine's Concrete Pioneer." MA Thesis, Cooperstown Graduate Program, 1990.

Clemens, Samuel. *Mark Twain's Correspondence with Henry Huttleston Rogers, 1893–1909.* Berkeley: University of California Press, 1909.

Colburn, David R. *Racial Change and Community Crisis: St. Augustine, Florida, 1877–1980.* Gainesville: University of Florida Press, 1991.

Collins, J.F.L. *Collins' Both Sides of Fifth Avenue: A Brief History of the Avenue with Descriptive Notes Containing over Two Hundred Photographs of Residences, Churches, Hotels, Public Buildings, Clubs, Monuments, 1910.* New York: J.F.L. Collins, 1910.

Condit, Carl W. *American Building Art: The Nineteenth Century.* New York: Oxford University Press, 1960.

Conway, John. *Remembering the Sullivan County Catskills.* Charleston: The History Press, 2008.

Craig, Robert Michael. *Bernard Maybeck at Principia College: The Art and Craft of Building.* Layton: Gibbs Smith, Publisher, 2004.

Cram, Ralph Adams, Thomas Hastings, and Claude Bragdon. *Six Lectures on Architecture.* Chicago: University of Chicago Press, 1917.

Crawford, William G., Jr. *Florida's Big Dig: The Atlantic Intracoastal Waterway, 1881–1935*. Cocoa: Florida Historical Society Press, 2006.

Crespo, Rafael Agapito. "Florida's First Spanish Renaissance Revival." (Volumes I–III). PhD diss., Harvard University, 1987.

Cunningham, Erin. "Preserving with Purpose: Narratives of Settlement Women and Historic Interiors at Hull House and on Henry Street." PhD diss. University of Florida, 2010.

Davis, Jack E. *An Everglades Providence: Marjory Stoneman Douglas and the American Environmental Century*. Athens: University of Georgia Press, 2009.

Deagan, Kathleen. "Discover First America; Legacies of La Florida." Presentation, Flagler College Auditorium, November 23, 2009.

Denby, Elaine. *Grand Hotels: Reality & Illusion*. London: Reaktion Books, 1998.

Derby, George, and James Terry White. "Auguste Pottier." In *The National Cyclopedia of American Biography*. vol. 6. New York: James T. White & Co., 1896.

Derr, Mark. *Some Kind of Paradise: A Chronicle of Man and the Land in Florida*. New York: William Morrow and Company Inc., 1989.

Dewhurst, William W. *History of Saint Augustine, Florida*. New York, New York: G. P. Putnam's Sons, 1881.

Diamonstein, Barbaralee. *Buildings Reborn: New Uses, Old Places*. New York: Harper & Row, 1978.

Dickson, William Kennedy Laurie, and Antonia Dickson. *The Life and Inventions of Thomas Alva Edison*. New York: Thomas Y. Crowell & Co., 1894.

Duncan, Alastair. *Tiffany Windows: The Indispensable Book on Louis C. Tiffany's Masterworks*. New York: Simon and Schuster, 1980.

Dunkle, John Robert. "St. Augustine, Florida: A Study in Historical Geography." PhD diss., Clark University, 1955.

Dunlop, Beth, and Joanna Lombard. *Great Houses of Florida*. New York: Rizzoli, 2008.

"Edison and Ford Winter Estates." Guide. Kansas City: Terrell Creative, 2006.

Edwards, Virginia. *Stories of Old St. Augustine*. Jacksonville: Paramount Press, 1973.

Emerson, Edward W., and Waldo E. Forbes. *Journals of Ralph Waldo Emerson, 1820–1872*. New York: Houghton Mifflin Company, 1909.

Favis, Roberta. *Martin Johnson Heade in Florida*. Gainesville: University Press of Florida, 2003.

———. "Martin Johnson Heade and the Flagler Artists' Colony." Unpublished typescript, 2006.

Federal Writers Project. *Florida: A Guide to the Southernmost State*. New York: Oxford University Press, (1939), 1947.

Flynn, G. Hutchinson. *The Life of Henry Bradley Plant*. New York: G. P. Putnam's Sons, 1904.

Flynn, John T. *God's Gold: The Story of Rockefeller and His Times*. New York: Harcourt, Brace and Company, 1932.

Fosdick, Raymond B. *John D. Rockefeller, Jr.: A Portrait*. New York: Harper & Brothers, Publishers, 1956.

Freudenheim, Leslie M. *Building with Nature: Inspiration for the Arts and Crafts Home*. Salt Lake City: Gibbs Smith, Publisher, 2005.

Fry, Joseph A. *Henry S. Sanford: Diplomacy and Business in Nineteenth-Century America*. Reno: University of Nevada Press, 1982.

Graham, Thomas. *The Awakening of St. Augustine: The Anderson Family and the Oldest City: 1821–1924*. St. Augustine: St. Augustine Historical Society, 1978.

———. "The Flagler Era." In *The Oldest City: St. Augustine Saga of Survival*, edited by Jean Parker Waterbury, 181–209. St. Augustine: St. Augustine Historical Society, 1983.

———. *Flagler's St. Augustine Hotels*. Sarasota: Pineapple Press, 2004.

———. *Mr. Flagler's St. Augustine*. Gainesville: University Press of Florida, 2014.

Graham, Thomas, and Leslee F. Keys. *Hotel Ponce de Leon: The Architecture & Decoration*. St. Augustine: Flagler College, 2013.

Gray, David. *Thomas Hastings, Architect: Collected Writings Together with a Memoir*. Boston: Houghton Mifflin Company, 1933.

Griffin, Patricia C. "The Impact of Tourism on Ritual and Festival: St. Augustine, 1821–1987." PhD diss., University of Florida, 1988.

Grunwald, Michael. *The Swamp: The Everglades, Florida, and the Politics of Paradise*. New York: Simon & Schuster, 2006.

Hamer, David. *History in Urban Places: The Historic Districts of the United States*. Columbus: Ohio State University Press, 1998.

Handler, Richard, and Eric Gable. *The New History in an Old Museum: Creating the Past at Colonial Williamsburg*. Durham: Duke University Press, 1997.

Hardy, Lady Duffus. *Down South*. London, England: Chapman and Hall, 1883.

Harr, John Ensor, and Peter J. Johnson. *The Rockefeller Century: Three Generations of America's Greatest Family*. New York: Charles Scribner's Sons, 1988.

Hatton, Hap. *Tropical Splendor: An Architectural History of Florida*. New York: Alfred A. Knopf, 1987.

Heaphy, Leslie A. *The Negro Leagues, 1869–1960*. Jefferson: McFarland & Company Inc., Publishers, 2003.

Hewitt, Mark Alan, Kate Lemos, William Morrison, and Charles D. Warren. *Carrère and Hastings: Architects*. New York: Acanthus Press, 2006.

Hoffman, Joel. "From St. Augustine to Tangerine: Florida at the U.S. World's Fairs," in "Florida Theme Issue." *The Journal of Decorative and Propaganda Arts* (The Wolfsonian-Florida International University) 23 (January 1998): 48–85.

Hogan, Lawrence D. *Shades of Glory: The Negro Leagues and the Story of African-American Baseball*. Washington, D.C.: National Geographic Society, 2006.

Holmgren, Beth. *Starring Madame Modjeska: On Tour in Poland and America*. Bloomington: Indiana University Press, 2011.

Hosmer, Charles B., Jr. "Introduction to the New Edition." In *With Heritage So Rich*, edited by Albert Rains and Laurance G. Henderson, 9–15. Washington, D.C.: Preservation Press, 1983.

———. *The Presence of the Past: A History of the Preservation Movement in the United States before Williamsburg*. New York: G. P. Putnam's Sons, 1965.

———. 1981. *Preservation Comes of Age: From Williamsburg to the National Trust, 1926–1949*. Vols. I and II, Charlottesville: University Press of Virginia.

Hughes, Edan Milton. *Artists in California, 1786–1940*. San Francisco: Hughes Publishing Company, 1986.

Hughes, Jim. *The Birth of a Century: Early Color Photographs of America*. London: Tauris Parke Books, 1994.

Hurley, Andrew. *Beyond Preservation: Using Public History to Revitalize Inner Cities*. Philadelphia: Temple University Press, 2010.

Israel, Paul. *Edison: A Life of Invention*. New York: John Wiley & Sons Inc., 1998.

Jackson, William Henry. *Time Exposure: The Autobiography of William Henry Jackson*. New York: G. P. Putnam's Sons, 1940.

Jacksonville Historic Landmarks Commission. *Jacksonville's Architectural Heritage: Landmarks for the Future*. Gainesville, Florida: University Press of Florida, 1989.

James, Henry. *The American Scene*. New York, New York: Harper & Brothers Publishers, 1907.

Jandry, Clay. "Unplugging the Everglades." In *Government vs. Environment*, edited by Donald Leal and Roger E. Meiners, 79–86. Lanham: Rowman & Littlefield Publishers Inc., 2002.

Jehl, Francis. *Menlo Park Reminiscences*. Vol. 3, Dearborn: The Edison Institute, 1941.

Jones, Barry. "William Henry Jackson, Thomas Moran: Analysis of Photographic and Painterly Style and Attitude during Their Explorations of the American West." MA Thesis, East Tennessee State University, 1987.

Jones, Robert. D. *Maitland Armstrong: American Stained Glass Master*. Tallahassee: Sentry Press, 2004.

Jordy, William H. *American Buildings and Their Architects: Progressive and Academic Ideals at the Turn of the Twentieth Century*. Garden City: Doubleday, 1972.

Karas, Natalie. "Carrère and Hastings," unpublished typescript, Flagler College, 2008.

———. "Ponce de Leon Hotel, Flagler College, St. Augustine, Florida, Solarium Paint Stratigraphy Analysis," unpublished typescript, University of Pennsylvania, 2008.

Kelley, William D. *The Old South and the New: A Series of Letters*. New York: G. P. Putnam's Sons, 1888.

Kenan, William Rand, Jr. *Incidents by the Way: More Recollections*. Self-published, 1958.

Kenan, William Rand, Jr. Charitable Trust. Annual Report, 2011.

Keys, Leslee F. "PICO: Plant Investment Company, Developing the 'Southernmost Frontier,'" unpublished typescript, University of Florida, 2011.

———. "The St. Augustine Quadricentennial Anniversary," unpublished typescript, University of Florida, 2010.

———. "Tourism and Resort Heritage in St. Augustine, Florida," unpublished typescript, University of Florida, 2009.

Keys, Leslee F., ed. *Historic Jefferson County.* Louisville: Jefferson County Government, 1992.

Kidney, Walter. *The Architecture of Choice: Eclecticism in America 1880–1930.* New York: George Braziller, 1974.

Kimball, Fiske. *The Restoration of Colonial Williamsburg in Virginia.* Bound imprint of *Architectural Record*, New York: F.W. Dodge Corporation, 1935.

King, Moses. *King's Photographic Views of New York.* Boston, Massachusetts: 1895.

Kirwin, Bill. *Out of the Shadows: African-American Baseball from the Cuban Giants to Jackie Robinson.* Lincoln: University of Nebraska Press, 2005.

Kjellberg, Pierre. *Bronzes of the 19th Century: Dictionary of Sculptors.* Atglen: Schiffer Publishing Company, 1994.

Knetsch, Joe and Nick Wynne. *Florida in the Spanish-American War.* Charleston: The History Press, 2011.

Koch, Robert. *The Stained Glass Decades: A Study of Louis Comfort Tiffany (1848–1933) and the Art Nouveau in America.* Vol. I. PhD diss., Yale University, 1957.

———. *Tiffany: Rebel in Glass.* New York: Crown Publishers Inc., 1972.

Kornwolf, James D. *Architecture and Town Planning in Colonial North America.* Baltimore: The Johns Hopkins University Press, 2002.

Lamme, Ary J. *America's Historic Landscapes: Community Power and the Preservation of Four National Historic Sites.* Knoxville: University of Tennessee Press, 1989.

Lanctot, Neil. *Negro League Baseball: The Rise and Ruin of a Black Institution.* Philadelphia: University of Pennsylvania Press, 2004.

Lanier, Sidney. *Florida: Its Scenery, Climate and History.* Philadelphia: J.P. Lippincott and Co., 1876.

Larson, Erik. *Devil in the White City: Murder, Magic, and Madness at the Fair that Changed America.* New York: Random House, 2003.

Latham, Earl, ed. *John D. Rockefeller: Robber Baron or Industrial Statesman?* Boston: D.C. Heath and Company, 1949.

Lawson, Edward W. *The Saint Augustine Historical Society and Its Oldest House.* Nashville: Cullom & Ghertner Company, 1957.

Lee, Antoinette. *Architects to the Nation: The Rise and Decline of the Supervising Architect's Office.* New York: Oxford University Press, 2000.

Lee, Henry. *The Tourist's Guide of Florida.* New York, New York: Leve & Alden Printing Company, 1885.

Libby, Gary R., ed. *Celebrating Florida: Works of Art from the Vickers Collection.* Gainesville: University Press of Florida, 1995.

Limerick, Jeffrey, Nancy Ferguson, and Richard Oliver. *America's Grand Resort Hotels*. New York: Pantheon Books, 1979.

Linebaugh, Donald W. *The Springfield Gas Machine: Illuminating Industry and Leisure, 1860s–1920s*. Knoxville: The University of Tennessee Press, 2011.

Lomax, Michael E. *Black Baseball Entrepreneurs, 1860–1901: Operating by Any Means Possible*. Syracuse: Syracuse University Press, 2003.

Long, Ellen Call. *Florida Breezes, or Florida Old and New*. Jacksonville: Ashmead Brothers, 1883.

Longstreth, Richard. *On the Edge of the World: Four Architects in San Francisco at the Turn of the Century*. Berkeley: University of California Press, 1998.

Loring, John. *Louis Comfort Tiffany at Tiffany & Co*. New York: Harry N. Abrams, 2002.

Lumadue, Richard Thomas. "History and Demise of the University Foundation in St. Augustine, Florida: An Institutional Autopsy." PhD Diss., University of North Texas, 2007.

MacDonald, J. A. *Plain Talk about Florida*. Eustis: J. A. MacDonald, Printer, 1882.

MacKay, Robert B., Anthony K. Baker, and Carol A. Traynor, eds. *Long Island Country Houses and Their Architects, 1860–1940*. New York: Society for the Preservation of Long Island Antiquities and W. W. Norton & Company, 1997.

Mann, Maybelle. *Art in Florida: 1564–1945*. Sarasota: Pineapple Press Inc., 1999.

Manucy, Albert. *The Houses of St. Augustine: Notes on the Architecture from 1565 to 1821*. Gainesville: University Press of Florida, 1991.

———. *Sixteenth Century St. Augustine: The People and Their Homes*. Gainesville: University Press of Florida, 1997.

Marcosson, Isaac F. *Marse Henry: A Biography of Henry Watterson*. New York: Dodd, Mead & Company, 1951.

Martin, Sidney Walter. *Flagler's Florida*. Athens: University of Georgia Press, 1977.

———. *Henry Flagler: Visionary of the Gilded Age*. Lake Buena Vista, Florida: Tailored Tour Publications, 1998.

Mathews, Nancy Mowll. *Moving Pictures: American Art and Early Film, 1880–1910*. Manchester: Hudson Hills Press & Williams College Museum of Art, 2005.

McCarthy, Kevin. *A Book Lover's Guide to Florida*. Sarasota: Pineapple Press, 1992.

McCash, William Barton, and June Hall McCash. *The Jekyll Island Club: Southern Haven for America's Millionaires*. Athens: University of Georgia Press, 1989.

McCoy, Esther. *Five California Architects*. New York: Reinhold Book Corporation, 1960.

McGreevy, Patrick. *Stairway to Empire: Lockport, the Erie Canal, and the Shaping of America*. Albany: SUNY Press, 2009.

McIver, Stuart B. *Touched by the Sun: The Florida Chronicles*. Vol. 3. Sarasota, Florida: Pineapple Press, 2005.

McKee, Harley J. *Introduction to Early American Masonry, Stone, Brick, Mortar, and*

Plaster. Washington, D.C.: National Trust for Historic Preservation and Columbia University, 1973.

McMakin, Dorothy Primrose. "General Henry Shelton Sanford and His Influence on Florida." MA Thesis, John B. Stetson University, 1938.

Mendez, Jesus. "Henry Flagler: Florida Wizard and Bahamian Magician." Presentation, Florida Historical Society Annual Conference, May 24, 2013.

Messinger, Cheryl, and Terran McGinnis. *Images of America: Marineland*. Charleston: Arcadia Publishing, 2011.

Moe, Richard, and Carter Wilkie. *Changing Places: Rebuilding Community in the Age of Sprawl*. New York: Henry Holt and Company, 1997.

Montgomery, Horace, ed. *Georgians in Profile: Historical Essays in Honor of Ellis Merton Coulter*. Athens: University of Georgia Press, 1958.

Mormino, Gary. *Land of Sunshine, State of Dreams: A Social History of Modern Florida*. Gainesville: University Press of Florida, 2005.

Morrone, Francis. *The Architectural Guidebook to New York City*. Layton: Gibbs Smith, 1998.

Morton, W. Brown III. "What Do We Preserve and Why?" In *The American Mosaic: Preserving a Nation's Heritage*, edited by Robert E. Stipe and Antoinette Lee, 145–77. Washington, D.C., US/ICOMOS, 1987.

Mueller, Edward A. *Steamships of the Two Henrys: Being an Account of the Maritime Activities of Henry Morrison Flagler and Henry Bradley Plant*. DeLeon Springs: E. O. Painter Printing Co., 1996.

Murtagh, William J. *Keeping Time: The History and Theory of Preservation in America*. Hoboken: John Wiley & Sons Inc., 2006.

Nevins, Allan. *John D. Rockefeller: The Heroic Age of American Enterprise*. New York, New York: Charles Scribner's Sons, 1941.

———. *Study in Power: John D. Rockefeller Industrialist and Philanthropist*. New York, New York: Charles Scribner's Sons, 1953.

Nolan, David. *Fifty Feet in Paradise: The Booming of Florida*. New York: Harcourt Brace Jovanovich Publishers, 1984.

Osborne, Ray. *Presidential Visits to Florida: Grover Cleveland 1888*. A1A Computer Professionals Inc., n.p.

Ossman, Laurie. "Carrère and Hastings." Presentation, Flagler College, May 21, 2006.

———. "Carrère & Hastings and the Reinvention of St. Augustine." Presentation, Flagler College, March 19, 2013.

Ossman, Laurie, and Heather Ewing. *Carrère and Hastings: The Masterworks*. New York: Rizzoli, 2011.

Page, Max. *The Creative Destruction of Manhattan, 1900–1940*. Chicago: University of Chicago Press, 1999.

Page, Max, and Randall Mason. *Giving Preservation a History: Histories of Historic Preservation in the United States*. New York: Routledge, 2004.

Phillips, Morris. *Abroad and at Home: Practical Hints for Tourists*. New York: Brentano's, 1891.

Platt, Frederick. *America's Gilded Age: Its Architecture and Decoration*. South Brunswick: A.S. Barnes and Company, 1976.

Pollack, Deborah C. *Laura Woodward: The Artist Behind the Innovator who Developed Palm Beach*. Singapore: Blue Heron Press, 2009.

Rains, Albert, and Laurance G. Henderson, eds. *With Heritage So Rich*. Washington, D.C.: Preservation Press, 1983.

Rajtar, Steve, and Kelly Goodman. *A Guide to Historic St. Augustine*. Charleston: The History Press, 2008.

Ralph, Julian. *Dixie or Southern Scenes and Sketches*. New York: Harper & Brothers Publishers, 1896.

Reed, Henry Hope, and Francis Morrone. *The New York Public Library: The Architecture and Decoration of the Stephen A. Schwarzman Building*. New York: W. W. Norton & Company, 2011.

Reinhardt, Richard. "Bernard Maybeck." In *Three Centuries of Notable American Architects*, edited by Joseph Thorndike, 232–47. New York: American Heritage, 1987.

Reynolds, Charles B. *The Standard Guide: St. Augustine 1892*. Reprint. St. Augustine: Historic Print & Map Company, 2004.

———. *A Tribute*. St. Augustine: n.p., 1910.

Reynolds, Kelly. *Henry Plant: Pioneer Empire Builder*. Cocoa: Florida Historical Society, 2003.

Ribowsky, Mark. *A Complete History of the Negro Leagues, 1884–1955*. New York: Carol Publishing Group, 1995.

Rockefeller, John D. *Random Reminiscences of Men and Events*. New York: Doubleday, Doran & Company Inc., 1933.

———. "Some Old Friends." *World's Work, XVII*, n.p., November 1908.

"Roosevelt Rests in Flowery Lands," *The Arizona Republican*, October 22, 1905.

"Rotunda." Grant Records, Flagler College Archives.

Rowland, Monica. "Menendez Versus Mickey: A Study of Heritage Tourism in Florida." MA Thesis, University of South Florida, 2006.

Rybczynski, Witold, Laurie Olin, and Steven Brooke. *Vizcaya: An American Villa and Its Makers*. Philadelphia: University of Pennsylvania Press, 2006.

Segall, Grant. *John D. Rockefeller: Anointed with Oil*. New York: Oxford University Press, 2001.

Severens, Kenneth. *Southern Architecture: 350 years of Distinctive American Buildings*. New York: Elsevier-Dutton Publishing Co. Inc., 1981.

Shaplen, Robert. *Toward the Well-Being of Mankind: Fifty Years of the Rockefeller Foundation*. Garden City: Doubleday & Company Inc., 1964.

Shaughnessy, Joseph. "Crises of Authenticity in Saint Augustine's Early Preservation History, 1840–1955." MA Thesis, University of Florida, 2009.

Shepherd, Anne Dale, ed. *St. Augustine Boy*. Dartford: Xlibris Corporation, 2009.

Shreve, Sara Denise. "A History Worth Saving: The Palace of Fine Arts and the Interpretation of History on a Reconstructed Site." MA thesis, Cornell University, 2006.

Simmon, Scott. *The Films of D. W. Griffith*. Cambridge: Cambridge University Press, 1993.

Small, Herbert, comp. *Handbook of the New Library of Congress in Washington*. Boston: Curtis & Cameron, 1931.

Smyth, G. Hutchinson. *The Life of Henry Bradley Plant: Founder and President of the Plant System of Railroads and Steamships and also of the Southern Express Company*. New York: G. P. Putnam's Sons, 1898.

St. Augustine Record. "St. Augustine Remembers: Through the Eyes of Those Who Lived It." Augusta: Scrapbook Video Production, 2006.

Standiford, Les. *Last Train to Paradise: Henry Flagler and the Spectacular Rise and Fall of the Railroad that Crossed an Ocean*. New York: Crown Publishers, 2002.

Stebbins, Theodore, Jr. *The Life and Work of Martin Johnson Heade: A Critical Analysis and Catalogue Raisonne*. New Haven: Yale University Press, 2000.

Stipe, Robert E., ed. *A Richer Heritage: Historic Preservation in the Twenty-First Century*. Chapel Hill: University of North Carolina Press, 2003.

———. "Historic Preservation: The Process and the Actors," in *The American Mosaic: Preserving a Nation's Heritage*, edited by Robert E. Stipe and Antoinette J. Lee. Washington, D.C., US/ICOMOS, 1987.

Strock, G. Michael. *The Stained Glass Windows of Trinity Episcopal Church*. St. Augustine: Trinity Episcopal Church, 1995.

Strong, William B. *The Sunshine Economy: An Economic History of Florida since the Civil War*. Gainesville, Florida: University Press of Florida, 2008.

Tarbell, Ida M. *The History of the Standard Oil Company*. New York: McClure, Phillips & Company, 1904.

Taylor, James. "History of Terra Cotta in New York City." *The Architectural Record*, Vol. II, July 1892 to July 1893.

Tebeau, Charlton W. *A History of Florida*. Coral Gables: University of Miami Press, 1971.

Tilden, Freeman. *Interpreting Our Heritage: Principles and Practices for Visitor Services in Parks, Museums, and Historic Places*. Chapel Hill: University of North Carolina Press, 1957.

Todd, Frank Morton. *The Story of the Exposition: Being the Official History of the International Celebration Held at San Francisco in 1915 to Commemorate the Discovery of the Pacific Ocean and the Construction of the Panama Canal*. Volumes 1–5. New York: G. P. Putnam's Sons, The Knickerbocker Press, 1921.

Tolles, Bryant F., Jr. *The Grand Resort Hotels of the White Mountains*. Jaffrey: David R. Godine, Publisher, 1998.

———. *Resort Hotels in the Adirondacks: The Architecture of a Summer Paradise, 1850–1950*. Hanover: University Press of New England, 2003.

————. *Summer by the Seaside: The Architecture of New England Coastal Resort Hotels, 1820–1950*. Hanover: University Press of New England, 2003.

Tomlan, Michael A., ed. *Preservation of What, for Whom?: A Critical Look at Historical Significance*. Minneapolis: University of Minnesota for National Council for Preservation Education, 1998.

Truman, Benjamin C. *History of the World's Fair: Being a Complete and Authentic Description of the Columbian Exposition from Its Inception. 1893*. Reprint. New York: Arno Press, 1976.

Turkel, Stanley. *Great American Hoteliers: Pioneers of the Hotel Industry*. Bloomington: AuthorHouse, 2009.

Turner, Gregg. *Florida Railroads in the 1920s: Images of Rail*. Charleston: Arcadia Publishing, 2005.

————. *A Journey into Florida Railroad History*. Gainesville: University Press of Florida, 2008.

Turner, Gregg M., and Seth H. Bramson. *The Plant System of Railroads, Steamships, and Hotels: The South's First Great Industrial Enterprise*. Laurys Station: Garrigues House, Publishers, 2004.

Twain, Mark. The Mark Twain Papers & Project. The Bancroft Library, University of California, Berkeley.

Tyler, Norman, Ted J. Ligibel, and Ilene R. Tyler. *Historic Preservation: An Introduction to Its History, Principles, and Practice*. New York: W. W. Norton & Company, 2009.

Varner, Elizabeth Chantale. "Bolstering a National Identity: President Andrew Johnson's Pottier and Stymus Furniture in the United States Treasury Department." MA Thesis, Smithsonian Associates and the Corcoran College of Art + Design, 2008.

Ward, George Morgan, comp. *In Memoriam: Henry Morrison Flagler*. Buffalo, New York: Matthews Northrup, 1914.

Warren, Dan R. *If It Takes All Summer: Martin Luther King, the KKK, and States' Rights in St. Augustine, 1964*. Tuscaloosa: The University of Alabama Press, 2008.

Waterbury, Jean Parker. *The Treasurer's House*. St. Augustine: St. Augustine Historical Society, 1994.

————. *Where Artillery Lane Crosses Aviles Street: The Segui/Kirby Smith House*. St. Augustine: St. Augustine Historical Society, 1987.

Watters, Sam. *Gardens for a Beautiful America, 1895–1935*. New York: Acanthus Press, 2012.

Waugh's Blue Book of Leading Hotels and Resorts of the World. Boston, Massachusetts: W. Wallace Waugh & Son, Publishers, 1907.

Weeter, Joanne. *Louisville Landmarks: A Viewbook of Architectural and Historic Landmarks in Louisville, Kentucky*. Louisville: Butler Books, 2004.

Whiffen, Marcus. *American Architecture since 1780: A Guide to the Styles*. Cambridge: MIT Press Inc., 1965.

White, James E. *A Life Span and Reminiscences of Railway Mail Service.* Philadelphia: Deemer and Jaisohn, 1910.

White, Sol. *History of Colored Baseball with Other Documents on the Early Black Game, 1886–1936.* Reprint. Lincoln, Nebraska: University of Nebraska Press, 1995.

Wiencek, Henry. *The Moodys of Galveston and Their Mansion.* China: Everbest Printing Co. and the Mary Moody Northern Endowment, 2010.

Wilkins, Thurman, and Caroline Lawson Hinkley. *Thomas Moran: Artist of the Mountains.* Norman: University of Oklahoma Press, 1998.

Wilson, Mark Anthony. *Bernard Maybeck: Architect of Elegance.* Layton: Gibbs Smith, 2011.

Woodbridge, Sally Byrne. *Bernard Maybeck: Visionary Architect.* New York: Abbeville Press, 1996.

Woods, Mary N. *Beyond the Architect's Eye: Photographs and the American Built Environment.* Philadelphia: University of Pennsylvania Press, 2009.

———. *From Craft to Profession: The Practice of Architecture in Nineteenth-Century America.* Berkeley: University of California Press, 1999.

INDEX

LESLEE F. KEYS is assistant professor of history and director of historic preservation at Flagler College in St. Augustine, where she lives in a 1928 bungalow. She is the coauthor with Thomas Graham of *Hotel Ponce de Leon: The Architecture and Decoration*; editor of a book featuring historic properties in Louisville, Kentucky, *Historic Jefferson County*; and author of a design guidelines book for Dayton, Ohio, *Blueprint for Rehabilitation: A Positive Approach to Guidelines*.